ABOUT

FACE

FOR MY PARENTS

• • •

O K A G E S A M A   D E

ABOUT FACE

PERFORMING RACE
IN FASHION AND THEATER

FACE

Dorinne
Kondo

ROUTLEDGE: NEW YORK AND LONDON

Published in 1997 by

Routledge
29 West 35th Street
New York, NY 10001

Published in Great Britain in 1997 by

Routledge
11 New Fetter Lane
London EC4P 4EE

Printed in the United States of America
Designer: Mark Abrams

ISBN 0-415-91140-0.(cl.)
ISBN 0-415-91141-9 (pbk.)

Library of Congress Cataloging-in-Publication Number: 96-43837

contents

a c k n o w l e d g m e n t s

DURING THE COURSE of researching and writing this book, my life has been touched by the generosity of many. First, to those in the fashion and theater worlds who inspired this inquiry and made it possible, my warm appreciation. Fieldwork for the fashion project occurred at periodic intervals between 1989 and 1993, including trips to view the collections in Paris and Tokyo, attendance at sales exhibitions, and interviews with designers' representatives, fashion professionals, and, at Comme des Garçons, the designer herself. My thanks to: Designer Rei Kawakubo and the Press Department at Comme des Garçons, especially Jan Kawata and Miki Higasa; Marion Greenberg and her staff in New York; Jun Kanai of Issey Miyake; Chiaki Yamamura at Yohji Yamamoto. For introductions and advice, Vincent Crapanzano and Jane Kramer; Holly Brubach; Diana Crane; Valerie Steele; for their time, the people who graciously consented to interviews: Jeff Weinstein of the *Village Voice*; Jean Drusedow, then of the Costume Institute at the Metropolitan Museum of Art; Harold Koda, then of Fashion Institute of Technology in New York and now of the Costume Institute at the Met; designer Diane Pernet; Susan Sidlauskas; Barbara Weiser. For availing me of their knowledge of photography and magazine layout, thanks to Erwin Ferguson and Amy Bass-Wilson. Laura Brousseau offered her acute analytic insight on the *Kyoto étrangère* section.

In theater, my appreciation to East West Players and to the David Henry Hwang Writers' Institute, especially teachers R. A. Shiomi, David Henry Hwang, and Brian Nelson, as well as the other writers in the playwriting class, for galvanizing my passion for theater. During the course of fieldwork for this book, I importuned many for interviews, and they responded generously: thanks to the playwright Perry Miyake and cast of *Doughball*. To David Román goes a special acknowledgment for the inspiration of his work and for sharing with me his wit, scholarly expertise, passion for theater, and love of laughter.

Funding for the research and fieldwork on which this book is based was granted by the Northeast Asia Council of the Association for Asian Studies, the American Philosophical Society, and especially the Research Committee at Pomona College and the research funds from my MacArthur Chair. The Rockefeller Foundation supported a year on leave at the Center for Cultural Studies at Rice University, where I was able to begin research on the fashion project. Thanks to Director Michael Fischer and to colleagues in Cultural Studies and the Department of Anthropology at Rice, including George Marcus, Julie Taylor, Sharon Traweek, and Stephen Tyler, for fostering the inauguration of this project. The Institute of American Cultures funded a year on leave at the Asian American Studies Center at UCLA, providing resources that enabled me to make substantial progress toward finishing this book. Don Nakanishi, Enrique de la Cruz, Catherine Castor, and other members of the faculty and staff offered helpful support and the freedom to pursue my project free of other responsibilities. Concurrently, I spent a quarter on leave at the University of California at Irvine Humanities Research Institute. Mark Rose, Deborah Massey, Sauni Hawes, Linda Arias, and Chris Aschan provided a congenial environment for academic work. In our seminar, colleagues at UCHRI offered their insightful comments on the book proposal. Thanks to Kum Kum Bhavnani, Edward Chang, Kimberle Crenshaw, Angela Davis, Gina Dent, Avery Gordon, Neil Gotanda, Herman Gray, Melvin Hall, Jacqueline Leavitt, Maria Ochoa, Linda Vo, Devra Weber, Tekle Woldemikael, Kristal Brent Zook. At Pomona College, Gail Orozco was exemplary in her efficiency and professionalism, enabling teaching and research to run smoothly. During my years at Pomona and a year on leave at UCLA, I was blessed with hyper-competent research assistants who helped me keep body and soul together: Genevieve Siri, Maria Gorsuch, Daniel Ziblatt, Stacey Hirose, Melissa Cushman, Mei Zhan, Teresa Hernández, Rachael Joo, Nancy Luna, Araceli Pérez, Steve Ou. Their intelligence and political commitment give me hope that our society is indeed transforming for the better.

Some years ago, over dinner at a Chinese restaurant in San Francisco, Sylvia Yanagisako gave me the idea of collecting my essays on fashion and theater in a single volume—a notion I embraced, abandoned, then re-embraced. The editors at Routledge supported this project enthusiastically: thanks to Max Zutty, Marlie Wasserman, Eric Zinner, William Germano. Over the years, many friends and colleagues have offered their comments on these essays or have given other crucial forms of support: Karen Blu, Donald Brenneis, Judith Butler, Steven Feld, Clifford Geertz, Deena González, Matt Hamabata, Elaine Kim, Smadar Lavie, Elizabeth Long, Lisa Lowe, Lynne Miyake, Marcyliena Morgan, Clyde Nishimoto, Cecelia Pang, Elliott Shore, Anna Deavere Smith, Ted Swedenburg, Dana Takagi, Samuel Yamashita, Kamala Visweswaran. Steven Gregory provided emotional and intellectual companionship during the last stages of finishing the manuscript. Miriam Silverberg offered her generous friendship and insightful comments on the final draft. Lisa Rofel sustained me with her keen intellectual engagement and unfailing encouragement throughout the vicissitudes of book-making. It is difficult to imagine writing without her as interlocutor. Lisa also introduced me to Kerry Walk's indispensable writing consultation. Kerry's human insights, her brilliant time management strategies, her counsel and her enthusiasm inform this book at every turn. And it was she who came up with the title. Without her, this book would have been far, far longer in the making.

Versions of these essays have appeared in the following anthologies and journals. "*M. Butterfly*: Orientalism, Gender, and a Critique of Essentialist Identity" is reprinted from *Cultural Critique* (16) Fall 1990, Oxford University Press. Portions of "Orientalizing" and "The Limits of the Avant-garde?" appeared in "The Aesthetics and Politics of Style in the Japanese Fashion Industry," in Joseph Tobin, ed. *Remade in Japan: Everyday Life and Consumer Taste in a Changing Society*. New Haven: Yale University Press, 1992. "The Narrative Production of 'Home,' Community and Identity" first appeared in Smadar Lavie and Ted Swedenburg, eds. *Dislocation, Diaspora, and Geographies of Identity* (Durham: Duke University Press, 1996). Permission to reprint is appreciatively acknowledged.

Though authors rarely mention "place," I must acknowledge Los Angeles, a city that has allowed me and my work to thrive. Its daunting sprawl, glaring contradictions, and bristling tensions cannot erase the sense of unprecedented historical possibility animating the cultural and political work here by people of color. It keeps me strong and alive and happier than I would have ever dreamed possible.

Finally, my parents have, over the years, provided staunch and unstinting support in countless ways. As with my first book, I am sure they have been wondering what has taken so long. Amidst the hard work, I too have sometimes wondered—and can only, in response, dedicate this volume to them as a token of gratitude for their love and patience. Once again, *okagesama de.*

We write about what moves us. As positioned subjects with particular stakes in our work, this is both inevitable and necessary. Here, then, I write about Asian American theater and Japanese fashion, to acknowledge the different yet related ways each has touched my life.

For many years Asian American theater has been a powerful force in keeping alive my racial and ethnic identities. I am back in graduate school, working at my first job, living on the East Coast. As the years pass, I find myself acutely missing a large Asian American—specifically, Japanese American—community. It is as though without nourishment this Japanese American part of my identity— not Japanese, not white—slowly wastes away. So the moment I hand in my grades, I jump onto the next plane for San Francisco, stay in Japan Town, and feed body and soul: eat my favorite foods and see the latest in Asian American performance. The play needs work, I might think, but my enduring memories are of empowerment: the pride and wonder I feel seeing live Asian American actors on stage in plays written by Asian Americans. After years of starving for images of ourselves, wanting to see ourselves as something more than dragon ladies, lotus blossoms, despotic tyrants, or desexualized servants, here are three-dimensional, live actors who look like we do, performing right before our eyes.

Theater becomes a place where we can recognize ourselves, be ourselves, perform ourselves, seemingly apart from the oppressive gaze of the dominant—though I now know this "safe space" is always provisional, always partial. Asian American theater touches my life with an empowerment that awakens me to a vision of cultural possibility.

Seeing David Henry Hwang's M. Butterfly *on a Broadway stage was like a searing touch—empowering, to be sure, and profoundly moving. It is 1988, and I am spending the year at Princeton. Accustomed to the underfunded productions of nonprofit theater, I go to a matinee in the belly of the beast. The rococo casements, the red carpet, the audience filled with white matrons. . . It is an unlikely site for an Asian American voice. I glance around, tense with anticipation. What will it be like? What on earth will this audience think? The curtain rises. A spectacular curving ramp sweeps from one side of the stage to the other. John Lithgow launches into his monologue. And B. D. Wong, splendidly clad, glides down the ramp. It is an afternoon of revelations: Wong's acting tour de force, Eiko Ishioka's stunning sets and costumes, Lucia Hwong's engaging music. Most of all, there is the brilliance of the writing: the smart, sassy dialogue, the incisive political critique, the profound insights into the plight of Asian and Asian American women and gay men, the trenchant observations on the power-laden discourses of "love." The words penetrate straight through skin, mind, heart: a touch that is steady, painful, yet replete with recognition. It is as though David Henry Hwang, this person I have never met, knows my life intimately. And of course this feeling is possible precisely because the structures of Orientalism, male dominance, and heterosexism continue to shape geopolitics and Asian and Asian American lives. In 1988* M. Butterfly *marks a moment of Asian American arrival on the mainstream stage.*

And what of fashion? Can it move so profoundly? I write in other vignettes about clothing and racial pride, about clothing as a vehicle for political awakening. Above all there is the matter of pleasure: intellectual, sensuous, aesthetic. In high fashion, the garments themselves provoke such pleasures, but perhaps they are at their most seductive in one of late capitalism's emblematic spectacles: the fashion show.

November 1990, Tokyo, the Comme des Garçons show. I am in the section toward the foot of the stage, choice seats reserved for foreign visitors. Last season in Paris, CDG had shown a collection that was uncharacteristically lighthearted, even jaunty, yet marked by CDG's distinctive stylistic oddities—the extra sleeve, the tortured shirring, the use of interfacing fabrics on the outside of the garment.

This time the show begins lyrically, with the sound of birds. Designer Rei Kawakubo says she wants to create an atmosphere of nostalgic beauty to distract us, if only momentarily, from our troubled worlds. Women file down the runway with powdered hair, enrobed in diaphanous layers of fabric printed with shapes of rocks and minerals or the patterns of stained glass. Some appear in soft shades of apricot and green, others in the CDG signature colors of black and navy. The tailoring innovation for this collection: hems that are gently rolled, instead of cut and stitched, producing a softer, unfinished look. Always there is the distinctive CDG asymmetry: one short sleeve and one long, hems that are off balance. The parade of soft shapes leads to the grand finale: Comme des Garçons Noir, the evening collection. White Grecian columns with sleeves that join in the back, brilliant red ball gowns with a voluminous pouch in front or dipping provocatively almost to the tailbone, sway down the runways. The combination of sturdiness and fragility, the surprise of such gentle beauty from a designer known for her uncompromising asceticism and intellectual toughness, the allure of a red so saturated it throbs—at moments like these, when staging and design come together, I feel Kawakubo can open up the audience, take our expectations and wrench them so that we leave disoriented and off balance. Again, Kawakubo has forced us to reappraise our assumptions about what counts as clothing, what counts as beauty.

The empowering touch. The searing touch. The wrenching touch.

ABOUT

PERFORMING RACE
IN FASHION AND THEATER

FACE

INTRODUCTION

the politics of pleasure

1 .

IT IS A BLEAK historical moment in which I write. Progressive forces seem increasingly embattled: affirmative action, the arts, public television, immigration, abortion rights, are being assailed with unprecedented brutality. Again, California stands at the vanguard of movements both progressive and regressive. Demographically, people of color will soon outnumber whites, and in response, the backlash to this statistical reality has been savagely "cutting-edge." Proposition 187, a de facto anti-Latino, anti-Asian move that enjoins the withholding of services to "illegal immigrants," resoundingly passed in the last election. The California Civil Rights Initiative, designed to protect the "civil rights" of straight white men against the evils of affirmative action, is on the ballot for the fall. White (usually male) students and colleagues seem to feel increasingly free to say and do the offensive, no doubt empowered by the muscular rhetoric of Gingrich and crew. Is this the last gasp of a threatened power structure whose days are numbered, or the beginning of the end of the progress hard won by disempowered groups—women, people of color, gays and lesbians, among others—since the 1960s?

On the level of the everyday, the situation seems overwhelming, and for me, this particular semester, with its constant battles against the forces of regression

3

in its many guises, has been especially exhausting. All of my colleagues of color, and perhaps especially the women of color, seem drained by the line of students outside our doors, by work speed-ups, by constant meetings and committees, and by the hostile political turn to the right. On one such exhausting day, I made my way to a reception for Chicana artists, part of a two-day conference organized by Chicana writer and cultural critic Alicia Gaspar de Alba. As I walked, I grumbled to myself that surely none of my white male counterparts was obligated to attend so many events. Yet upon finding some of my favorite colleagues at the reception, my mood began to brighten. As the multiple video monitors began to flicker, and as image after stunning image appeared on the central screen, my exhaustion melted. The work was riveting: Carmen Lomas Garza's depictions of everyday life, imbued with a mythic quality; Yolanda López's witty, subversive appropriations of La Virgen de Guadalupe; Delilah Montoya's provocative, disturbing photomontages of jars floating askew in panoramic landscapes or urban scenes. By the end of the show, the artists had transformed my disgruntlement into delight, fascination, intellectual and sensuous pleasure, a sense of renewed purpose. Critical, visually stunning, politically subversive, this art made me remember what is at stake when we talk about representation and aesthetic/political contestation. It is about challenging the dominant; it is about creating ourselves; it is about pleasure and joy; it is about empowerment; it is about giving life in a world bristling with so much that would kill the spirit.

In the present political climate, such life-giving moments seem increasingly few, and all the more precious for their rarity. The work of these Chicana artists, the feeling of community I treasure from Asian American theaters such as East West Players in Los Angeles, the strong voices of Asian American playwrights and actors, even Comme des Garçons's play with aesthetic convention, provide some of those moments of pleasure, shimmering moments full of life. As many analysts have noted, and as many people on the margins in one way or another know from experience, the world of representation and of aesthetics is a site of struggle, where identities are created, where subjects are interpellated, where hegemonies can be challenged. And taking seriously that pleasure, that life-giving capacity of aesthetics, performance, bodies, and the sensuous is, within our regime of power and truth, an indisputably political act.

4

In these essays, vignettes, and interviews, I explore the ways Japanese fashion and Asian American theater illuminate the politics of pleasure, the performance of race, and the possibilities for intervention in a regime of commodity capitalism. Conventionally, the disparate sites of fashion and theater, Japan and Asian Americans, would be the basis for two different books.[1] Though informed by ethnographic methods and attention to historical and cultural specificity, the juxtaposition of these multiple sites disrupts the premises of ethnographic writing defined by object of study and area, highlighting instead the theoretical frame, the political stakes, and the questions that animate my project. These questions center on the performance of identities and cultural politics: what counts as an effective intervention in our regimes of truth and, more specifically, how we disrupt an Orientalist hegemony; how we engage the complex politics of pleasure and of "resistance" when nothing is beyond commodification or beyond the dominant; how we theorize, live, and contest race, nation, and other collective identities in a world where these boundaries are being continuously transgressed, problematized, yet reasserted for complicated political ends.

Fashion and theater provide illuminating points of entry into this complex nexus of issues. At first glance each could be dismissed as a problematic domain of elite culture, yet these essays contend that both can offer opportunities for aesthetic/political contestation. Both are key arenas for the performance of identities, from the "individual" to the "national." Spectacle and staging are necessarily elements of each, whether on the theatrical stage, on a runway, or in the more mundane settings of everyday life, as we perform ourselves with the costumes, props, and theatrical conventions at our disposal. Accordingly, both fashion and theater highlight the performativity of gender, race, and nation. And through enacting/subverting familiar tropes of these and other identities, Japanese fashion and Asian American theater in turn become interventions—contestatory and/or problematic—in circulating Orientalist discourses.

In bringing together these disparate sites, this book writes a moment of transition. Just as my first book traced a movement from British social anthropology and interpretivism to poststructuralist theorizing of identities constructed in and through relations of power, so this book traces another set of transitions. *Crafting Selves* examined aesthetics, politics, and the production of identities on the shop floor, where production of artisanal and manufactured goods was simultaneously constitutive of gender and work identities. *About Face* retains those concerns with the aesthetics/politics nexus and the performance of identities in the realm of *cultural* production. The essays mark out shifting spaces in and between Asian and Asian American Studies, Anthropology, Cultural Studies, Performance Studies, and Theater. Motivated by ethnographic concerns and methods, this collection eschews the conventions of ethnographic writing and claims instead a site between Anthropology and Cultural Studies. Rhetorically, I engage the shorter form of the essay, interspersed with vignettes and an interview in order to disrupt the holistic pretensions of ethnography and to explore related issues at multiple levels, in multiple voices. My forays into theater speak all too eloquently of the limitations of academese, and these other modes of writing provide other registers in which to illuminate common themes. Throughout, *About Face* is predicated on an activist mode of inquiry, where academic writing as well as my creative work as dramaturge and fledgling playwright are intended as interventions in power-laden discourses.

Those interventions occur within a field defined by the hegemonic discourses of race and Orientalism. Though perhaps belaboring the obvious, it must be emphasized that Orientalist discourses are racial discourses, for Orientalist tropes figure "race" for Middle Eastern, Asian and Asian American subjects in the U.S. context. When "race" is enunciated at the contemporary historical moment, the black-white binary is immediately invoked, and race becomes the marked term designating "black" or "people of color," while "white" remains the unmarked site of privilege. Indeed, so deeply inscribed in the dominant imaginary is the black-white binary and the association of race with "blackness" that several readers suggested that the term "race" in my book title would lead the audience to believe that the book was about African Americans. There are, of course, important historical and ideological reasons for the persistent power of this binary,[2] but even though the constitution of the racial field in the U.S. cannot be thought without the defining polarity of black and white, its unquestioning reproduction inevitably erases the complexity of what is better figured as a changing matrix of racialization. Racial, gender, class, sexual, and national identities, among others, should be thought through together, as mutually constitutive and defining. In addressing the performative dimensions of Asian and Asian American identities and the racializing discourses they reproduce/undermine, *About Face* implicitly problematizes the black-white binary and essentialist notions of racial hierarchy, which create separate, bounded racial groups and place them on a single continuum along the black-white axis.

In addressing issues of race and performance one necessarily engages recent social constructivist, poststructuralist, and deconstructive approaches to identity formation that subvert fixed, essentialist notions of identity—a critically important political move if one's goal is to effect social transformation.[3] In such approaches, the forces constitutive of "the subject," including race, gender, and sexuality, are seen as socially, culturally, and historically specific categories that are always contested and in flux, rather than natural, foundational, or biological essences. The process of subject formation has in turn been described by Judith Butler (1990), redeploying the work of linguistic philosopher J. L. Austin (1975), as one of "performativity,"[4] where the enacting of identities in fact brings those identities into being, rather than expressing some predetermined essence. Butler proposed the notion of gender, sex, and sexuality as performatives that are constitutive—not merely attributes—of identity. These identities are reproduced or, as Derrida (1988) notes, cited, as repetitions of normative injunctions without which identities would be unthinkable. Performative citations are thus never merely the voluntary choices of a humanist subject; rather, they are the product of constitutive constraints that create identities, creative performances elicited under duress. Repeated iterations of identity can both consolidate its force and provide the occasion for its subversion (Butler 1993).

De-essentializing moves such as these historicize and politicize identity formation, and open up the processes of subject formation—themselves inseparable from gendering, racialization, sexualization, class formation—to potential change within the discursive possibilities present at a given historical moment. Within such a theoretical frame, identities such as "race" are unmoored from their seemingly biological foundations, becoming instead "an unstable and 'decentered' complex of social meanings constantly being transformed by political struggle" (Omi and Winant, 68). The most sophisticated of these approaches follows the articulation of multiple axes of power. Ann Stoler (1995), for example, reappraised the work of Foucault in order to make the crucial argument that the sexualized bourgeois subject described in *The History of Sexuality* is in fact an always already racialized subject. Indeed, the formation of this bourgeois subject is inextricable from—cannot be thought without— systems of colonial domination, for he/she is always already defined against the colonized, colored "others."

Some of the most vigorous theorizing of such multiplicity within historically specific power relations has come from the work of women of color; strikingly,

7

many of these analysts highlight the performativity of identity.[5] Gloria Anzaldúa's concept of the new *mestiza* (1987) as the "crossroads" where multiple lines of force meet, and her performative writing strategies that deploy multiple languages and genres have inspired a generation of feminist scholarship. Among more recent studies, Marta Savigliano demonstrates the complex imbrications of gender, class, race, sexuality, nation, colonialism, and political economy as they are brought to bear in the historical formation and global circulation of the tango. Here, both subject and text are performative. Some chapters take on the structure of a play or a memoir, others follow the conventions of analytic and theoretical academic writing. The book ends with an inspiring naming of women that acts as a rousing call to action and a performance of political solidarity. These works eloquently demonstrate that historically specific, political identities such as "race" and "nation" are themselves performative;[6] that is, they bring to life that to which they refer, rather than merely naming something already present.

Sue-Ellen Case (1995) further explores the political implications of the intersections of performance and identity. Invoking distinctions between "performance" and "performativity," "lesbian" and "queer," she marks the discursive shift between "performing lesbian," that assumes and invokes the "live" body and collective, grassroots political action premised on a politics of visibility, and "queer performativity," that would problematize assumptions of identity and visibility politics as essentialist, based on spurious ontological claims and a metaphysics of presence. Case wittily dissects two theorists of queer performativity, Eve Sedgwick and Judith Butler, arguing that for them, queer performativity evacuates politics of collective efficacy, replacing it with writing as performance and political action as writing. Though perhaps overstated—neither Sedgwick nor Butler eschew collective political action and both view political transformation as a goal of their theoretical work—Case highlights the dangers of confining one's interventions to academic textual production.

Further, Case marks a related shift in the fields of performance and theater studies: the critic's gaze, she argues, has moved from that of practitioner to that of spectator. If theatrical production as a collective project can be taken as a form of political action, then this is indeed a major cause for concern. My own experiences as a playwright and dramaturge illuminate for me the differences in what is at stake for the practitioner and for the academic critic. A practitioner's goal is an activist one: to create a better production within a set of limitations, including budget, time constraints, venue, and casting possibilities. The goal of how to make things better is uppermost; hers is not an exercise in criticism for the sake of demonstrating intellectual prowess. This stance informs my claim that Asian American theater can be a site for the performance of potentially enabling political identities, which should not be disdained as representing the end of the political, despite those critics who would dismiss social movements based on race, gender, and sexuality as mere identity politics. Rather, "the social construction of identity or the 'fixing' of racialized, gendered, and other subject positions within a given social order is not only political, it is also the precondition of politics" (Gregory, forthcoming). And the stakes we have in performing those identities arise from specific historical conditions and the specific social contexts within which we mount our interventions.

The identity "Asian American" is one instantiation of such specificity. It arose in the 1960s in conjunction with student activism around civil rights, New Left politics, and the Vietnam War. "Asian American" emerged as a political coalition that united under a single banner people from many different nations (including former historical rivals, antagonists, and colonizer/colonized), who were marked by different immigration histories and positioned differently with regard to class, gender, and sexuality, in order to combat the specific racisms that face "Asian Americans" in the United States.[7] In part, the term is a more politically vigorous replacement for "Oriental" and the latter's racist mystifications and exoticisms. The performative "Asian American" calls for a coalition; it interpellates new kinds of political subjects who are no longer "Orientals." In so doing, it names a utopian political hope articulated within a particular historical horizon.

Ineluctably, the racialized histories of Asian American subjects in this country shape what is at stake in this book. In particular, the "relocation" of Japanese Americans in concentration camps during World War II remains the signal historical event that informs my intellectual/political practice. Speaking about it at any length provokes profound feelings of rage and sorrow and defiance that are in and of the body in ways difficult to describe in words. My family and many others I know are all too familiar with Orientalist discourses that confuse "Japan" and "Japanese Americans" and the resulting destruction of Asian American lives. The conflation of Asian with Asian American and the racism Asian Americans face—one that, among its effects, fixes us in our seemingly ineffable foreignness—continues as one aspect of the reproduction

9

of larger structures of racial domination. Figurations of and violence against Asian Americans occur within specific geopolitical histories including the Korean War, the Vietnam War, the emergence of Japan as economic super-power, and postwar anti-Communist ideologies. Given this legacy, that which heightens the possibility of the confusion of Asian with Asian American raises for me the specter of relocation in truly visceral terms. Japan-bashing in any form does so even more obviously. Inevitably, my own political antennae are highly attuned to any of these moves.

Yet precisely because of this elision, the project of this book centers around the ways hegemonic representations, mostly of Japan, reverberate in both Asian and Asian American lives. Why, after all, must Asian Americans deny that there might be connections, in multiple forms, to their nations of origin? Are Americans of European descent compelled to deny these possible links? Yet so enduring is the legacy of racisms deployed against Asian Americans— again, relocation looms large here—even publicly admitting those possibilities can feel politically dangerous. The Orientalisms deployed vis-à-vis Asia still produce transnational effects, as continuing anti-Asian violence in the U.S. graphically demonstrates.

Consequently, for this particular authorial subject, the stakes are clear, and they lie in the potential for interrupting Orientalist hegemonies. Since the struc-tures of Orientalism have been widely described elsewhere,[8] I am concerned primarily with what I call counter-Orientalisms: specifically, the ways in which Asian American theater and Japanese fashion might mobilize this subversive potential. They create sites for the production and performance of contestatory wish-images in the form of racial, gender, national, and transnational identities. But the ways power works means that nothing can be pristinely separated from the dominant; consequently, one of the most inevitable, poignant, and problem-atic effects of domination occurs when subaltern peoples reproduce forms of their own oppression through self-Orientalizing[9] or what Marta Savigliano (1995) aptly termed "autoexoticizing." This autoexoticizing is never *merely* a reinscription of the dominant. Homi Bhabha (1987) argues that even when col-onized peoples imitate the colonizer, the mimesis is never complete, for the specter of the "not quite, not white" haunts the colonizer, a dis-ease that always contains an implicit threat to the colonizer's hegemony. This complexity—a con-tradictory contestation and reinscription of power that occurs simultaneously, in multiple registers—is critically important when we talk about the politics of pleasure.

10

Perhaps it is no accident that those who have written of the politics of pleasure are often people on the margins of race, sexuality, gender, class, and that our work occupies the margins of what counts as intellectually serious. In the early 1980s, Tania Modleski (1982) and Janice Radway (1984) initiated landmark investigations of women's pleasures in popular genres such as soap opera and romance fiction. These pastimes are far from purely contestatory—Modleski, for example, argues that soap opera and Harlequin romances may in fact interpellate women as appropriately gendered subjects through mobilizing utopian fantasies that at once provide tools for critique and reinforce patriarchal nuclear family structures. Furthermore, the soap format's interruption of continuity conditions the housewife/subject through the mimicry of the rhythms of her day. Yet these programs also supply what Modleski calls a negation of conventionally masculine modes of pleasure. Such feminist inquiry and work in cultural studies by analysts such as Stuart Hall (1992) convincingly problematize the idea of cultural politics as a zero-sum game, where any oppositional gesture is inevitably recuperated in the juggernaut of commodity capitalism. Modleski and others show the levels at which opposition can be both contestatory and complicit, and yet still constitute a subversion that matters. While avoiding an uncritical celebration of the popular, these analysts write against the pessimistic and ultimately, elitist moves of those who take their cue from the Adornian strains of the Frankfurt School and later Baudrillard, who exhibit an "anxiety of contamination" from the masses and whose dismissive stance indexes their own sites of privilege. Equally important, Modleski and Radway show us the ways gender has defined what counts as a worthy object of study.

Pleasure, when introduced into academic discourses, suggests the subversion of the intellectual privilege accorded to logic and abstraction. In the early 1970s, Roland Barthes attempted to theorize this oppositionality through an erotics of reading in *Le plaisir du texte*, among other works. A reaction to the confident systematicity of early "high" semiotics, including his own *Elements of Semiology* and *Writing Degree Zero*, Barthes sought to undermine the logic of the binary and the closed relation of signifier and signified, to focus instead on multiple meanings and the play of signifiers. In *Le plaisir du texte*, he explores reading as an exemplary site for this play, making an argument for reading strategies that subvert conventions and hence power relations. Tellingly, he differentiates *plaisir* (pleasure) and *jouissance* (bliss, "coming") according to the degree to which each disrupts convention; *le texte de plaisir* "contents, fills, grants euphoria; the text that comes from culture and does not break with it, is linked to a comfortable practice of reading," whereas *le texte de jouissance* "imposes a state of loss, the text that discomforts . . . unsettles the reader's historical, cultural, psychological assumptions, the consistency of his tastes, values, memories, brings to a crisis his relation with language" (14). Barthes links this distinction to the subject's experience of self as consistent, on the one hand (*plaisir*), and as enjoying and seeking the loss of self-consistent subjectivity on the other (*jouissance*). Barthes's strategy here is not the simple reinscription of a binary; rather, he refuses to posit an ontological gulf between pleasure and bliss, asserting them as polemical, heuristic distinctions that themselves can be mutable, blurry, incomplete (4). Further, both pleasure and bliss can disrupt assumptions about what counts as political and what counts as serious. In a witty critique of the hegemonies of psychoanalysis and orthodox Marxism, Barthes speaks of the political policeman and the psychoanalytical policeman:

> Futility and/or guilt, pleasure is either idle or vain, a class notion or an illusion. . .Pleasure is continually disappointed, reduced, deflated, in favor of strong, noble values: Truth, Death, Progress, Struggle, Joy, etc. Its victorious rival is Desire: we are always being told about Desire, never about Pleasure; Desire has an epistemic dignity, Pleasure does not. It seems that (our) society refuses (and ends up by ignoring) bliss to such a point that it can produce only epistemologies of the law (and of its contestation), never of its absence, or better still: of its nullity. Odd, this philosophical permanence of Desire (insofar as it is never satisfied): doesn't the word itself denote a "class notion"? (A rather crude presumption of proof, and yet noteworthy; the "populace" does not know Desire—only pleasures.) (57–8).

We can find Barthes's notions of *plaisir* and *jouissance* useful for theorizing an erotics of the production of meaning that disrupts the univocality of the sign, the reification of binarisms as the foundation for a science of meaning, the conventions of what counts as politically and intellectually serious, and the psychoanalytic and philosophical privileging of Transcendental Desire. However, we must eschew the next step Barthes himself made: projecting these zones of resistance to univocal meanings and hermeneutic desires onto the "Orient" as "antitext to the West" (Lowe 159) in new permutations of Orientalism, developments Lisa Lowe analyzes in her *Critical Terrains*. In his struggles to transcend the strictures of conventional signification, Barthes figures the Orient as a space of resistance to logical binarisms, redeploying overdetermined, power-laden Orientalist tropes of inscrutability, mysticism, and imperviousness to rationality in service of his critique of semiology. Precisely by engaging with contradictions such as those exemplified in Barthes's work, *About Face* compels scrutiny of the complexities of a cultural politics of pleasure.

Such a politics clearly animates the construction of racialized identities for people of color. Paul Gilroy (1993) and Stuart Hall (1992) make a passionately convincing case for the centrality of music, performance, movement, and the inscription of bodies through dress and style as sites of pleasure and of identity formation in the Black diaspora. In a regime of plantation slavery and forced labor, these were among the few domains of creativity permissible, and their legacy remains vibrant. Cornel West (in Dent 1992) and Gina Dent (1992) speak of Black pleasure, Black joy, as generative of Black identities and Black popular culture through its articulation of critical consciousness. West contrasts pleasure, associated with the individual, the sexual, the market and commodification, to joy, a collective experience suffused by the nonmarket values of love and care. Dent locates West's formulations within a larger feminist and psychoanalytic discussion of pleasure, as an intervention that places those discussions "within a black progressive context" (2). I would agree with West that the "pleasures" provided by the culture industries are inextricable from the forces of the market and of commodification, but I am suspicious of the attempt to posit a domain of precapitalist, nonmarket values. This pastoral trope oversimplifies for rhetorical purposes, missing both the potential contestation implicit in pleasure and the fact that even "joy" now occurs fully within a commodity capitalist regime. Consequently, I seek to reclaim pleasure as a site of potential contestation that might engage, and at times be coextensive with, the critical impulse. How we dress, how we move, the music that accompanies our daily activities and that we create and refashion, our engagement with—and not simply the passive consumption of—media or commodities, do matter and can be included in a repertoire of oppositional strategies.

Pleasure, aesthetics, and popular culture can all motivate a cultural politics that makes a difference. They can be part of what gets you through the day, what my mother calls "giving you a lift." All those who analyze so-called popular culture, moral and political evaluations notwithstanding, must minimally attempt to account for the "fun" and the "lift" that such activities provide. To treat "pleasure" seriously is not to say that all pleasures are equal. Nor is it to stifle critical appraisals; indeed, my intent is the opposite. The term "subversion" itself implies that transcendent "liberation" from power relations is illusory, for some degree of complicity with the dominant is inevitable. Criticism thus

13

becomes even more necessary as a way to understand our complicities and the effectiveness of our interventions. For example, we are inevitably enmeshed in consumer capitalism, but this should not prevent us from pushing ourselves to create more vigorous and contestatory representations on-stage or to work on multiple fronts to transform hegemonic structures. Such modes of critique are essential in studying fashion and theater. The "pleasure" we experience in images, spectacle, narrative, among other domains, can be seductive, insidious, empowering. Sometimes these qualities are mutually exclusive; most often, they coexist in varying degrees in the same work. A strategically deployed critical consciousness would require a sensitivity to this complexity, and to the multiple, contradictory levels at which we appropriate these cultural forms.

Critical sensitivity becomes especially urgent when we speak of fashion and theater, requiring careful attention to both their commonalities and their specificities. It is fashion that is the more obviously problematic, a highly fraught arena for a discussion of cultural politics and pleasure. The moral indignation on all sides regarding questions of clothing and cosmetics, the disciplines and punishments surrounding ideals of beauty, clearly index a (barely acknowledged) preoccupation with fashion, appearance, and bodily surfaces. Two recent examples offer eloquent testimony to the persistence of familiar preconceptions about fashion as a purely problematic domain: Robert Altman's film *Prêt-à-Porter* (*Ready to Wear*), and my own encounters with numerous colleagues around the idea for this book.

Prêt-à-Porter presents a conventionally masculinist take on fashion. A farce set amidst the high dramas of the Paris collections, Altman portrays the fashion world as motivated by vanity, greed, and status-seeking; the film's recurrent motif of people inadvertently stepping into dog feces symbolizes their corruption. Various plots and subplots emphasize superficiality, corporate rapacity, and homophobic stereotypes, culminating in a fashion show put on by a designer played by Anouk Aimée, whose company has just been sold against her will. She sends a parade of naked women out onto the runway. At first, this shocks the audience into silence. Tentatively, they begin to applaud and then burst into cheers in a 1990s version of "The Emperor's New Clothes." Here Altman tells us quite literally that there is nothing to fashion. Kim Basinger's character, a fashion reporter, stands in for Altman as she exclaims to the camera in exasperation, "What the hell am I talkin' about? What the hell is going on here? . . . Is

14

that fashion? Is there a message out there? I've been forever trying to find out what this bullshit is all about, and you know what? I have had it!" Altman has "had it" and doesn't understand "what this is all about" precisely because he never ventures beyond the conventional wisdom. Superficiality, status jockeying, greed, and vanity of course abound among the fashion pack, making it ripe for parody; indeed, some of the most interesting examples have been mounted from within, as the work of the late Franco Moschino testifies. Tellingly, Altman pays no attention whatsoever to the clothes, which become mere elements of set decoration. He cannot see the craft of fashion, that garments can actually have intellectual, aesthetic, and sensuous dimensions. And it is this contradiction—that aesthetics, craft, and intelligence can coexist with, because of, or in spite of superficiality and commercialism—that makes fashion so compelling an object of study, emblematic of cultural production in late capitalism. In the end, *Prêt-à-Porter* is a film made by a man who knows and cares nothing about clothing, an ignorance itself overdetermined in terms of gender and sexuality. This masculine gaze reinscribes the conventional binaries of surface and depth, appearance and reality, and holds in suspicion those of us who are recognizably feminine gendered subjects. Can you wear lipstick and still think? Can you care about design, color, texture, cut, draping, drafting techniques, display—that is, about clothes—and still be political? Of course, concern with the aesthetic production of the subject reinscribes certain class and gender stereotypes. The mistake is in thinking that the other position—ostensibly not caring about clothing or appearance, which in itself is a form of preoccupation with appearance—is politically innocent. Such a position is overdetermined in terms of its reinscription of masculinities, and, as some women of color (both gay and straight) would argue, of race. After all, who can afford to be unconcerned about his/her appearance? Who is *allowed* to ignore it with impunity?

That fashion marks a terra incognita for some academics was vividly brought home to me when I discussed with various colleagues my intentions to bring together essays on fashion and theater in a single book. Some were completely nonplussed. "What do fashion and theater have to do with each other?" they mused. Another common variation on a theme went something like this: "Theater is definitely interesting, but *fashion*. . ." Strikingly, most of the negative reactions came from straight men. My conjecture is that they are the members of our culture who are less accustomed to thinking of fashion as performance. This is not to say that all heterosexual men were unsupportive of this project—far from it. Yet the pattern seems too insistent simply to ignore.

Gender, sexuality, and race may condition the degree to which we are conscious of the ways we perform ourselves in everyday life, of the ways fashion and theater perform *us*.

Challenging conventional presuppositions, I make political claims in this book specifically for the work of the "Japanese designers." Especially in the early 1980s, they led us to question what counts as clothing: rethinking the relationship of clothing to bodies; disrupting the boundaries between fashion and art, fashion and architecture, fashion and sculpture; enabling different kinds of gender performances. Clothing can have a political edge as signifiers of subcultural style and as components of ethnic/racial pride; indeed, I would argue that in the early 1980s Japanese clothing design enabled a valorization and eroticizing of Asian bodies as stylish in a contemporary way, rather than merely exotic or an inadequate imitation of Western bodies. Speaking of Asian design rather than Asian production interrupts some of the Eurocentric assumptions most Europeans and Americans hold about the primacy of European design and the "imitativeness" of the Japanese and other Asians. Indeed, this is in part responsible for my focus on production at the level of design. More generally, at times the surfaces of the body are the most readily available sites for inscribing resistance, and some of us on the margin want to say that style is one battleground among many others.

Yet of course the fashion world is politically problematic. The battleground of style is suffused, indeed constituted, by commodification. The garment industry is deeply enmeshed in an intense semiotics of distinction and a global assembly line on which many Third World women and men toil—both in the Third World and in the implosive diaspora of the Third World in the first, as the recent raids on Southern California sweatshops only further confirm. The fashion and cosmetics industries promote aesthetic ideals that often oppressively reinscribe normative codes of gender, race, class, and sexuality. Fashion's planned obsolescence is inseparable from complicity with capitalist production and the mobilization of desire. Such complications demand a critical, multilayered consideration of fashion's contradictory implication in a politics of pleasure, avoiding the temptations of dismissive condemnation, on the one hand, and power-evasive celebration, on the other.

16

Like fashion, theater is a contradictory site of pleasure and contestation. "Theater" is itself a diverse phenomenon, encompassing many kinds of venues, artists, and levels of accessibility; it matters centrally who is writing, who is performing in what venue for what audience. With the present cuts in funding for the arts, mainstream theater has become increasingly safe, conservative, geared to please the upper-middle-class white audiences who are its principal supporters. The Tony Awards for 1995 were an example; only two new musicals were nominated in the Best Musical category, while nominees proliferated in the categories for Best Revival of a Play and Best Revival of a Musical. Two new hits and major Tony award winners of the 1996 season are notable exceptions: *Bring in 'Da Noise, Bring in 'Da Funk* and *Rent*. Both have been heralded as potentially revitalizing the creatively moribund Broadway stage. Both plays claim origins "downtown": the Public Theater/New York Shakespeare Festival and the New York Theater Workshop, respectively. However, despite the claims for novelty made in critical commentary on these plays, both belong to a genre—the musical—that tends to deflect attention from the political and from sharp social criticism through mobilizing the seductive pleasures of music, spectacle, and dance. Indeed, this may even be more obvious when the themes of the play are overtly political.[10] In *Rent*, the devastation of AIDS and the oppressive poverty of many who live in the East Village are romanticized and commodified as "style" in this modern reprise of *La Bohème*,[11] while *Bring in 'Da Noise, Bring in 'Da Funk*, a refiguration of the American musical that brilliantly stages a political history of African Americans through music and tap, inevitably re-presents the safely contained spectacle of African American men dancing. Despite the appearance of these new works on Broadway, mainstream theater's reliance on the relatively sure bet and the deemphasizing of the political often results in aesthetic and political conservatism, producing entertaining spectacles that cater to the largely white, middle-class audience's comfortable expectations. Such conservatism has heightened as entertainment industry conglomerates move into Broadway; exemplary here is Disney's *Beauty and the Beast*. Mainstream theater and its association with "high culture" can give audiences the titillating sense that they are viewing something on a higher plane than either Hollywood movies, Las Vegas, or television, while in reality relying on the devices of spectacle and on familiar tropes and narratives, rarely providing work that challenges either artist or audience.

A similar disturbing tendency has emerged given current discourses on multiculturalism. Though arts funding may still be available for work of this kind, mainstream regional theaters seem to garner the lion's share of the grants, while smaller theaters run by artists of color remain in precarious financial straits. Mainstream theaters may present work authored by such artists, but more often work about people of color is written and/or directed by white play-wrights and directors. Though one might see this optimistically as a step in a historical process, such a policy has unfortunately acted to reinforce dominant views of people of color. Multicultural initiatives of this kind can provide jobs for many actors of color, yet all too often they are employed in the service of a vision not of their own making. Further, the historical climate is such that even uttering this criticism can and is used to argue against mounting any produc-tions that involve multiracial diversity. Caught between appropriation of "our stories," on the one hand, and a retreat into whiteness and Eurocentricity in the guise of "universality" on the other, self-authored representations by people of color are still painfully rare in mainstream theater.

This is the larger context in which we must view Asian American theater and productions such as David Henry Hwang's *M. Butterfly* and Anna Deavere Smith's *Twilight: Los Angeles 1992*. No production is ever perfect or beyond complicity; in these cases, one could argue that *M. Butterfly* inevitably rein-scribes the very trope it is contesting, while *Twilight* appeals to a liberal humanist notion of telling all sides of a story. Yet in a milieu deadened by safe revivals, sheer spectacle, digestible entertainment, and the erasure or margin-alization of minority-discourse perspectives, these productions make key inter-ventions. They mount political critiques from the points of view of artists of color, who tell stories from those of us who have been erased from representa-tion on a major stage. This edge of critique heightens the importance of work done in smaller theaters dedicated to producing work by artists of color. For Asian Americans, these include venues such as East West Players in Los Angeles, Asian American Theater Company in San Francisco, Northwest Asian American Theater in Seattle, Theater Mu in Minneapolis, and Pan-Asian Repertory in New York. Often, these theaters have a community base; all serve as sites for the performance and production of Asian American identities.[12]

Perhaps this is especially true for theater specifically: for all the difficulties of funding and the potential high price of a ticket, it remains a relatively wel-coming site for *artists*. Performance artists, for example, need little more than their voices, bodies, and a few props, making this performance genre far more realizable than even the lowest-budget film. Despite the disturbing tendencies toward conservatism overall, theater can also accommodate work that is more aesthetically and politically cutting-edge than can the mainstream film indus-try. For example, Tony Kushner's *Angels in America*, an epic play about history, AIDS, compassion, and new forms of kinship, enjoyed a long run on Broadway and has been widely produced in mainstream regional theaters across the country, but it is inconceivable that it would have first been made as a Hollywood film. Theater and performance constitute a prime site for intervention from people "on the margins": formally, through disrupting generic conventions, but more important, through subverting hegemonic figurations of race, gender, and sexuality.[13]

Finally, a focus on fashion and theater compels a scrutiny of our own assumptions as subjects constructed through a particular disciplinary apparatus. In the disciplines of theater and drama, for example, Asian American performance and Japanese fashion can offer valuable critiques of the concept of universality that remains pervasive in the arts. Too often, "universality" is reified as the ultimate aesthetic goal, enshrining conventional notions of art as a transcendent realm apart from history, politics, and society. Indeed, despite the many extant academic critiques of universality, invoking issues of social context and power in theater circles still can elicit counterclaims that such issues are merely "sociological" and fail to grasp the purity of the aesthetic domain. The reification of the aesthetic and its separation from the "practical" stuff of economics, politics, and history have quite material consequences when the values imputed to that binary are reversed: for example, the dismissal of the arts as nonfunctional, a view that justifies the general impoverishment of artists, Federal budget cuts and the draconian downsizing of the National Endowment for the Arts.[14] The discourse of aesthetic transcendence, then, can possess highly repressive political and material effects.

"Universality" is further deployed in drama to signify a notion of the transhistorically Human, emblematized by the work of Shakespeare or classic Greek drama. Such a position reifies the liberal humanist subject and forecloses understandings of the historically, culturally specific contexts in which plays and other aesthetic forms are produced. Rather than fixed and universal, such work might better be understood as *translatable* and *appropriable* in the present historical moment. Plays conventionally deemed to have universal appeal are those that can attract large (i.e., white) audiences. The discourse on universality in theater, like its analogues in other disciplines, operates to disguise the elision of "universal" with "white" or "European." The universal as a transhistorical category marks the place of the Master Subject and deflects critical consideration of such a Subject's always already historically, culturally, and racially specific meanings and positionings. Though both "Japanese designers" and "Asian American theater artists"—formed as they/we are by such discourses—themselves deploy notions of universality to indicate wide appeal, our inquiry will interrogate such notions, suggesting that the work of these cultural producers in fact problematizes notions of the universal as a place of transcendence and as a place of whiteness.

For anthropology, fashion and theater provoke reflection on disciplinary conventions, including the defining disciplinary practice of ethnographic field-work. Neither site constitutes "the field" as the faraway site of "the primitive." Both are phenomena of metropolitan centers around the globe: the field here becomes our everyday lives. Each subverts the dynamic of "studying down"— focusing on a place/group/class "less developed" than one's own—so integral to contemporary social science and conventionally, at least, to anthropological practice. Though in each case the ethnographer has the final authority of inscription, the upper-class milieu of high fashion and the sense of collective struggle in Asian American theater construct power relations very different from the archetypal neocolonial anthropological fieldwork project.

Such challenges to foundational categories and practices can bear further implications for the way we write. I have elsewhere (1990) problematized the binaries theory/experience, theory/ethnography, arguing instead for the notion of theory as enactment, locating theory in writing practices and in what we call style. Recently (1996), I advocated a move to performative ethnography, in which performance is accorded status as ethnographic practice, and in which ethnographies, through performance conventionally defined and through per-formative writing strategies, can count as theory and as political. For example, the ephemerality of performance in theater and fashion reveal the limits of aca-demic discourses premised on fixity and the primacy of the written text. For adherents of poststructuralist theory, the dictum of "no fixed text," philosophical verities such as the intentional fallacy, in which authorial intention never guar-antees meaning, take on material weight in the context of fashion and theater. Performance onstage or on the runway can never be captured fully by the text, the camera, or the word; for example, even a videotape of a performance frames it in ways particular to the framing apparatus itself and to the circumstances of filming. Ephemerality distinguishes theatrical performance from film and video, our mechanically reproduced, high-tech texts. Similarly, in its ceaseless changes, fashion resists any attempt at totalization or at fixing an analytic object. By the time these words appear in published form, some features of fashion will already be out of date, and the object of investigation will have shifted. This defining elusiveness gives rise to what Peggy Phelan (1993) tellingly calls *mourning*, born of the yearning to recapture the evanescent.[15] Writing about performance is inevitably an attempt to assuage this yearning. In short, both theater and fashion occasion reflection on the totalizing gesture implicit in all attempts at writing about performance, including ethnographic ones,[16] and on the academic privilege accorded the textual object.

Similarly, theater and fashion disrupt the notion of fieldwork as a continuous sojourn in a single locale. Instead, both require intensive, short-term investigations, sometimes in widely scattered parts of the globe. For me, this meant spending time between 1989 and 1993 in Tokyo, New York, Paris, San Francisco, and Los Angeles, among other sites, engaging in intensely focused activities as a fashion professional might: sales exhibitions, the collections in Paris and Tokyo, visits to boutiques and other retail outlets, interviews, fashion and video archives, in addition to the traditional anthropological fieldwork practice of "hanging out." Geographic dispersal shifts the focus from a single culture, anthropology's Master Trope, to what has been called the transnational, especially to transnational circuits of capital, and to cultures in the plural. *About Face* attempts to recapitulate through the invocation of multiple sites and voices the dispersed yet interconnected movements of fashion, and the intensive, sporadic nature of fieldwork required to study both fashion and theater.

A more radical development in ethnographic practice is the emergence of feminist, minority, and postcolonial critiques, which refigure the field in both senses: the constitution of the discipline itself, and its defining practice, fieldwork. The notion of fieldwork as a long sojourn in a distant and "primitive" place is even further problematized when those who were formerly objects of study become its authors. In such cases, fieldwork can become, in Kamala Visweswaran's words, "homework" (1994), a critical scrutiny of our own sites of enunciation. *About Face* is intended precisely as a kind of homework, an intervention in Orientalist discourses that shape Asian and Asian American subjectivities, racial formations, and the horizon of our possibilities.

Historical shifts in the academy, including the critiques of objectivity mounted in many disciplines, the emergence of ethnic studies, feminist theory, postcolonial critiques, cultural studies, neo-Marxism and some forms of post-structuralism and deconstruction, mark the recognition that all scholarship is political, embedded in systems of knowledge/power. I noted elsewhere (1986) that the position of the so-called objective observer is often merely distant, unsympathetic, and far from innocent with respect to power. Poststructuralist theory shows us that performance, in its moves to unfix, historicize, and render contingent the Transcendental Signified, can be deployed in the service of progressive political aims. However, I want to push these claims further, to argue that performance can be part of a radical political practice in other ways. For example, as the final essay argues, theatricality and hyperbole can animate protest, becoming one strategy in a repertoire of political action. Above all, this book argues for theater and performance as sites for political intervention and the articulation of new kinds of political identities. The claiming of a political identity such as Asian American, queer, woman of color, can be both subversive of the dominant and dangerous, even life-threatening, for those who make those claims. Yet, critically important as these articulations can be, Angela Davis (1996) reminds us that it is not enough simply to inhabit an identity, no matter how contestatory. Rather, these political subjectivities should be mobilized in ways that enable us to work in alliance for social transformation, as the last chapter explicitly argues.

In this light, I view my work with Asian American and multiracial theater as that of a partner in struggle, where I am both participant and observer, both an analyst and someone who has worked on theatrical productions. Writing ethnography in such a context becomes an inscription of Asian American and multiracial cultural production into official, scholarly histories, while critical appraisal becomes all the more urgent in order to make things better collectively. Far from compromising one's (always already spurious) "objectivity," I would argue that such a stance simply renders explicit the political stakes we all have in our projects, wittingly or not.

Certainly, my own experiences in the theater highlight for me the urgency of what is at stake. For example, my work as a dramaturge on Anna Deavere Smith's *Twilight: Los Angeles 1992*—a play about the L.A. uprisings[17]—mirrored for me the possibilities for multiracial collaboration in a nation increasingly "of color." Our collaborative process eloquently addressed the possibilities for creative oppositional ethnography across races, invoking a model of political coalition fraught with difficulty and hard work, a struggle by turn daunting, painful, and inspirational, but above all necessary. Given this historical horizon, scholarly writing and my creative work as fledgling playwright and as dramaturge become multiple modalities for forming urgently necessary political alliances, emblematized in terms such as Asian American and people of color. In that spirit of collective work and collective struggle I offer the essays in this book.

The sequential logic of the following chapters is shaped by questions of cultural politics. The first section, "Orientalisms," introduces the complex contestations/reinscriptions of the racialized discourses of Orientalism as they circulate in the domains of theater and fashion. I argue that David Henry Hwang's *M. Butterfly* made a critical intervention in American theater at the moment of its appearance on the Broadway stage in 1988. It subverts the insistent Orientalist trope of *Madama Butterfly*, providing an acute refiguration of the humanist subject upon which the Puccini opera is based, supplying us with critical tools we can use in order to appraise currents in feminist deconstructive literary criticism. The companion piece, "Orientalizing: Fashioning 'Japan,'" articulates the contradictory cultural politics suffusing tropes of race, nation, and the transnational in the fashion industry. Japanese designers find themselves essentialized in racial and national terms, while they themselves both contest and reproduce these identities. Orientalisms, counter-Orientalisms, self-Orientalizing, circulate and intertwine in multiple transnational sites. I examine the construction of what counts as *Paris*, Wim Wenders's film on Yohji Yamamoto, and Japanese fashion journalism in order to explore these multiplicities.

Section Two, "Consuming Gender, Race, and Nation" focuses on fashion as exemplifying a cultural politics rife with paradox, emblematic of commodity capitalist regimes. "The Limits of the Avant-garde" examines the enmeshment of avant-garde aesthetic contestation with capitalist appropriation through an analysis of the historical trajectory of the runway shows mounted by Comme des Garçons. In many ways, Comme des Garçons and the other so-called avant-garde designers offered possibilities for different figurations of gender and forced a rethinking of clothing conventions in the early 1980s. They mounted an always already racialized critique of European assumptions about bodies, about the relation between fashion and other domains, about clothing itself. Yet these challenges cannot escape more general problems that haunt the avant-garde, for its claims of originality, revolution, and novelty are both necessarily limited and readily appropriated as forms of elitist, marketable difference. "Fabricating Masculinity" articulates the constitutive contradictions of Japanese identity through a striking ad campaign for domestic business suits mounted by Comme des Garçons. Japan in the late 1980s and early 1990s was indisputably a first-world, capitalist power. Nonetheless, it remains racially marked, and those markings are in turn inseparable from gender and nation. The ad campaign for a "Japanese suit" adroitly links a specifically Japanese masculinity and masculine body with a place in the geopolitical order, provid-

23

ing us a point of entry into an extended analysis of race, gender, nation, and recent theoretical writings on transnationalism, especially the work of Paul Gilroy and Arjun Appadurai. In these two sections, I intersperse illustrative vignettes among the essays in order to underscore arguments made in the more analytic chapters and to raise questions of cultural politics in a vivid, more experiential register.

Like Japanese fashion, Asian American theater inevitably highlights figurations of race and more obviously opens possibilities for subverting hegemonic racial tropes. Accordingly, "Strategies of Intervention" come to the fore in Part Three. Each essay deploys a different tactic.[18] In the first, Perry Miyake's *Doughball* discursively creates the "authenticity" of "home" and "community" for Japanese Americans. As in the first essay on *M. Butterfly*, my analysis of *Doughball* becomes a point of entry into arguments against forms of feminist theorizing that would marginalize issues of race, nation, Orientalism, and geopolitics. An interview with playwright David Henry Hwang looks at theater, politics, and the creative process from the point of view of a prominent Asian American artist. The final chapter examines organized political activism and the critique of the politics of representation in several cultural productions: Asian American interventions around the Orientalist plays *Miss Saigon* and *The Mikado*, and the novel and film *Rising Sun*. At issue here is the construction of "Asian American" as an explicitly political subjectivity mobilized in service of organized efforts to effect political change. The stage and the screen are sites for the insidious, historically specific recirculation of dominant representations of Asian Americans, and they also offer possibilities for interrupting and challenging such hegemonies. Yet performance in the sense of cultural practice requires a wider critical ambit. I go on to argue that ongoing battles over the politics of representation must be carried on in multiple registers on multiple fronts: from the transnational to the local, from creative and critical work to organized protest and local institutional interventions.

Finally, what about "face"? To capture succinctly my concerns with Japan, Asian Americans, fashion, theater, identity, and cultural politics seemed virtually impossible, but after months of pondering *About Face* seemed both polysemous and suggestive. Face can be taken as the stereotypic "Oriental" trope, signifying a presumed Asian preoccupation with social reputation; this is the title's most problematic aspect. Perhaps its problematic nature is especially appropriate given the book's emphasis on the contradictory (contestatory and complicit) nature of cultural politics. Face simultaneously evokes the fashion world, beauty, and cosmetics, and thus the socially constructed persona: think of Madonna's assertion in "Vogue," "Rita Hayworth gave good face." Indeed, I was recently amused to see three uses of "about face" in the cosmetics industry: an "E!"-Entertainment Network broadcast on facials and skin care; an advertisement for a local plastic surgeon, whose "patient supermodel" urges readers to call in for "About Face," a video on facial surgery; and a *Los Angeles Times* article on a new line of cosmetics promoted by makeup artist Laura Mercier (Drake 1996). Face is our primary external, bodily locus of identity, as David Henry Hwang's farce of mistaken racial identities, *Face Value*, suggests. For him, face as skin color literally masks a more genuine and vulnerable self. In its more liberatory senses, face signifies the construction of new, contestatory identities by people on the margins, as exemplified in Gloria Anzaldúa's anthology, *Haciendo Caras/Making Face, Making Soul* (1990). Chinese Filipino gay playwright and performance artist Han Ong further elaborates this concept:

> One of the reasons I write is because I want to create images or versions of myself and confer upon them a kind of earthbound, weighty, specific, dirt-under-the fingernails reality. I don't see myself or anyone like me in the literature and TV and movies that I see . . .
> I feel like a Magritte painting of a bowler hat and a suit with no face. I feel that with each piece I write, I'm giving myself shape and weight and dimension. I'm so invisible right now that I have to write and write and keep writing—there's never enough.
> I have an Asian schoolboy's face. I'd like to have a face that represents me better. My face is "cute" and boyish, and I'm cynical and grainy and have an edge to me. I wish I had Leonard Cohen's face—or Marianne Faithfull's. Or Abbey Lincoln's. I think one of the reasons I write so much is that I don't have the face I deserve.
> Or I don't have the physicality I deserve. So I'm trying to give myself what I feel I deserve by dint of writing. I'm writing my face. Does that make sense? (Huygen, 39–40).

I would suggest that it does, and that those of us on the margins are trying to "write our faces" with the tools at our disposal: theater, design, cultural production, political organizing, academic writing. Our faces, in turn, can speak back to Orientalist hegemonies. Finally, about-face denotes a one-hundred-eighty-degree reversal of direction during a military march. Perhaps we can appropriate this term in our own battles over representation. Our utopian desire is that writing "about face" could trip up the continuing forward march of the hegemonies shaping our lives, forcing them to veer slightly, stumble, and perhaps eventually make a full "about-face." At stake is the hope that our interventions, however small, will one day enable subversions that matter.

ENDNOTES

1. A few works have begun to explore the interconnections among these sites. See Joel Kaplan and Sheila Stowell (1994), who examine the interconnections between theater and fashion in Britain at the turn of the century up to World War I. This book treats topics such as actresses' wardrobes, plays that thematize fashion, and contemporary (Edwardian) feminist takes on the interrelations of theater, fashion, and gender construction. A variety of works have begun to explore the links between Asians and Asian Americans, including Aihwa Ong (1995) and a special forthcoming issue of *positions: east asia, cultures, critique*, edited by Elaine Kim and Lisa Lowe.

2. For more extended discussions in recent writings on race, see Tricia Rose and Andrew Ross, eds. (1995) and Steven Gregory and Roger Sanjek, eds. (1995).

3. For an excellent account of what is at stake politically in poststructuralist theory, see Chris Weedon, *Feminist Practice and Poststructuralist Theory* (1987). See also my "Poststructuralist Theory as Political Necessity" (1995).

4. Numerous recent works in theater and performance studies take up questions of performance and performativity. Among the anthologies organized around these themes are: Sue-Ellen Case, ed. *Performing Feminisms* (1990); Case, Brett, and Foster, eds. *Cruising the Performative* (1995); Case and Reinelt, eds. *The Performance of Power* (1991); Hart and Phelan, eds. *Acting Out: Feminist Performances* (1993); Roach and Reinelt, eds. *Critical Theory and Performance* (1992). An anthology that considers the relationship between literary/philosophical appropriations of "performativity" and studies of performance is Andrew Parker and Eve Sedgwick, eds. *Performativity and Performance* (1995). For another insightful analysis of performance and performativity, see Jill Dolan, "Geographies of Learning: Theater Studies, Performance, and the 'Performative,'" in *Theater Journal* (December 1993).

5. For a more extended discussion of such work in anthropology, see Kondo (1996).

6. On this point, see Judith Butler's discussion of the work of Slavoj Žižek: "Arguing with the Real" in *Bodies That Matter*. See also Ernesto Laclau and Chantal Mouffe, *Hegemony and Socialist Strategy*.

7. For a history of the Asian American movement, see William Wei (1993). He notes that the conventional genealogy attributing a singular origin to the Third World strike at San

Francisco State in 1968 elides a far more complex history with multiple points of origin. Sucheng Chan (1991) also notes the bureaucratic usage of the term, in addition to its links to student activism. "Asian American" was taken up by the government census bureau and combined with "Pacific Islander"; consequently, the term "Asian Pacific American" or "Asian/Pacific Islander" is sometimes used in both bureaucratic and extra-bureaucratic settings.

8. In the wake of Edward Said's *Orientalism* (1978), numerous related works have appeared, detailing the processes of contesting/reinscribing Orientalisms in the Middle East and South Asia. For East Asia, see especially Lisa Lowe, *Critical Terrains*.

9. Some might argue that such a concept is an impossibility; i.e., that Orientalism is a power-laden discourse overdetermining the processes of so-called "self-Orientalizing," and to deploy such a term would be a form of blaming the victim.

10. For example, the issues of homosexuality and political repression in *Kiss of the Spider Woman* become subordinated to the dazzling theatricality of Chita Rivera's dancing and singing. And as Kerry Walk pointed out to me, Dickens's acute social commentary in *Oliver Twist* becomes similarly sanitized and romanticized in the musical *Oliver*.

11. Bloomingdale's recently advertised a line of clothing worn by the cast of *Rent*. The complicity of fashion and theater in the service of commodification could not be more eloquently enacted; in the advertising photographs and copy, East Village poverty is coded as young, hip style. The ad states: "It's the hands-down hit of the season. An anthem for hope, love and living in the city. . . See our Necessary Objects clothes by Ady Gluck-Frankel, worn here by members of the cast, Only at Bloomingdale's, on 2, 59th Street & Lexington Avenue," in the *New York Times*, May 8, 1996: A7.

12. For critical work on the staging of Asian American identities, see James Moy (1993) and Karen Shimakawa (1995).

13. Numerous analysts have analyzed and documented such interventions, taking various stands on their effectiveness. See, for example, Jill Dolan (1988), David Román (forthcoming), James Moy (1993), Kondo (1995), and special issues of *Theater Journal* on theater of color (38.4, December 1986), theater and hegemony (41.4, December 1989) and feminism (40.2, May 1988), among others.

14. For an historical analysis of the place of the arts and the aesthetic in Western societies, see Janet Wolff, *The Social Production of Art* (1981).

15. There is a danger here of reifying performance as a form of the transcendental sublime, one Henry Sayre (1989) notes in relation to the oral poetry movement and their enshrining of the human breath as that which could never be reproduced. It is a classic instantiation of the metaphysics of presence so aptly critiqued in the work of Jacques Derrida (1976). Moreover, W. B. Worthen argues that the celebratory notions of performance promulgated in Performance Studies themselves depend upon conventional notions of the relationship between text and performance, which contrast "performance (transgressive, multiform, revisionary) to the (dominant, repressive, conventional, and canonical)

27

domain of the 'text' " (14). At issue, Worthen points out, is the way that texts "are construed as vessels of authority, of canonical value, of hegemonic consensus" (ibid.). It is this hegemonic valorization of the text in literary studies, drama, philosophy, and other disciplines, that prompts my own strategic emphasis on performance as a privileged site of study.

16. There is of course an extensive anthropological literature on performance, primarily the study of ritual, and in ethnomusicology, a list far too long to cite exhaustively. The work of Victor Turner (see 1966, 1982, 1986) has been highly influential, as has the related work of Richard Schechner in Performance Studies (1985, 1990). S. J. Tambiah's analyses of ritual critically deployed the notion of Austinian performativity long before the current fascination with this notion in Cultural Studies (1979). Geertz (1973) is another classic formulation. See Beeman (1993) for an extensive review of anthropological work on theater and performance. A recent review of anthropological studies of performance (Palmer and Jankowiak 1996) illustrates some general problems with many anthropological approaches. Focusing on "imagery," the authors remain within power-evasive paradigms of cognition/emotion and metaphor, rather than analyzing images as coextensive with power relations. References to developments in poststructuralist theories of subject formation and their relationship to performance are virtually absent.

17. I worked on *Twilight* when it premiered at the Mark Taper Forum in Los Angeles in 1993, with Emily Mann as director. In 1994, George C. Wolfe directed a different version at the Public Theater/New York Shakespeare Festival and on Broadway; Tony Kushner and Kimberly Flynn were dramaturges. *Twilight* and Anna Deavere Smith received Obie Awards and a Tony nomination for this New York version in 1994. A third production, substantially revised from the original, opened in 1996 at the Berkeley Repertory Theater, directed by Sharon Ott.

18. Here, I am choosing not to follow DeCerteau's distinction between "strategies" and "tactics."

ORIENTALISMS

PART ONE

m . b u t t e r f l y :
o r i e n t a l i s m , g e n d e r ,
a n d a c r i t i q u e
o f e s s e n t i a l i s t i d e n t i t y [1]

IN DAVID HENRY Hwang's Tony award-winning play, *M. Butterfly*, Broadway audiences encounter a dazzling spectacle, in which a tale of seemingly mistaken gender identities and delusions perpetuated over decades occasions a richly textured production moving in and around the spaces of global politics, gender and racial identities, and the power relations inevitably present in what we call love. A close examination of *M. Butterfly* has profound implications for our assumptions about identity, including anthropological theories of the self or the person, the ways gender and race are mutually implicated in the construction of identity, and the pervasive insidiousness of gender and racial stereotypes.

The story intrigues through its sheer improbability. The playwright's notes cite the *New York Times*, which in May of 1986 reported the trial of a "former French diplomat and a Chinese opera star" who were "sentenced to six years in jail for spying for China after a two-day trial that traced a story of clandestine love and mistaken sexual identity. . . . Mr. Bouriscot was accused of passing information to China after he fell in love with Mr. Shi, whom he believed for twenty years to be a woman."[2] In asking himself how such a delusion could be sustained for so long, Hwang takes us through the relations between France and Indochina, and most especially, through the terrain of written images of "the Orient" occupied most centrally by that cultural treasure, *Madama Butterfly*. These already written images—the narrative convention of "submissive Oriental woman and cruel white man"—are played out in many different arenas, including, perhaps most tellingly, the space of fantasy created and reproduced by the Frenchman himself.

An analysis of *M. Butterfly* suggests the ways Hwang challenges our very notions of words like "truth," our assumptions about gender, and most of all, how *M. Butterfly* subverts and undermines a notion of unitary identity based on a space of inner truth and the plenitude of referential meaning. Through its use of gender ambiguity present in its very title—is it Monsieur, Madame, Mr., Ms. Butterfly?[3]—through power reversals, through constituting these identities within the vicissitudes of global politics, Hwang conceals, reveals, and then calls into question so-called "true" identity, pointing us toward a reconceptualization of the topography of "the self." Rather than a bounded essence, filled with "inner truth," separated from the world or "society" by an envelope of skin, *M. Butterfly* opens out the self to the world, softening or even dissolving those boundaries, where identity becomes spatialized as a series of shifting nodal points constructed in and through fields of power and meaning. Finally, *M. Butterfly* intertwines geography and gender, where East/West and male/female become mobile positions in a field of power relations. It suggests that analyses of shifting gender identity must also take into account the ways gender is projected onto geography, and that international power relations and race are also, inevitably, inscribed in our figurations of gender.

II

Perhaps the creative subversiveness of Hwang's play best emerges in contrast to the conventions of the opera *Madama Butterfly*, to which it provides ironic counterpoint. This cultural "classic"—music by Giacomo Puccini, libretto by Giuseppe Giacosa and Luigi Illica, based on a story by John Luther Long— debuted at La Scala in 1904. It remains a staple of contemporary opera company repertoire, one of the ten most performed operas around the world. As we will see, Hwang reappropriates the conventional narrative of the pitiful Butterfly and the trope of the exotic, submissive Oriental woman, rupturing the seamless closure and the dramatic inevitability of the story line.

The conventional narrative, baldly stated, goes something like this. Lieutenant Benjamin Franklin Pinkerton is an American naval officer, stationed on the ship *Abraham Lincoln* in Nagasaki during the Meiji period, the turn of the century when Japan was "opened" to the West. The opera begins with Pinkerton and Goro, a marriage broker, as they look over a house Pinkerton will rent for himself and his bride-to-be, a fifteen-year-old *geisha* named Cho-Cho-san ("butterfly" in Japanese). American consul Sharpless arrives, and Pinkerton sings of his hedonistic philosophy of life, characterizing himself as a vagabond Yankee who casts his anchor where he pleases. "He doesn't satisfy his life/if he doesn't make his treasure/the flowers of every region. . .the love of every beauty."[4] Pinkerton toasts his upcoming marriage by extolling the virtues of his open-ended marriage contract: "So I'm marrying in the Japanese way/for nine-hundred-ninety-nine years/Free to release myself every month" (189). Later, he toasts "the day when I'll marry/In a real wedding, a real American wife" (191). When Butterfly arrives with an entourage of friends and relatives, Pinkerton and Sharpless discover that among the treasures Butterfly carries with her into her new home is the knife her father used for his *seppuku*, or ritual suicide by disembowelment—and music foreshadows the repetition that will inevitably occur. Friends and relatives sing their doubts about the marriage, and in a dramatic moment, Butterfly's uncle, a Buddhist priest, enters to denounce her decision to abandon her ancestors and adopt the Christian religion. Rejected by her relatives, Butterfly turns to Pinkerton. The couple sing of their love, but Cho-cho-san expresses her fear of foreign customs, where butterflies are "pierced with a pin" (215). Pinkerton assures her that though there is some truth to the saying, it is to prevent the butterfly from flying away. They celebrate the beauty of the night. "All ecstatic with love, the sky is laughing" (215), says Butterfly as they enter the house and Act One closes.

By the beginning of Act Two, Pinkerton has been gone for three years. Though on the verge of destitution, Butterfly steadfastly awaits the return of her husband, who has promised to come back to her "when the robin makes his nest" (219). And, known only to her servant, Suzuki, Cho-cho-san has had a baby, a son with *occhi azzurini*, "azure eyes," and *i ricciolini d'oro schietto*, "little curls of pure gold"—truly a stunning genetic feat. The consul Sharpless comes to call, bearing a letter from Pinkerton, and he informs Butterfly that her waiting is in vain, that Pinkerton will not return and that she should accept the marriage proposal of the Prince Yamadori who has come to court her. Still sure of her husband, she will have none of it. In Cho-cho-san's eyes,

33

she is no longer Madame Butterfly, but Mrs. Pinkerton, bound by American custom. In desperation, hoping the consul will persuade Pinkerton to return, Cho-Cho-san brings out her son. At that point Pinkerton is in fact already in Nagasaki with his American wife. Knowing that he is in port, Butterfly and Suzuki decorate the house with flowers, and Butterfly stays awake all night, awaiting Pinkerton's arrival. In the morning, when Suzuki finally persuades her mistress to rest, Sharpless and Pinkerton arrive. Pinkerton has decided to claim his son and raise the boy in America, and he persuades Suzuki to help him convince Butterfly that this is for the best. Later, Cho-cho-san sees Sharpless and an American woman in the garden. Now, realizing that Pinkerton has in fact married again, Cho-cho-san cries out with pain, "All is dead for me!/All is finished, ah!" (253) and she prepares for the inevitable. She tells Sharpless to come with Pinkerton for the child in half an hour. Cho-cho-san unsheathes her father's dagger, but then spies her son, whom Suzuki has pushed into the room. In her agony, the music forces her higher and higher, as her voice threatens to soar out of control and then sinks to an ominous low note. Cho-cho-san blindfolds her child, as if to play hide-and-seek, goes behind a screen to insert the knife and emerges, staggering toward the child. The brass section accompanies her death agony, trumpeting vaguely Asian-sounding music until finally, climactically, a gong signals her collapse. We hear Pinkerton's cries of "Butterfly!" as Pinkerton and Sharpless run into the room. Butterfly points to the child as she dies, and the opera resolves in a swelling, tragic orchestral crescendo.

In *Madama Butterfly* Puccini draws on and recirculates familiar tropes: the narrative inevitability of a woman's death in opera,[5] and most especially, the various markers of Japanese identity: Butterfly as *geisha*, that quintessential Western figuration of Japanese woman, the manner of Butterfly's death, by the knife—the form of suicide conventionally associated in the West with Japan, the construction of the Japanese as a "people accustomed/to little things/humble and silent" (213). And little is exactly what Butterfly gets. In Western eyes, Japanese women are meant to sacrifice, and Butterfly sacrifices her "husband," her religion, her people, her son, and ultimately, her very life. The beautiful, moving tragedy propels us toward narrative closure, as Butterfly discovers the truth—that she is, indeed, condemned to die as her identity as a Japanese geisha demands—an exotic object, a "poor little thing," as Kate Pinkerton calls her. In Puccini's opera, men, women, Japanese, Americans, are all defined by familiar narrative conventions.[6] And the predictable happens: West wins over East, Man over Woman, White over Asian. The music, with its soaring arias and bombastic orchestral interludes, amplifies the points and draws us into further complicity with convention. Butterfly is forced into tonal registers that edge into a realm beyond rational control, demanding a resolution which arrives, (porno)graphically, with the crash of the gong.[7] Music and text collaborate, to render inevitable this tragic—but oh-so-satisfying—dénouement: Butterfly, the little Asian woman, crumpled on the floor. The perfect closure.

Identities, too, are unproblematic entities in Puccini's opera; indeed, Puccini reinforces our own conventional assumptions about personhood. Butterfly's attempts to blur the boundaries and to claim for herself a different identity—that of American—are doomed to failure. She is disowned by her people, and she cleaves to Pinkerton, reconstituting herself as American, at least in her own eyes. But the opera refuses to allow her to "overcome" her essential Japanese womanhood. The librettists have Butterfly say things and do things that reinforce our stereotyped notions of the category "Japanese woman": she is humble, exotic, a plaything. Pinkerton calls her a diminutive, delicate "flower," whose "exotic perfume" (199) intoxicates him. His bride, this child-woman with "long oval eyes" (213), makes her man her universe. And like most Japanese created by Westerners, Butterfly is concerned with "honor" and must kill herself when that honor has been sullied. Death, too, comes in stereotypical form. Her destiny is to die by the knife—metaphorically, via sexual penetration, and finally, in her ritual suicide.[8] Butterfly is defined by these narrative conventions; she cannot escape them.

I would like to suggest that this view of identity—a conventional view familiar to us in our everyday discourses and pervasive in the realm of aesthetic production—is based on a particular presupposition about the nature of identity, what philosophers call "substance metaphysics."[9] Identities are viewed as fixed, bounded entities containing some essence or substance, expressed in distinctive attributes. Thus Butterfly is defined by attributes conventionally associated in Western culture with Asian—or even worse, "Oriental"—women. Furthermore, I would go to on to argue that a similar view of identities underlies the burgeoning anthropological literature on what we call the self or the person. "The self" carries a highly culturally specific semantic load and presents a picture of unitary totality. According to our linguistic and cultural conventions, "self" calls up its opposing term, "society," and presupposes a particular topography: a self, enclosed in a bodily shell, composed of an inner

essence associated with truth and real feelings and identity, standing in opposition to a world that is spatially and ontologically distinct from the self.[10] A self
is closed, fixed, an essence defined by attributes. Typically, the many anthropological analyses of *la notion de personne*,[11] the concept of self in this or that
culture, abstract from specific contexts certain distinctive traits of the self
among the Ilongot, the Ifaluk, the Tamils, the Samoans, the Americans. And
even those analyses which claim to transcend an essentialist notion of identity
and a self/society distinction by arguing for the cultural constitution of that self
tend to preserve the distinction in their rhetoric. That one can even talk of a
concept of self divorced from specific historical, cultural, and political contexts
privileges the notion of some abstract essence of selfhood we can describe by
enumerating its distinctive features. This self/society, substance/attribute view
of identity underlies anthropological narratives just as it informs aesthetic productions like *Madama Butterfly*.[12]

III

The self/society, subject/world tropes insidiously persist in a multiplicity of
guises in the realms of theory and literature, but in anthropology, the literature on
the self has transposed this opposition into another key: the distinction between
a person—a human being as bearer of social roles—and self—the inner, reflective essence of psychological consciousness, recapitulating the binary between
social and psychological, world and subject.[13] Yet anthropology deconstructs this
binary even as it maintains its terms, for in demonstrating the historical and cultural specificity of definitions of the person or the self, we are led to a series of
questions: Are the terms "self" and "person" the creations of our own linguistic
and cultural conventions? If "inner" processes are culturally conceived, their
very existence mediated by cultural discourses, to what extent can we talk of
"inner, reflective essence" or "outer, objective world" except as culturally meaningful, culturally specific constructs? And how is the inner/outer distinction itself
established as the terms within which we must inevitably speak and act?

Early studies of the person, like the classic Marcel Mauss essay, take as a
point of departure *la notion de personne* as an Aristotelian category, an example of one of the fundamental categories of the human mind. Traversing space
and time, Mauss draws our attention to different ways of defining persons and
selves in different cultures in different historical moments, but posits the evo-

lutionary superiority of Western notions of the same. In a key passage, Mauss discusses the notion of the self:

> Far from existing as the primordial innate idea, clearly engraved since Adam in the innermost depths of our being, it continues here slowly, and almost right up to our own time, to be built upon, to be made clearer and more specific, becoming identified with self-knowledge and the psychological consciousness.[14]

Western conceptions of self as psychological consciousness and a reflexive self-awareness, based on a division between the inner space of selfhood and the outer world, are held up as the highest, most differentiated development of the self in human history. Though Mauss's insights have been elaborated in richly varied ways, most anthropological analyses leave in place the rhetoric of the self as psychological consciousness and self-knowledge, continuing to impart the impression of implicit ethnocentric superiority, essential unity, and referential solidity.

I have used the term "referential solidity," for it is clear that this rhetoric/ theory of the self pivots around a spatialized ideology of meaning as reference. Saussure's influential formulation of the sign as the relation between signifier (the sound-image, "the impression it makes on our senses") and signified (the concept inside the head, "the psychological imprint of the sound")[15], links the speaking subject to assumptions about meaning as plenitude, a fullness occupied by certain contents, located inside the self. Here we find another permutation of the Cartesian dichotomy between reason and sense perception. Self is constituted culturally, but in its presence, supported by the solidity of referential meaning, "the self" takes on the character of an irreducible essence, the Transcendental Signified, a substance which can be distilled out from the specificities of the situations in which people enact themselves. Such an essence of inner selfhood preserves the boundaries between the inner space of true selfhood and the outer space of the world.

The many anthropological accounts reliant on characterizations of *la notion de personne*, "the concept of self," with no reference to the contradictions and multiplicities within "a" self, the practices creating selves in concrete situations, or the larger historical, political, and institutional processes shaping those selves, decontextualize and reify an abstract notion of essential selfhood, based on a metaphysics of substance. Echoing *Madama Butterfly*'s familiar narrative conventions and satisfying sense of closure, anthropological narratives recirculate tropes of a self/world boundary and a substance/attribute configuration of identity.

37

However, when we move from the conventions of fixed, essentialist identities in *Madama Butterfly* to the subversion of those conventions in *M. Butterfly*, we might go on to ask how selves in the plural are constructed variously in various situations, how these constructions can be complicated and enlivened by multiplicity and ambiguity, and how they shape and are shaped by relations of power. Such an approach would open out the space of selfhood to the world, dissolving the boundaries and emptying the inner self of its plenitude, spatializing selves as conjunctions of forces produced by history, politics, culture, and narrative conventions, within a changing, complicated, and open discursive field. From clear boundaries between inner and outer, fixed identities characterized by distinctive attributes, and narrative closure to an open, shifting multiplicity of meanings, constituted in and by a changing field of discourses and forces of power, where selves in the plural are empty of reference in an essentialist sense: these are the moves suggested by an analysis of David Henry Hwang's *M. Butterfly*.

IV

The play opens with ex-diplomat René Gallimard in prison. (His last name, the name of a famous French publishing house, already resonates with notions of narrative and of textual truth, and his first name, which sounds the same in its masculine and feminine forms, underlines the theme of gender ambiguity). "It is an enchanted space I occupy" (8), he announces, and indeed, it is enchanted—a space of fantasy, a prison of cultural conventions and stereotypes where Gallimard's insistence on reading a complex, shifting reality through the Orientalist texts of the past make him the prisoner and eventually, the willing sacrificial victim of his own culturally and historically produced conventions.

Gallimard will be seduced, deluded, imprisoned by clinging to an ideology of meaning as reference and to an essentialist notion of identity. For him, clichéd images of gender and of race and geography unproblematically occupy the inner space of identity, enabling opera star Song Liling to seduce him through the play of inner truth and outer appearance. The first encounter between Song and Gallimard occurs in a performance at the home of an ambassador, where Song plays the death scene from *Madama Butterfly*. Clothed as a Japanese woman, wearing a woman's makeup, Song is "believable" as Butterfly. This "believability" occurs on the planes of gender, size, and geography, when Gallimard gushes to Song about her/his wonderful performance, so con-

John Lithgow and B.D. Wong in *M. Butterfly*
Joan Marcus, photographer

vincing in contrast to the "huge women in so much bad makeup" (18) who play Butterfly in the West.

Gallimard adheres to stereotyped images of women and of the Orient, where he assumes a transparent relationship between outer appearance and the inner truth of self. The signs of this identity are clothing and makeup, and since Song is dressed as a woman, Gallimard never doubts Song's essential femininity. Gallimard's equally essentialized readings of the Orient enable Song to throw Gallimard off balance with her/his initial boldness, when s/he describes the absurdity of *Madama Butterfly*'s plot, but for the geographic and racial identities of its protagonists:

> Consider it this way: what would you say if a blonde homecoming queen fell in love with a short Japanese businessman? He treats her cruelly, then goes home for three years, during which time she prays to his picture and turns down marriage from a young Kennedy. Then, when she learns he has remarried, she kills herself. Now, I believe you would consider this girl to be a deranged idiot, correct? But because it's an Oriental who kills herself for a Westerner—ah!—you find it beautiful (18).

Later, Song becomes flirtatious, and strategically exhibits the appropriate signs of her inner, essential Oriental female self: modesty, embarrassment, timidity. Gallimard responds, "I know she has an interest in me. I suspect this is her way. She is outwardly bold and outspoken, yet her heart is shy and afraid. It is the Oriental in her at war with her Western education" (25). Thus, Gallimard reads Song's Westernized, masculine exterior as mere veneer, masking the fullness of the inner truth of Oriental womanhood. However she may try to alter this substance of identity, in Gallimard's eyes, she—like Madame Butterfly—will never be able to overcome her essential Oriental nature.

This conventional reading of identity enables Song to manipulate the conventions to further her/his ends, to become more intimate with Gallimard, and eventually, to pass on to the government of the People's Republic of China the diplomatic secrets s/he learns in the context of their relationship. When Song first entertains Gallimard in her/his apartment, s/he appeals to Orientalist stereotypes of tradition, modesty, unchanging essence, invoking China's two-thousand-year history and the resulting significance of her actions: "Even my own heart strapped inside this Western dress . . . even it says things. . . . things I don't care to hear" (27).

Her/his appeal finds a willing audience in Gallimard, who finds *this* Song far more to his liking, and shares with the audience his delighted discovery that "Butterfly," as he has begun to call her, feels inferior to Westerners. Seeing Song supposedly revealed—paradoxically, in the moment of her greatest concealment—in her feminine/Oriental inferiority, behaving with appropriate submissiveness and docility, Gallimard for the first time finds what he believes to be his true self, as a Real Man defined in opposition to Song. Wondering whether his Butterfly, like Pinkerton's, would "writhe on a needle" (28), he refuses to respond to her increasingly plaintive missives, and for the first time feels "that rush of power—the absolute power of a man" (28), as he cleans out his files, writes a report on trade, and otherwise enacts confident masculine mastery in the world of work. In the phrase "the absolute power of a man," Hwang highlights the connection between this power and the existence of a symmetrical but inverted opposite, for though presumably Gallimard was by most people's definitions a man before he met his Butterfly, he can only acquire the "absolute power of a man" in contrast to her. In love with his own image of the Perfect Woman and therefore with himself as the Perfect Man, Gallimard reads signs of dissimulation—that Song keeps her clothes on even in intimate moments, with appeals to her "shame" and "modesty"—as proofs of her essential Oriental womanhood. In so doing, he guards his inner space of "real, masculine" identity.

Gallimard begins with a conception of gender and racial identity based on an ideology of the inner space of selfhood. The audience, however, is allowed a rather different relationship between inner truth and outward appearance, one that initially preserves the distinction between real, inner self and outer role. That Song is a Chinese man playing a Japanese woman is a "truth" we know from an early stage. Song plays ironically with this "truth" throughout. Its subtleties are powerfully articulated in a scene where Song is almost unmasked as a man. Gallimard, humiliated by the failure of his predictions in the diplomatic arena, demands to see his Butterfly naked. Song, in a brilliant stroke, realizes that Gallimard simply desires her to submit. S/he lies down, saying, "Whatever happens, know that you have willed it . . . I'm helpless before my man" (47). Gallimard relents, and Song wins. Later, Song triumphantly recounts the crisis to Comrade Chin, the PRC emissary and then rhetorically asks her: "Why, in the Peking opera, are women's roles played by men?" Chin replies, "I don't know. Maybe, a reactionary remnant of male. . ." Song cuts her off. "No. Because only a man knows how a woman is supposed to act" (49).

Irony animates these passages. On the one hand, Song is surely a man playing a woman—and his statement is a clear gesture of appropriation. However, Hwang suggests that matters are more complicated, that "woman" is a collection of cultural stereotypes connected tenuously at best to a complex, shifting reality. Rather than expressing some essential gender identity, full and present, "woman" is a named location in a changing matrix of power relations, defined oppositionally to the name "man." So constructed by convention and so oppositionally defined is woman, that according to Song, only a man really knows how to enact woman properly. And because man and woman are oppositionally defined terms, reversals of male and female positions are possible. Indeed, it is at the moment of his greatest submission/humiliation as a woman that Song consolidates his power as a man. S/he puts herself "in the hands of her man," and it is at that moment that Gallimard relents—and feels for the first time the twinges of love, even adoration. The vicissitudes of the Cultural Revolution and the signal failure of Gallimard's foreign-policy predictions send Gallimard home to France, but he keeps a shrine-like room waiting for his Perfect Woman. And in his devoted love, his worship of this image of Perfect Woman, Gallimard himself becomes like a woman.

A dramatic reversal is effected in the play in Act Three through a stunning confrontation, where Song reveals his "manhood" to Gallimard. By this time Song is dressed as a man, but he strips in order to show Gallimard his "true" self. Gallimard, facing Song, is convulsed in laughter, finding it bitterly amusing that the object of his love is "just a man" (65). Song protests in an important passage that he is not "just a man," and tries to persuade Gallimard that underneath it all, it was always him—Song—in his full complexity. Gallimard will not be persuaded, however. Clinging to his beloved stereotypes of Oriental womanhood, now supposedly knowing the difference between fantasy and reality, he declares his intention to "choose fantasy" (67). Song announces his disappointment, for his hope was for Gallimard to "become. . . something more. More like . . . a woman" (67). Song's efforts are to no avail, and Gallimard chases Song from the stage.

Gallimard returns to his prison cell in a searing finale and launches into a chilling speech as he paints his face with geisha-like makeup and dons wig and kimono. He speaks of his "vision of the Orient" (68), a land of exotic, submissive women who were born to be abused. He continues:

> . . . the man I loved was a cad, a bounder. He deserved nothing but a kick in the behind, and instead I gave him . . . all my love.
>
> Yes—love. Why not admit it all. That was my undoing, wasn't it? Love warped my judgment, blinded my eyes, rearranged the very lines on my face . . . until I could look in the mirror and see nothing but . . . a woman (68).

Gallimard grasps a knife and assumes the *seppuku* position, as he reprises lines from the Puccini opera:

> Death with honor is better than life . . . life with dishonor (68).

He continues:

> The love of a Butterfly can withstand many things . . . unfaithfulness, loss, even abandonment. But how can it face the one sin that implies all others? The devastating knowledge that, underneath it all, the object of her love was nothing more, nothing less than . . . a man. It is 1988. And I have found her at last. In a prison on the outskirts of Paris. My name is René Gallimard—also known as Madame Butterfly (68, 69).

Gallimard plunges the knife into his body and collapses to the floor. Then, the coup de grâce. A spotlight focuses dimly on Song, "who stands as a man" (69) atop a sweeping ramp. Tendrils of smoke from his cigarette ascend toward the lights, and we hear him say "Butterfly?" as the stage darkens.

This stunning gender/racial power reversal forces the audience toward a fundamental reconceptualization of the topography of identity. "True" inner identity is played with throughout, then seemingly preserved in the revelation of Song's "real" masculinity, then again called into question with Gallimard's assumption of the guise of Japanese woman.[16]

Whereas the death of Madame Butterfly in Puccini's opera offers us the satisfaction of narrative closure, Gallimard's assumption of the identity of a Japanese woman is radically disturbing, for in this move Hwang suggests that gender identity is far more complicated than reference to an essential inner truth or external biological equipment might lead us to believe. As Foucault has noted,[17] sex as a category gathers together a collection of unrelated phenomena in which male and female are defined oppositionally in stereotyped terms and posits this discursively produced difference as natural sexual difference. *M. Butterfly* deconstructs that naturalness, opening out the inner spaces of true gender identity to cultural and historical forces, where identity is not an inner space of truth but a location in a field of shifting power relations.

Perhaps what Hwang might further emphasize is the inadequacy of either gender category to encompass a paradoxical and multiplicitous reality. The key statement here is Song's, that he is more than "just a man." In the stage directions, Song at the end "stands as a man" (69) (my emphasis) in the clothing and the confident, powerful guise of a man. But we cannot say with certainty that he *is* a man, for man is an historically, discursively produced category which fails to accommodate Song's more complex experience of gender and subverts that ontological claim. Song attempts to persuade Gallimard to join him in a new sort of relationship, where Song is more like a man, Gallimard more like a woman. At precisely this point Hwang suggests the inability of the categories of man and woman to account for the multiple, changing, power-laden identities of his protagonists. Gallimard refuses, saying that he loved a woman created by a man, and that nothing else will do. Song thereupon accuses him of too little imagination. Gallimard immediately retorts that he is pure imagination, and on one level, he is right. In his obsession with the Perfect Oriental Woman, he truly remains the prisoner and then the willing sacrificial victim of his Orientalist cultural clichés—a realm of pure imagination indeed. But this distinction between imagination and reality itself erects the bar between categories and fails to open those mutually exclusive spaces to irony, creativity, and subversion. The last word rests with Song, and in the end, his interpretation prevails: that Gallimard has too little imagination to accept the complexity and

43

ambiguity of everyday life, too little imagination to open himself to different cultural possibilities, blurred boundaries, and rearrangements of power.

One might also argue that Gallimard's refusal arises from his attempt to keep erect his boundaries as a heterosexual man. Gallimard's lack of imagination appears in part to be a homophobic retreat, and there is a level at which Hwang seems to suggest that gay relationships offer the greatest potential for gender subversion. Yet, upon inquiry, Hwang further complicates matters by refusing us the comfort of conventional binaristic categories:

> To me, this is not a 'gay' subject because the very labels heterosexual or homosexual become meaningless in the context of this story. Yes, of course this was literally a homosexual affair. Yet because Gallimard perceived it or chose to perceive it as a heterosexual liaison, in his mind it was essentially so. Since I am telling the story from the Frenchman's point of view, it is more specificially about 'a man who loved a woman created by a man.' To me, this characterization is infinitely more useful than the clumsy labels 'gay' or 'straight.'[18]

Hwang once again forces us to confront the pervasive, essentialist dualisms in our thinking and argues instead for historical and cultural specificity that would subvert the binary.

V

Literary critics and readers of French literature will note the striking parallels between the tale of *M. Butterfly* and the Balzac short story, "Sarrasine," the object of Roland Barthes's *S/Z* and of Barbara Johnson's essay, "BartheS/BalZac."[19] Both Sarrasine and Gallimard commit the same errors of interpretation in pursuing their objects of desire. Sarrasine, a sculptor, falls in love with an Italian opera singer, his image of the perfect woman. But La Zambinella is a castrato. Sarrasine, a newcomer to Italy, is ignorant of this custom, and he pays for his ignorance, his passion, and his misinterpretation with his life, victim to the henchmen of the powerful Cardinal who is La Zambinella's protector. Gallimard and Sarrasine are almost perfect mirrors for one another. Signs of beauty and timidity act as proofs to both men that the objects of their love are indeed women. Both flee strong women. In Gallimard's case, this takes the form of escape via a brief affair with another refraction of himself/his fantasy, a young Western blonde also named Renée, who enacts a symbolic castration

44

by commenting on his "weenie" and advancing her theory of how the world is run by men with "pricks the size of pins." But for Gallimard as for Sarrasine, "it is for having fled castration" (175) that they will be castrated. Both men are unmanned as the world laughs at their follies. And both are undone by their view of gender as symmetrical inversions of mirrored opposites. For both, their own masculinity is defined in contrast to a perfect woman who is a collection of culturally conventional images, and each crafts the Other to conform to those conventions. Neither Gallimard nor Sarrasine is capable of really recognizing another, for in their insistence on clinging to their cherished stereotypes, both love only themselves.[20] In both cases, the truth kills.

Clearly, the parallels are stunning. But Hwang does not allow us to stop there. Like these literary critics, Hwang offers us a provocative reconsideration of the construction of gender identity as an inner essence. But for him, a challenge to logocentric notions of voice, of referentiality, of identity as open and undecidable, is only a first step. Hwang opens out the self, not to a free play of signifiers, but to a play of historically and culturally specific power relations. Through the linkage of politics to the relationship between Song and Gallimard, Hwang leads us toward a thoroughly historicized, politicized notion of identity, not understandable without reference to narrative conventions, global power relations, gender, and the power struggles people enact in their everyday lives. These relations constitute the spaces of gender, but equally important, the spaces of race and imperialism played out on a world stage.

A double movement is involved here. As Hwang deploys them, Song's words open out the categories of the self and the personal or private domain of love relationships to the currents of world historical power relations. Simultaneously, Hwang associates gender and geography, showing the Orient as supine, penetrable, knowable in the intellectual and the carnal senses. The play of signifiers of identity is not completely arbitrary; rather it is overdetermined by a constitutive history, a history producing narrative conventions like *Madama Butterfly*. Hwang effects this double movement and plays with the levels of personal and political by situating Gallimard and Song historically, during the era of the Vietnam War and the Cultural Revolution, taking them up to the present. In so doing, he draws parallels between the relations of Asian woman and Western man and of Asia and the West.

Act One ends by intertwining these two levels, as Gallimard's triumph in the diplomatic arena—his promotion to vice-consul—coincides with his "conquering" of Song. Act Two continues these parallels, as Song appeals to Gallimard's

45

Orientalism in order to further his/her spying activities for the People's Republic. Extolling the progressiveness of France and exclaiming over his/her excitement at being "part of the society ruling the world today" (36), Song cajoles Gallimard into giving him/her classified information about French and American involvement in Vietnam. In *his* work, Gallimard uses his new-found masculine confidence and power and the opinions of Orientals he forms in his relationship with Song to direct French foreign policy. We reencounter in the diplomatic arena the exchange of stereotypes pervading the relationship between Gallimard and his Butterfly. "The Orientals simply want to be associated with whoever shows the most strength and power"; "There's a natural affinity between the West and the Orient"; "Orientals will always submit to a greater force" (37). Not surprisingly, Gallimard's inability to read the complexities of Asian politics and society leads to failure. Gallimard's predictions about Oriental submission to power are proved stunningly wrong during the Vietnam War: "And somehow the American war went wrong too. Four hundred thousand dollars were being spent for every Viet Cong killed, so General Westmoreland's remark that the Oriental does not value life the way Americans do was oddly accurate." "Why weren't the Vietnamese people giving in? Why were they content instead to die and die and die again?" (52, 53). And as the political situation in China changes, so does the relationship between Gallimard and Song change. Gallimard is sent home to Paris for his diplomatic failures; Song is reeducated and sent to a commune in the countryside as penance for his/her decadent ways.

Act Three begins with Song's transformation into a man, as he removes his makeup and kimono on stage, revealing his masculine self. It is a manhood based on a collection of recognizably masculine conventions: an Armani suit; a confident stance, with feet planted wide apart, arms akimbo; a deeper voice; a defiant, cocky manner as he strides back and forth on the stage, surveying the audience. He brings together the threads of gender and global politics in a French court. Questioned by a judge about his relationship with Gallimard, Song offers as explanation his theory of the "international rape mentality": "Basically, her mouth says no, but her eyes say yes. The West believes the East, deep down, wants to be dominated. . . You expect Oriental countries to submit to your guns, and you expect Oriental women to be submissive to your men" (62). And then Song links this mentality to Gallimard's twenty-year attachment to Song as a woman: ". . .when he finally met his fantasy woman, he wanted more than anything to believe that she was, in fact, a woman. And second, I am an Oriental. And being an Oriental, I could never be completely a man" (62).

Thus, Hwang—in a move suggestive of Edward Said's *Orientalism*[21]—explicitly links the construction of gendered imagery to the construction of race and the imperialist mission to colonize and dominate. Asia is gendered, but gender in turn cannot be understood without the figurations of race and power relations that inscribe it. In this double movement, *M. Butterfly* calls into question analyses of race and colonialism which ignore links to gender, just as it challenges theories of gender which would ignore the cultural/racial/global locations from which they speak. In *M. Butterfly*, gender and global politics are inseparable. The assumption that one can privilege gender, in advance, as a category, setting the terms of inclusion without fully considering those for whom gender alone fails to capture the multiplicity of experience, is itself an Orientalist move.[22] *M. Butterfly* would lead us to recognize that if the Orient is a woman, in an important sense women are also the Orient, underlining the simultaneity and inextricability of gender from geographic, colonial, and racial systems of dominance. And this is the "critical difference" between the implications of an *M. Butterfly*, on the one hand, and on the other, deconstructive analyses of gender identity. For Hwang, the matter surpasses a simple calling into question of fixed gender identity, where a fixed meaning is always deferred in a postmodern free play of signifiers. He leads us beyond deconstructions of identity as Voice, Logos, or the Transcendental Signified, beyond refigurations of identity as the empty sign, or an instantiation of "writing inhabited by its own irreducible difference from itself" (Johnson 11). And the difference lies in his opening out of the self, not to a free play of signifiers but to a power-sensitive analysis that would examine the construction of complex, shifting selves in the plural, in all their cultural, historical, and situational specificity.[23]

In sum, *M. Butterfly* enacts what I take to be a number of profoundly important theoretical moves for those engaged in cultural politics. It subverts notions of unitary, fixed identities, embodied in pervasive narrative conventions such as the trope of "Japanese woman as Butterfly." Equally, it throws into question an anthropological literature based on a substance-attribute metaphysics which takes as its foundational point of departure a division between self and society, subject and world. *M. Butterfly* suggests to us that an attempt to exhaustively describe and to rhetorically fix a concept of self abstracted from power relations and from concrete situations and historical events, is an illusory task. Rather, identities are constructed in and through discursive fields, produced through disciplines and narrative conventions. Far from bounded, coherent, and easily apprehended entities, identities are multiple, ambiguous, shifting locations in matrices of power.

Moreover, *M. Butterfly* suggests that gender and race are mutually consti-tutive in the play of identities; neither gender nor race can be accorded some *a priori* primacy over the other. Most important, they are not incidental attrib-utes, accidents ancillary to some primary substance of consciousness or ratio-nality that supposedly characterize a self.[24] In *M. Butterfly*, we find a nuanced portrayal of the power and pervasiveness of gender and racial stereotypes. Simultaneously, Hwang de-essentializes the categories, exploding conventional notions of gender and race as universal, ahistorical essences or as incidental features of a more encompassing, abstract concept of self. By linking so-called individual identity to global politics, nationalism, and imperialism, Hwang makes us see the cross-cutting and mutually constitutive interplay of these forces on all levels. *M. Butterfly* reconstitutes selves in the plural as shifting positions in moving, discursive fields, played out on levels of so-called indi-vidual identities, in love relationships, in academic and theatrical narratives, and on the stage of global power relations.

Finally, perhaps we can deploy the spatial metaphor once more, to place *M. Butterfly* in a larger context and to underline its significance. The play claims a narrative space within the central story for Asian Americans and for other people of color. Never before has a dramatic production written by an Asian American been accorded such mainstream accolades:[25] a long run on Broadway; a planned world tour; Tonys and Drama Desk Awards for both Hwang and B. D. Wong, who played Butterfly; a nomination for the Pulitzer Prize.[26] For me, as an Asian American woman, *M. Butterfly* is a voice from the Borderlands, to use a metaphor from Gloria Anzaldúa and Carolyn Steedman,[27] a case of the "other speaking back,"[28] to borrow Arlene Teraoka's phrase. Hwang's distinctively Asian American voice reverberates with the voices of others who have spoken from the borderlands, those whose stories cannot be fully recognized or subsumed by dominant narrative conventions, when he speaks so eloquently of the failure to understand the multiplicity of Asia and of women.[29] "That's why," says Song, "the West will always lose in its encoun-ters with the East," and his words seem especially resonant given the history of the post-World War II period, a history including the Vietnam War and the eco-nomic rise of Asia. The future Hwang suggestively portrays is one where white Western man may become Japanese woman, as power relations in the world shift and as the West continues to perceive the East in terms of fixity and essentialist identity. And, when Gallimard's French wife laments Chinese inability to hear *Madama Butterfly* as simply a beautiful piece of music, Hwang further suggests that his own enterprise, and perhaps by extension, ours, requires a committed, impassioned linkage between what are conventionally defined as two separate spaces of meaning, divided by the bar: aesthetics and politics. Those like Gallimard who seek to keep the bars erect run the risk, Hwang implies, of living within the prison of their culturally and discursively produced assumptions in which aesthetics and politics, the personal and the political, woman and man, East and West form closed, mutually exclusive spaces where one term inevitably dominates the other. It is this topography of closure *M. Butterfly*—by its very existence—challenges.

ENDNOTES

1. A preliminary version of this paper was presented at the 1988 Annual Meetings of the American Anthropological Association, Phoenix, Arizona at the panel, "The Culture and Politics of Space." The version reprinted here first appeared in 1990 and remains virtually unchanged. The tone of the essay is strategically celebratory, given contemporary mainstream reception and impassioned accusations, especially from heterosexual Asian American men, that *M. Butterfly* merely represented stereotypes of Asian American exoticism and effeminacy. My analysis is highly inflected through the original Broadway production directed by John Dexter, starring John Lithgow and B. D. Wong. After viewing many productions, it is clear to me that one's reading of power relations between Song and Gallimard depends crucially upon the casting of the central actors and on other staging elements. For example, in other versions it has sometimes been easier to view the relationship as one of simple vengeance and power reversal in which Song becomes Pinkerton, rather than allowing for the possibility of love between the two. Wong's nuanced performance, in particular, preempted the reading of mere reversal.

   Since 1988, numerous critical works on *M. Butterfly* have appeared. I make no claims for exhaustiveness in this short summary of key articles in which the play's political valences are read quite differently. Some critics find *M. Butterfly* to be highly problematic. James Moy sees the play as a reinscription of Orientalist stereotypes and as a disfigurement of the Asian American subject, citing the Orientalist motifs represented onstage and the "racial and sexual confusion" (123) embodied by the character of Song. I would argue that the play, depending in part on the production—can also profoundly and simultaneously problematize those Orientalisms. On closer scrutiny, the trope of disfigurement in Moy's criticism reveals its foundational presupposition: a normative subject who is always already masculine and heterosexual. From this perspective, Song's complex sexuality can only seem "confused." Holding different assumptions about normativity would give one a different view on the possibility of an Asian American "whole subject," and therefore on the tropes of disfigurement and confusion. Colleen Lye's objections arise when *M. Butterfly* is taken out of its original U.S. context. She argues that in Singapore, *M. Butterfly* was appropriated by the state as a celebration of Chinese culture that ultimately served to buttress the interests of the repressive regime. Such a reading is convincing, but does not necessarily contradict the kinds of arguments I make for *M. Butterfly* in the context of U.S. mainstream theater. Lye opposes the two readings, arguing for the primacy of transnational and imperial circuits of power over the claims of minority discourse and the specific histories of race and civil-rights struggles in the U.S., which are dismissed as mere identity politics. My views are of course quite different, as the introduction to this volume makes clear. Rey Chow (1995) analyzes the film *M. Butterfly* and appropriately reads it in terms of Lacanian lure and misrecognition. As David Henry Hwang notes in his interview in this volume, the director David Cronenberg clearly subordinated the Orientalist critique in the play to a story about misrecognition in love. Chow too goes on to argue against a notion of identity politics that would foreground issues of race, gender, and sexuality, advocating that we attend "not simply to homosexuality, heterosexuality, or race, but also to the larger, open-ended question of the limits of human vision" (64–5). This represents one kind of intervention, in which marked subjects claim a universal humanity. The danger in this case is that the reinscription of the psychoanalytic master narrative as the universally human both masks the racialized, historical specificity of that narrative and runs the risk of reintroducing a substance-attribute metaphysics in which the "embarrassed etc." (Butler 1990) of race, gender, and sexuality become mere attributes ancillary to the universal substance of human consciousness. I would argue that the category "human" is never without its racial and other markings, even—or especially—in its psychoanalytic guise. For other views on the importance of taking careful account of the specificity of political histories, see Mani and Frankenberg; for an illuminating analysis of the differences in postcolonial and minority discourse positions, see Tsing; for a thoughtful appraisal of what is at stake in cultural production, see Lipsitz.

Other critics argue for *M. Butterfly*'s contestatory potential. Angela Pao engages an innovative study of reception to explore this question. Using published critical reviews of *M. Butterfly*, she argues that on balance, the play subverted the critics' cultural competencies, forcing them to appraise their conventions of reading/viewing plays. Marjorie Garber highlights the issue of transvestism and argues that the play instigates category crisis through the figure of the transvestite/spy. Her interpretation emphasizes the border crossings of gender, nation, and sexuality. Garber argues that the play acts to deconstruct notions of character and the essentialisms on which such a notion is based. However, her discussion of Asian theatrical convention (the use of the *kurogo* from Kabuki or Peking Opera, for example) elides what is at stake given a specifically *Asian American* subject-position. Shimakawa offers a reading that argues for *M. Butterfly*'s (inevitably compromised) challenge to theatrical convention and "the 'obscenity' of a subject who does not wholly submit to its construction by that audience. . ." (362).

2. *M. Butterfly* appeared in *American Theater* 5 (July/August 1988) in a special pull-out section. The actors' edition was later published in 1988 by the Dramatists Play Service, 440 Park Avenue South, New York, NY 10016. All quotations cited are from this latter source. My thanks to William Craver Associates, literary agents for David Henry Hwang, for permission to quote from the play.

3. If the play were in French, the answer would be clear—Monsieur Butterfly. But since it is a play written in English by an Asian American, about a Frenchman, which utilizes an Italian opera as a narrative foil, the matter is rather more vexed and ambiguous.

4. William Weaver, translator, *Seven Puccini Librettos.* New York: W.W. Norton, 1981, 189. All quotations from the libretto are from this translation.

5. Treated so eloquently in Catherine Clément's work, *Opera, or the Undoing of Women,* Betsy Wing, translator. Minneapolis: University of Minnesota, 1988.

6. Indeed, both Butterfly and Pinkerton are exotic caricatures for Puccini and his librettists. See Arthur Groos, "Lieutenant F. B. Pinkerton: Problems in the Genesis of an Operatic Hero," *Italica* 64 (1987): 654–675.

7. Many thanks to Susan McClary for pointing out the ways in which the music collaborates with the textual narrative.

8. See Catherine Clément, 45.

9. For critiques of the metaphysics of substance, see Judith Butler (1990), and Lucius Outlaw, "African 'Philosophy': Deconstructive and reconstructive challenges," In *Contemporary Philosophy: A New Survey.* Edited by G. Fløistad and G. H. von Wright, Dordrecht: Martinus Nijhoff Publishers, 1987, 9–44.

10. See Judith Butler (1990) on the insidious persistence of the subject-world trope in object-relations theory and in hermeneutics.

In slightly different disciplinary languages, anthropologists have articulated similar critiques. James Clifford, for example, in *Person and Myth: Maurice Leenhardt in the Melanesian World* argues: "Orienting, indeed constituting, the person, this complex spatial locus is not grasped in the mode of narrative closure by a centered, perceiving subject" (7). Leenhardt uses the notion of "plenitude" to describe a person consituted through relationships to the cosmos, to nature, to other persons. The notions of "presence" and the plenitude of referential meaning I deploy in this paper owe more to the deconstructionist tradition, where plenitude is associated with the centered, whole subject. One could argue that Leenhardt's work, though rooted in evolutionary perspectives and silent on the question of power, presages the emphasis on decentered subjects in this historical moment.

11. The foundational essay here is by Marcel Mauss, "La notion de personne, celle de 'moi'," *Journal of the Royal Anthropological Institute* 68 (1938), 263–82.

12. The arguments I outline in this and the following section are more fully elaborated in my *Crafting Selves: Power, Gender and Discourses of Identity in a Japanese Workplace.* My thanks to the University of Chicago Press for permission to recapitulate those arguments in this essay.

13. For another critique of the self/person distinction, see Michelle Rosaldo, "Toward an anthropology of self and feeling," in Richard Shweder and Robert LeVine, editors, *Culture Theory: Mind, Self, and Emotion*. Cambridge: Cambridge University Press, 1984.

14. Marcel Mauss, "A Category of the Human Mind: the notion of person; the notion of self." In *The Category of the Person: Anthropology, Philosophy, History*. Edited by Michael Carrithers, Steven Collins, Steven Lukes. Translated by W. D. Halls. Cambridge: Cambridge University Press, 1985.

15. Ferdinand de Saussure, *Course in General Linguistics*. New York: McGraw-Hill, 1966.

16. The television promo for the play recapitulated these power reversals. It begins with a shot of B. D. Wong as the demure Butterfly, who turns around to reveal a confident B. D. Wong, in suit and tie. Laughing, he puts his face in his hands and turns around once again. As the hands open, we see the sorrowful face of John Lithgow, painted in lurid Japanese whiteface and Kabuki-like makeup, dressed as Butterfly.

17. Michel Foucault, *The History of Sexuality*. New York: Vintage, 1980.

18. David Henry Hwang, personal communication, April 30, 1989.

19. Barbara Johnson, *The Critical Difference*. Baltimore: The Johns Hopkins University Press, 1980.

20. Barbara Johnson (10–11) offers an incisive analysis of Sarrasine's interpretive errors, which turn on logocentric assumptions of meaning as referentiality and presence.

21. Edward Said, *Orientalism*. New York: Vintage, 1978.

22. Julia Kristeva's *About Chinese Women* is one of the most egregious examples. In related fashion, Roland Barthes in *L'empire des signes* reinscribes notions of the exotic Orient. Work by women of color contests this privileging of gender over all other social forces and forms of difference. The literature here is extensive; see, e.g., bell hooks (1984, 1990), Cherríe Moraga and Gloria Anzaldúa (1981).

   Some might argue that in many cases, the scope of inquiry could justifiably be narrowed to an internal reading of the West. However, in appraising the work of Foucault, Gayatri Chakravorty Spivak counters: "I am suggesting that to buy a self-contained version of the West is symptomatially to ignore its production by the spacing-timing of the imperialist project. . . .The clinic, the asylum, the prison, the university, seem screen-allegories that foreclose a reading of the broader narratives of imperialism" (210).

23. For one of the most compelling enactments of such a stance, see Gloria Anzaldúa, 1987. More conventionally academic arguments for this view can be found in Chris Weedon, *Feminist Practice and Poststructuralist Theory*, and in Julian Henriques, Wendy Hollway, Cathy Urwin, Couze Venn, Valerie Walkerdine, *Changing the Subject: Social Regulation and Subjectivity*.

24. See Outlaw, "African Philosophy", for an explication of this substance-accident configuration in philosophy, where gender and race are relegated to the status of accidental attributes.

25. This very mainstream success is the cause of considerable controversy among Asian American scholars, where success is seen by some as an index of sellout, pandering to mainstream stereotypes. A meeting of the Asian American Studies Association in 1989 hosted a panel on *M. Butterfly*, including a response by Hwang himself. The session was impassioned, with the most heated criticism hurled by the heterosexual Asian American men and their students (both male and female), who apparently felt their masculinity impugned by the stereotype of the effeminate Asian man or who felt that the play otherwise recirculated oppressive stereotypes. Hwang's rejoinder was to say that he saw nothing particularly admirable about aping "white, male, macho" notions of masculinity. The issue raised here is a difficult and poignant one for any artist in a marginal position. Must one reinscribe stereotypes in order to subvert them? And in so doing, doesn't one inevitably reinscribe other stereotypes—in this case, sneaky Oriental? Though the issue is vexed, I have argued elsewhere (1990) that there can be no pristine space of resistance, and that subversion and contestation are never beyond discourse and power. Consequently, there can never be a purely contestatory image, though we must remain sensitive to relative degrees of subversiveness.

The panel highlighted a second, and even more poignant, issue: the extraordinarily small—though growing—number of Asian Americans who are in the position of being able to represent the Asian American experience—as though there were only one. (Happily, in 1996 as I review this essay, a number of other Asian American playwrights have been produced in major venues, though Hwang is the only one to reach a Broadway stage.) As so often happens, the few carry the burden of representing a race, something no single work, or handful of works, could possibly do. Though artists' accountability to the community—a vexed collective identity—should always be a critical issue, perhaps the best strategy is to devote energies to opening more avenues for increasing numbers of artists/writers/scholars from diverse populations, rather than expecting the few to represent fully the experiences of any given group.

26. In a telling decision, the award was given to the play *Driving Miss Daisy*, a white Southerner's nostalgic apologia for the good old days when people of color knew their place.

27. For explorations of this metaphor of the "Borderlands", see Anzaldúa, *Borderlands*, and Carolyn Steedman, *Landscape for a Good Woman*. See also Renato Rosaldo, "Ideology, Place, and People Without Culture, *Cultural Anthropology* 3 (February 1988), 77–87, for a notion of the border or border zones.

28. Arlene Teraoka, "*Gastarbeiterliteratur*: The Other Speaks Back," *Cultural Critique* 7 (Fall 1987), 77–102.

29. Some critics note the lack of a "real" female presence in the play, and question whether Hwang has simply appropriated woman as something only a man really knows how to perform or create. Certainly, there is a sense in which woman, though not an essentialist category, does mark a position of subordination within a shifting field of power relations. It is also true that Hwang himself has seriously pondered the issues of the politics

of gender and representation here. In his notes for those who plan future productions of *M. Butterfly*, he suggests that having a "real" woman play the part of Song might have the undesirable consequence of inviting the complicity of the audience in yet again enjoying the humiliation of an Asian woman. Hwang feels the use of a woman in the part of Song "runs the risk of exploiting the very sexual oppression it seeks to condemn, in the same fashion as violent movies that pretend to be anti-violence. If a woman plays Song, then we are watching a woman being oppressed in a very seductive and pleasurable manner. If Gallimard were actually oppressing a man, the effect on the audience is much more subversive" (89). My own reaction is that the use of a man to play "woman" highlights the discursively constructed nature of the gender binary and the collection of stereotypes that pose as man and woman, and consequently *M. Butterfly* can become a searing indictment of the objectification of women and the Orient. That "real women" are not principal characters is precisely the point, and paradoxically this can render *M. Butterfly* an exceedingly effective critique of gender oppression and Orientalism. But subversion is never unproblematic or beyond power, as has already been noted—for example, an Asian American man rather than an Asian American woman gets an acting job—and as with any cultural product, the play can be read as simultaneously problematic and subversive, though I would argue that the subversive elements predominate.

3.
orientalizing:
fashioning "japan"

IN THE EARLY 1980s, Japanese fashion exploded onto the international scene. The work of designers such as Issey Miyake, Yohji Yamamoto, and Rei Kawakubo of Comme des Garçons was predicated on a revolutionary aesthetic vision—loose, architectural shapes, asymmetry, unusual textures and somber colors, "lace" made of holes and rips in fabric. To a Western public, these garments embodied unfamiliar notions of what counts as clothing and how clothing relates to human bodies. The fashion world reacted passionately. Detractors labelled it the "Hiroshima bag-lady look," while enthusiasts welcomed it as pathbreaking and subversive. Many dismissed it as destined only for shock value, a passing fad. Yet Japanese fashion and its influence have been pervasive at all levels of the industry.[1] The continuing success of designers such as Issey Miyake, Rei Kawakubo, and Yohji Yamamoto, among others, has forced Paris and New York to take notice, if sometimes grudgingly, and to recognize Tokyo and Asia more generally as sites of creation in the fashion industry, not merely as producers of designs conceived in the West.

Fashion provides us with an exemplary site for examining the constitutive contradictions of Japanese identity at a moment when Japan had assumed an acknowledged place as a global economic superpower. An advanced capitalist nation-state with an imperialist history and, arguably, imperial ambitions, it is nonetheless racially marked. Constitutive contradictions similarly animate the fashion industry: quintessentially transnational in its dispersal and reach, it is simultaneously rife with essentializing gestures that refabricate national boundaries. Consequently, for Japanese designers and others, what counts as Japanese is always a problematic issue. On the one hand, the entry of the Japanese into high fashion ready-to-wear indexes Japan's status as an advanced capitalist power and a cultural leader, for fashion is a global industry in which developed nations, and more specifically, major urban centers in those developed nations, assert hegemony as the sites of creation.[2] Yet, Japan's subordinate status as a late developer, forcibly compelled to modernize in Western terms, continues. Competition is still on someone else's ground, within an idiom and a tradition developed elsewhere. This history is materialized in the very designation of the medium in which Japanese designers work: *yōfuku*, "Western clothing," rather than *wafuku*, "Japanese clothing." Inevitably, the work of Japanese designers rearticulates a problematic of "Japanese" and "Western" identities.

At stake in these questions is a politics in a broad sense—economic power, cultural authority, world recognition, place in a world order[3]—at an historical moment when national boundaries are contested, problematic, and highly charged. Referentially unstable, defined through lack and difference as are all identities, "Japan" has been unthinkable historically outside its relations with the West and with other Asian nations.[4] An overly schematic narrative of relations with the West would mark a legacy of inferiority symbolized in the "opening" of Japan to Commodore Perry and the defeat in World War II, followed by a postwar economic boom and an increasing sense of Japanese political confidence as equal or, some might say, even superior to the West. At issue here are interimperial rivalries among advanced capitalist nation-states. Yet, because the Japanese are racially marked, the rivalry is laced with familiar Orientalist discourses whose tropes circulate in the fashion world as they do in the realms of politics. Even when some Japanese designers see themselves as part of a larger, transnational narrative field, the sedimented histories of nation-states and various essentializing practices resituate them in terms of their national, and often racial, identities. On the other hand, in its relations with other parts of Asia, Japan's mobilization as a nation-state in the late nineteenth century meant taking on the colonizing imperatives of the nation; specifically, projects of imperialist ambition and aggression manifested in the colonizations of Korea and Taiwan, wartime militarism, aggressions in China, as well as continuing economic imperialism in Southeast Asia. Western Orientalizing, counter-Orientalisms, self-Orientalizing, Orientalisms directed at other Asian countries: the interweavings of such constitutive contradictions produce "Japan".

This essay examines the fashioning of a Japanese national essence in a variety of sites in the garment industry. First, the industry's transnational complexity and the challenging of old forms of dominance emerge in the question of what counts as Paris, where Parisian hegemony in the fashion industry is simultaneously undermined and reasserted. This provides a broad context for the analysis of multiple Orientalisms. International fashion commentary tends to group Japanese designers on the basis of national essence rather than on individual design achievement, as is the usual case for European and American designers. "The Japanese" are termed "avant-garde" or "experimental," and the distinctive features of their work are often traced to origins in culture, such as a Japanese aesthetic, Zen, or regional costume.

Such essentializing gestures are for these designers centrally implicated in geopolitical power relations and in discourses of Orientalism, and the final section examines the reinscriptions and contestations of Orientalist discourses in three sites. The first is a moment of Western Orientalizing. Wim Wenders's documentary about designer Yohji Yamamoto, despite its celebration of postmodern identities, reinvokes a high modernist discourse of filmmaker as creator deity and recirculates familiar Orientalist tropes: Japan as miniature, aesthetic, feminized, exotic. A second moment examines processes of what Marta Savigliano (1995) calls "autoexoticizing," through the appropriation of Western gazes. Here I focus upon a 1989 feature entitled, "Kyoto snob resort" in a leading Japanese fashion magazine, *Ryūkō Tsūshin (Fashion News)*. The series of photographs and articles initiates a nostalgic search for the essence of Japaneseness as it simultaneously claims a strongly cosmopolitan identity through adopting/undermining a Western—usually French—gaze. It offers an exemplary instance of nostalgic essence fabrication, the provocation of consumer desire through commodity fetishism, and the construction of a feminine consumer-subject. The third moment enacts Japanese positioning as an imperialist, advanced capitalist nation-state in a position to Orientalize others. *Ryūkō Tsūshin Homme*, the men's issue of the same fashion magazine from the same month, provides a revealing point of entry into this colonizing male gaze, as its articles and fashion spreads perform Japanese male dominance over a feminized, Orientalized Thailand and an exoticized, mysterious Bali. Through an

examination of these disparate sites, the contradictions and mutually constitutive dialectics of nationalism/transnationalism and Japanese identity emerge in
their ambivalent complexity.

THE CENTER CAN(NOT?) HOLD

Questions of cosmopolitan and national identities are articulated in paradig-
matic form in the fashion world's complex relationship to Paris as the world
fashion capital. Strong contending sites of fashion design have arisen in recent
years in New York, Milan, and to a lesser extent, London and Tokyo. Yet even
as the fashion world proliferates and disperses, a strong centripetal force draws
designers to Paris. Compelling them is a sense that, after all is said and done,
only those designers who have made it in Paris have *really* made it. Certainly,
of the Japanese designers only the handful who regularly show in Paris can be
said to have achieved worldwide recognition: Hanae Mori, Issey Miyake, Rei
Kawakubo of Comme des Garçons, and Yohji Yamamoto notable among them.

To address the question of Parisian hegemony, however, one must also problematize what counts as French. Multinational financing, licensing, and the
hiring of foreign designers have wrought dramatic changes in the classic French
design houses, refiguring the boundaries of Paris. Chanel has been for years
the domain of German Karl Lagerfeld, who also designs for labels Chloé and
Lagerfeld and for the Milan design house Fendi. In 1989 Milanese Gianfranco
Ferre took over the House of Dior from the long regnant Marc Bohan. Last season, Ferre's successor, British designer John Galliano, showed his first haute-
couture collection for Dior. The venerable House of Grès was purchased by the
Japanese textile and apparel company Yagi Tsūshō in 1988. Yagi then hired
Takashi Sasaki, a Japanese who had worked for 15 years at Pierre Cardin, to
replace the ailing Madame Alix Grès. Sasaki presented his first collection for
Grès, 80 pieces for the spring and summer of 1990. In the same year Cacharel,
symbol of soft French femininity, hired a new head designer, Atsurō Tayama,
head of the Japanese fashion atelier A.T.[5] In 1995, hip London designer John
Galliano succeeded Hubert de Givenchy at the House of Givenchy, marking an
important shift in the traditions of haute couture. When Galliano moved to
Dior, Alexander McQueen took over the helm at Givenchy. Moreover, France's
"Others"—designers from former colonial territories and denigrated European
nations—have also made inroads into Paris, including the highly successful

Azzedine Alaia, of North African descent, the House of Xuly Bet, of Sene-
galese origin, and Belgian deconstructivist Martin Margiela.[6]

To complicate matters, a designer of one national origin may have an organization financed by one or more multi- or transnational corporations, and
employees in the boutiques, the showrooms, and the production lines may be
scattered across the globe. Certainly, Paris is the site for increasing numbers of
international alliances in which Japanese capital plays a key role. For example,
Romeo Gigli, the sensation of the late 1980s, opened a Paris boutique owned by
Japanese department store Takashimaya—which also owns the exclusive on the
production and marketing of Gigli in Japan. Onward Kashiyama, a Japanese
firm, distributes Jean-Paul Gaultier in Asia and the U.S. and owns Gaultier's
Italian production facilities. In 1995 they inaugurated their own house line
designed by American Michael Kors.[7] Production is also globally dispersed; for
example, Comme des Garçons and Yohji Yamamoto manufacture some of their
simple garments in their intermediately priced, or bridge lines, in France and
Italy. One can only guess what the origins of these workers might be: Turkish
Gastarbeiter? North African immigrants? If Paris is hegemonic, it is no longer
the Paris reigned exclusively by the French. Indeed, French fashion, itself
emblematic of French nationhood, is created by Germans, Italians, Japanese,
and North and West Africans, among many others.

On the Japanese side, the relation to the West is a complex mixture of
"mimicry" (Bhabha 1987), appropriation, synthesis, and "domestication"
(Tobin 1992). Western clothing has become the normative standard in Japan
after its introduction in the Meiji period (1868–1912), so that kimono either
mark special occasions or signify traditionalism. On the level of fashion design,
the 1990 Tokyo collections I attended were instructive. Mostly, designers
showed what I call "just clothes," garments indistinguishable from what you
might see on the streets of Paris, New York, or even middle America. The
mimetic reproduction of the West was further symbolized by the overwhelming
use of white models. One or two Asian models appeared in the shows of most
Japanese designers; only those from abroad, such as the recently deceased Bill
Robinson, featured numerous Asian models. In the Tokyo collections, when
Black models were used, they added "exotic" color, reproducing Western
industry practice. The predominance of white models and the just-clothes
quality of most of the collections can be thought of in multiple ways: one, as
poignant and racially marked. Another level might see in the collections a
thorough domestication of Western clothing, so that the garments Japanese

59

designers produce for the domestic market are no longer merely reproductions, but thorough appropriations of Western clothing conventions. Another, taking a cue from Bhabha's analysis of mimicry, would see the complex combination of "not quite"—the almost realized reproduction of Western clothing—and "not white," the racial marking that makes the notion of the Japanese entering the domain of Western clothing slightly disturbing, even ominous. Indeed, Japanese designers in their very entry into the domain of Western clothing destabilize the East-West binary even as, at another level, they reinscribe it through mimesis.

Given this aesthetic/political history and the context of an industry defined by cosmopolitanism, global dispersion, a contested European cultural hegemony, and mimetic/appropriative tendencies in the domestic fashion industry, what counts as "Japanese" is, for Japanese designers—a label many themselves eschew—a highly vexed issue. Many desire not to be lumped together, nor to be seen as designing out of a culture. Fashion, they say, should transcend nationality (*mukokuseki*). Perhaps Issey Miyake's well-documented career and his thoughtful disquisitions on the subject most eloquently illustrate these complexities and ambivalences. After graduating from Tama Art University in 1964, he went to Paris to work at the houses of Lanvin and Givenchy for four years. In an address at the Japan Today Conference, he describes his awakening to possibilities for synthesis of Japanese and Western forms in his creations:

> Away from the home country, living and working in Paris, I looked at myself very hard and asked, 'What could I do as a Japanese fashion designer?' Then I realized that my very disadvantage, lack of Western heritage, would also be my advantage. I was free of Western tradition or convention. I thought, 'I can try anything new. I cannot go back to the past because there is no past in me as far as Western clothing is concerned. There was no other way for me but to go forward.' The lack of Western tradition was the very thing I needed to create contemporary and universal fashion. But as a Japanese I come from the heritage rich in tradition . . . I realized these two wonderful advantages I enjoy, and that was when I started to experiment creating a new genre of clothing, neither Western nor Japanese but beyond nationality. I hoped to create a new universal clothing which is challenging to our time (Miyake 1984).

Predictably, Miyake feels uncomfortable with the label "Japanese designer" precisely because it enforces stereotyped limits to his vision of a design with universal appeal. He fears that his association with Japonaiserie will make the interest in his clothing simply a fad. Miyake wryly stated, "I have been trying to create something more than Japanese or Western for over ten years and, ironically, I find myself as one of the leaders of the new Japanese craze. I hope I will be around a lot longer than this sudden interest" (1984).

Miyake's claim on universality reproduces the contradictions animating Japanese identity formation from the 1970s. On the one hand, his appeal for universality fuels the forces of consumer capitalism. "Universality" means clothing that will sell anywhere in the world, and more specifically, in Europe and the United States. Claims for universality reveal desires for parity with the West as a nation-state, as a capitalist power and as a cultural producer. On the other hand, "universality" reaches for recognition outside essentialized Japanese identity. Here, the salient feature is racial marking, which preserves the unmarked category of universality for "white". Who, after all, is allowed the designation "designer," not "Japanese designer?" Miyake's move toward universality on this level is a common, if problematic, move to escape ghettoization.[8]

This dilemma, how to play on someone else's field as a racially marked, artistic, capitalist, geopolitical rival, faces all Japanese designers who have international reputations, and each deals with the dilemma somewhat differently. According to Harold Koda (1989), former curator at the Fashion Institute of Technology and currently costume curator at the Metropolitan Museum of Art, the arrival of the Japanese in Paris can be conceived in generational terms. The trailblazer in the field of international fashion design and a highly powerful force in the industry is Hanae Mori. She first went to Paris in 1961, showed for the first time overseas in New York in 1965, and in 1977 became the first Asian to be admitted to the Chambre Syndicale de la Haute Couture: the exclusive ranks of those who are allowed to design haute couture, garments made-to-order for the world élites.[9] Mori is known for her feminine, classic garments, clothing for the elegant, well-heeled, mature woman. The shapes of her clothing draw from classic draping and tailoring as much as from regional costume. The garment in the photograph exemplifies these influences. The coat echoes kimono in its flowing shape, but the sweater dress it covers is slim, recognizable in terms of Western clothing conventions as feminine, sexy, soigné. The Japanese elements in her work often lie in the patterns of the fabrics she uses: her well-known butterfly motif, for instance, in clothing and accessories in the late '70s and early '80s, or patterns on her luxurious evening gowns that evoke motifs from *kimono*.

Kansai Yamamoto's Japan draws on the stylishness of Edo townsman culture. Understated aestheticism has no place here; instead, Kansai boldly

61

1990–1 Autumn-Winter Ready-to-Wear Collection
Paprika cashmere turtleneck dress
Paprika wool long coat printed with black spots
Mamoru Sakamoto, photographer
Used by permission, Hanae Mori International

appropriates Edo stripes and Edo firemen's gear, among other motifs, to create wildly patterned tops, electric bright, multicolored sweaters with padded shoulders reminiscent of samurai armor, and dramatic combinations of strong colors and bold graphics in his space-age/Edo-retro look. Kenzo Takada has been resident in France since 1965 and showed his first Paris collection in 1970 (Sainderichin). Kenzo's bright, folkloric styles, his recreations of boxy kimono shapes in quilted and flowered fabrics in the 70s, his continued sporadic references to kimono in later collections allude to regional costume even as they modify it. Mitsuhiro Matsuda and to some extent Takeo Kikuchi of Bigi claim for Japan a different version of Japanese-ness that alludes to the Japanese appropriation of Western clothing in earlier parts of this century. One of Bigi's labels, Moga, explicitly invokes the heritage of the flapper, the *mo(dan) ga(aru)* (modern girl) of the 1920s. Matsuda stresses the romantic aspects of fashion in his work, through nostalgic evocations of prewar elegance in beautifully tailored suits, rich patterns and colors, embroidery, and passementerie. All these designers tend to use Western tailoring techniques or adaptations of regional costume for their work.

This tendency to group Japanese designers together—a move this chapter makes as well, even as I try to deconstruct that essentializing category—proves understandably frustrating to people who pride themselves on their distinctiveness and creativity. Certainly, to lump together Hanae Mori's lavishly printed silks, Miyake's technology of pleats, Matsuda's nostalgic retro mode, and Kawakubo's radically deconstructive vision, suppresses the differences within this highly diverse group. The fashion world and the larger cultural and historical discourses of which it is a part circulate the tropes of both individual creativity and national identity. For the moment, I am highlighting the racial/political elements at work in the construction of a national identity, but both the trope of individual genius and the trope of national essence must be interrogated.[10]

Indeed, essentialist national identities are most strongly asserted in the case of the so-called avant-garde of Japanese fashion. "Japanese designer" usually designates one of the three—Miyake, Kawakubo, Yamamoto—who, according to New York designer Diane Pernet, gave fashion its "last big shock" (1989). Fashion commentators categorize their related yet distinct work in terms of its experimental moves, which are then traced to Japanese aesthetics, traditions, and costumes, or to some overarching postmodernity. Generally, journalists and fashion analysts single out several distinctive features of

"Japanese fashion" in the early 1980s, and with some ambivalence about the essentializing effects of these discourses, I reproduce that commentary here.

First is the premium placed on the cloth as a point of departure for design. The fabrics themselves are often in-house designs, specially commissioned, artisanally produced textiles, or startling synthetics that draw on the best of available technology. Yohji Yamamoto speaks of *nuno no hyōjō*, the expression of the cloth, "displaying what is inherent in the cloth: wrinkles in linen, puckers along a seam, the texture of hand-washed silk satin" (Stinchecum 74). Miyake explicitly likens fabric to "the grain in wood. You can't go against it. I close my eyes and let the fabric tell me what to do" (Cocks 1986, 70). Like the others, Kawakubo experiments with new textures and dyes. Her inspiration "is different types of fabric she has seen in her lifetime—not necessarily clothing but perhaps a piece of paper or carpeting" (Sidorsky 18). She is known for her aesthetic of imperfection and asymmetry,[11] and has reportedly been known to loosen a screw on a loom in order to introduce the surprise of the imperfect, the trace of the handmade, into the process of mechanical reproduction. Yamamoto, like Miyake and Kawakubo, appreciates the playful and innovative use of a variety of unexpected materials. In an interview, Barbara Weiser of the boutique Charivari voiced to me her surprise at finding Yohji garments made from the fabric used to cover tennis balls (1989). Similarly, Issey Miyake both draws on artisanal production from Japan and other sites[12] and explores the technologies of synthetic fabrics. In recent collections, he has pursued the technology of pleats in garments that are often described as museum pieces, evoking images of Fortuny.[13] Kawakubo works closely with textile designers and producers; their innovations are often featured motifs in her collections. For example, in the 1990 spring-summer collection I saw in Paris, "non-woven, man-made" fabric was such a theme.

A second commonality costume curator Harold Koda labels "terse expression": that is, a respect for the integrity of the material and an aversion to cutting into the cloth. He links this aesthetic to the use of cloth in kimono and regional costume, where the bolt is used virtually in its entirety, with relatively little cutting and little waste. "The minimum is used to maximum effect" (1989). Examining the pattern pieces of one of these garments reveals this tendency toward terse expression. Even in constructing a simple skirt, Miyake uses one entire piece of cloth to achieve the draping (rather than depending, for example, on multiple pieces cut on the bias). A conventional Western skirt involves greater waste of the material, as pattern pieces are laid

Bonded cotton dress from 1986 collection
Photographed by Steven Meisel
Courtesy Comme des Garçons

out and then cut from fabric; if the pattern is arranged on the bias of the fabric, the waste will be even greater.[14] On the body, the two skirts may seem
similar, even identical, to the untrained eye; however, at the level of construction, the differences are stunning. For example, Miyake is said to work
with the fabric first, draping it over himself, then draping it on a model, and
only then making up sketches (Cocks 1986, 70).

A related innovation prevalent in the clothing of the early 1980s and less apparent in contemporary designs are garments in one size. This commentators link to the conventions of kimono, which come in a single size and are adjusted to fit the body of the wearer through wrapping and tying. Barbara Weiser (the owner, with her mother and brother, of the highly successful Charivari boutiques in Manhattan) described for me her first encounter with Yamamoto's work:

> It was. . .maybe 1979. . . What happened was that I was in Paris for the collections. . .rather disappointed and bored with what we saw that season, and I decided to go hunting. I went to Les Halles . . . into a shop on the rue du Cygne, and there were these garments that had the oddest look. They looked slightly like hospital gowns in fabrics and forms that I had never seen, and they were all one size, which was in itself radical, and they were moderately priced at that point. I took about 15 or 20 pieces into the fitting rooms, and tried them all on and found that they were *fascinating* when I put them on the body. Actually you couldn't tell how interesting the forms were when they were just hanging on the racks. I remember calling my mother at the hotel and said that she had to come immediately and see them, because they were the most interesting garments I had seen. I didn't know if I loved them or what: I just am utterly stunned. My mother and I, who are not the same size, she started trying on the exact same pieces, which was also odd in itself. And she immediately asked them if they had a collection, and it turned out that they had just opened the store, so it was in the back or upstairs. They wheeled out the racks, and we were buying the collection. (November 13, 1989)

Weiser is literally invested in Yamamoto's clothing as the retailer who introduced his line to the U.S., and she portrays them accordingly in the most laudatory terms. Still, her encounter is eloquent testimony to the shock Japanese garments provoked when they first appeared in Paris.

Finally, Japanese designers are credited with the predominance of the color black during the early 1980s. Indeed, in Japan the unrelenting black-on-black aesthetic earned devotees of Kawakubo and Yamamoto the nickname *karasuzoku*, the crow tribe. In the U.S. Kawakubo and Yamamoto's explorations of black defined the 1980s all-black, hip, downtown/art-world look in New York. Jeff Weinstein of *The Village Voice* argues that for Kawakubo " 'black' becomes a full spectrum, an examination of the relationship between fiber and dye" (1989). Certainly, the emphasis on black permeated fashion in advanced capitalist nations, as did the loose cuts of clothing prevalent during this period. In the early 1980s, then, the Japanese avant-garde are grouped through their experimentation with fabrication, the use of black, the innovation of one-size garments, and traditions of wrapping: layering the body in various configurations of cloth and using materials to form an architectural/sculptural space *around* the body, rather than tailoring clothing close to the body.

There is a level at which these observations from fashion commentators are perceptive and revealing of themes and continuities. Yet at another level the very act of labelling these designers and tracing their commonalities to cultural continuity remains problematic. In my interview with Comme des Garçons designer and president Rei Kawakubo, I explicitly asked about her take on primarily Western journalistic reactions to her work that emphasized its putative Japanese elements. Kawakubo responded with some asperity:

> DK: I'd like to ask in some detail about aesthetics. . . . In the foreign press, there's usually a lot of talk about Japanese aesthetics, like *sabi/wabi*.[15] . . . I'm wondering how you feel the clothing has been covered in the foreign press.
> RK: Do you feel *sabi/wabi*? About Japan? Something . . . that exists only in Japan, even though it doesn't exist in your country? Do you have that sense?
> DK: I wonder . . . I think it probably exists elsewhere . . .
> RK: So, I don't especially . . . feel it. It's not important. For me.
> DK: Others give that interpretation.
> RK: I've seen so-called 'traditional' culture maybe once in school, when I had to. Things like Kabuki, one time only, for a class in elementary school. (my translation)

In this interchange, Kawakubo impatiently resists definitions of Japanese identity that reinscribe conventional notions of traditional culture. Her world is transnational, more "Western" in conventional terms than "traditionally Japanese." More important, this new version of identity itself displaces and shifts the terms of an East/West dichotomy, in a Japan that is itself constituted through incorporation of the West.

Further, Kawakubo goes on to comment on the label "Japanese designer." Joining our discussions was the Comme des Garçons international press liaison Jan Kawata:

> DK: And what do you think of being grouped as a "Japanese designer"?
> RK: I wonder whether they say it elsewhere: "American designer, American designer."
> JK: They don't.
> RK: It's the individual's name, probably.
> JK: The top countries are America and France, and the other countries . . .
> RK: . . . are number two, so they use the name of the country.

Clearly, for Kawakubo and her staff, as well as for other Japanese designers, grouping on the basis of race and nationality undermines the distinctiveness of her work, assimilates it to an essentialized notion of tradition that she eschews, and indexes Japan's secondary status in the fashion world.

As Kawakubo's responses indicate, troping in terms of national essence can easily be turned toward Eurocentric and Orientalist ends. In these appropriations, the Japanese are "not quite/not white:" simultaneously inadequate "imitators" of Western fashion and a racial threat. Racial overtones emerge blatantly, in the Associated Press coverage of the Paris collections in the early '80s: "Rei Kawakubo for Comme des Garçons proved as usual to be the high priestess of the Jap wrap."[16] *Women's Wear Daily* and other unsympathetic gatekeepers dubbed the black, asymmetrical garments "the Hiroshima bag-lady look." Condescension and dismissal are sometimes shown in subtle ways. Writer and publisher James Nelson pointed out to me (1989) the frequent misspellings of the names of Japanese designers in early articles in *Vogue* and in British fashion magazines. He passionately contends that such mistakes would be neither committed nor tolerated with European or American designers. The misspellings, though seemingly trivial, are gestures that tell us who counts and who does not. In 1989, the year before I attended the Paris collections, the misattributions continued. The expensive ($300) trade publication *The Fashion Guide*—a supposedly comprehensive who's-who in the industry—contains numerous errors in their information on Japanese designers. Comme des Garçons, Rei Kawakubo's company, is listed as French. And Kawakubo's name is given, in the introduction to Japanese fashion, as "Hai Kawakube"! Misspellings proliferate: "Harajuku," a trendy Tokyo hangout, is rendered "Harajuka"; Hiromichi Nakano comes across as "Wakano," the Bigi group as "Higi," and so on (416). American, French, British, and Italian designers suffer no such orthographic indignities.

Reception among retailers seemed equally mixed. Jeff Weinstein of the *Village Voice* described to me the "shabby little Japanese design corners" in major department stores during the heyday of Bloomingdale's in Manhattan. "It's not treated well; you walk in and you look at their Ralph Lauren boutique—it's all very prim and proper. This they don't give a damn about" (1989). The marginalization of the work of Japanese designers he attributed to racism and to a climate of Japan-bashing.[17] Like Weinstein, in her interview Barbara Weiser noted the anti-Japanese reaction in the fashion world, linking it to wider issues of trade and economic competition during a period when Japan-bashing was (and continues to be) in the air.

Just as the daring of Japanese clothing has provoked virulent negative response, so has it attracted acclaim. Hanae Mori was awarded the Chevalier des lettres, from the French government. The Musée des Arts Décoratifs mounted an exhibition of Miyake's work in the winter of 1988, and costume curator at the Museum, Yvonne Deslandres, calls him "the greatest creator of clothing of our time" (Cocks 1986, 67). Innovative designers Claude Montana and Romeo Gigli acknowledge Issey Miyake as a major influence. The corps of French fashion journalists presented Miyake with an "Oscar" of fashion as the best international designer at their first awards ceremony in October 1985. Indeed, his work earns him the greatest accolade the fashion industry can bestow: "*son style dépasse les modes*" (*Elle*, Feb. 3, 1986, 58), "his style goes beyond fashion."[18]

But praise can be in the form of a backhanded compliment; it can also construct limits and create a colonizing distance, even as it celebrates. Take, for example, the trendy downtown magazine *Details* (before it became a Condé Nast publication and a mainstream men's magazine), which described the 1988 Mori haute-couture collections with this Orientalizing gesture:

> Hanae Mori happily returned to her roots with fabulously painted panels on silk crepe, their motif lifted from ancient Japanese art screens. The fabric, uncut, formed flowing kimono evening dresses. What a lovely surprise to see Madame Mori return to her original source of inspiration after years of misguided attempts to imitate European style (Cunningham 121).

Laudatory though this passage may seem to be, the subtext is "East is East and West is West," and attempts to blur the boundaries are "misguided." Only when the motifs are "ancient" and recognizable as *kimono* are they successful. Mori's transgression—designing Western clothes indistinguishable from the work of Western designers—produces Cunningham's anxiety and condescension. The racial menace of "not white" provokes the dismissive term "imitation," minimizing the racial threat by consigning her work to the "not quite." "Stay Japanese"—according to some stereotyped view of Japanese-ness—the passage tells us. This familiar operation of Orientalism typically results in a Western commentator's melancholia in the face of the Westernization of a Third World or racialized Other. Orientalist melancholia is in part a form of mourning the perceived impending loss of his/her object of study and the concomitant threat to the commentator's site of privilege, as Rey Chow (1993) acutely demonstrated in her critique of East Asian Studies in the U.S. In a similar vein, an editor with a major French fashion magazine told me that many fashion professionals in France are fascinated with Japan, for they consider it to be the only country truly able to appreciate and understand French fashion on an aesthetic level. What appears to be a lavish compliment seems less flattering on closer examination. In fact, the utterance reasserts the centrality of French fashion as standard which only Japan can appreciate or approach. Surely the elevation of Japan to the position of France's appreciative audience scarcely constructs the relationship as an equal one. In both cases, Japan is "not quite/not white," almost but not quite France's equal in the latter example, contained within a "culture garden" (Chow 1990) of kimonos, butterflies, and silk in the former.

Recirculated Orientalist discourses and racial marking provoke counter-Orientalist responses. The late Tokio Kumagai offered this view:

> I'm working in the "fashion" world, but I also have hopes for political trends and such to go a certain way. In the latter half of the twentieth century, there exist many different. . .ways of life. But I think it is wrong to invade or to negate another culture. . .in other words, another way of life, through an economic system or political might, simply because of the fact that one part of the population has more power. I think we have to make a world where different cultures can cooperate and move forward. Even in Japanese fashion, the inclination toward white people has been strong. There's something wrong with thinking that white people's culture created at the end of the nineteenth century is more beautiful and powerful than any other. "Beauty" is something found in different ways among Japanese, in Chinese, in Black people; the notion that a fixed proportion is beautiful is nothing more than a prejudice. Because "beauty" is not something you can dictate from a position of authority.[19] (1986)

In this statement, Kumagai explicitly links the present state of the Japanese fashion world to political events such as the "opening" of Japan in the Meiji period, and he passionately argues against the enshrinement of "white people's culture" in Japan, where power and standards of beauty are directly related. In arguing for a multiplicity of definitions of beauty, Kumagai enacts an oppositional gesture, contesting hegemonic European and American aesthetic canons.

The passionate and ambivalent reactions to Japanese fashion from all players suggest that the stakes exceed the purely aesthetic, as though such a realm could exist beyond history, politics, economics, or the Law of the Father. At issue are global geopolitical relations, where the historically sedimented terms "Japan/Europe" and "Japan/U.S." bristle with significance. Though this essay can but gesture toward these wider contests for power, surely the arrival of Japanese fashion in Paris in the early 1980s, when the Japanese economy was burgeoning, cannot have failed to engender both admiration and fear in the fashion industry as elsewhere. The rhetoric of war recurs in fashion trade papers and popular fashion magazines just as it does in the popular press and in mainstream business journals. For example, in *Vogue*'s retrospective of the major fashion influences of the 1980s, Japanese designers are grouped together in a series of photos labelled "the Japanese invasion." They were the only designers to be categorized on the basis of nationality, even as their work was acknowledged to be classic. Similarly, a French article on Japanese fashion trumpets its headline "*L'offensif japonais*," demonstrating that the language of war and race circulates in Europe as it does in the U.S. The use of martial metaphors reminiscent of other such terms deployed in "the trade war," reminds us of the inextricability of fashion from capitalist accumulation and interimperial rivalry.

The positioning of Japan on the present fashion scene arises directly from these geopolitical histories. Miyake Design Studio representative Jun Kanai foregrounded the salient issues when she linked the interest in Japanese culture and design to Japan's economic success:

> Just as Japan emerged as an economic power, there is cultural or aesthetic power that developed. That will be (architect Arata) Isozaki, (furniture designer) Kuramata Shiro, Issey in fashion or Comme des Garçons's Rei Kawakubo, or Hanae Mori a little bit earlier, or the music of Kitaro. So there's a whole group of artists that emerged at the same time. . .that had to do with the wealth of the nation and also the power, that sort of energy (1989).

Kanai resisted easy Orientalizing by describing Miyake's generation as one for whom Rin Tin Tin and Coca Cola were as Japanese as, say, Kabuki. Her insights lead us into Japan's sedimented relations with the West. The incorporation of American popular culture and Western clothing as part of a contemporary Japanese identity does not arise in a vacuum via spontaneous generation, simple diffusion, or the arrival of a postmodern information/consumer society in a free play of genres and cross-references in a ludic site beyond power. Rather, it is directly linked to historically specific geopolitical relations and the forces of advanced capitalism: Western cultural, economic, and military dominance, on the one hand, and the increasing power of Japanese capital and the Japanese nation-state on the other. The appropriation of Western popular culture is inseparable from the "opening" of Japan in the Meiji period and the outcome of World War II, centrally including the American Occupation of Japan, and the postwar emergence of Japan as a capitalist superpower.

71

These complex positionings are visible in the establishment of the Tokyo collections themselves. In an attempt to make room for themselves in world arenas, a consortium of well-known Japanese designers, including Miyake, Kawakubo, Yamamoto, Matsuda, Yamamoto Kansai, and Mori, initiated the first such collections in 1985. Their goal was "to wedge the country's talent into the traditional fashion route: Milan, Paris, New York" (Cocks, May 19, 1986, 92). Four international designers were invited to Tokyo for a "Tokyo summit," creating a meeting of "world powers" on the fashion scene. And the analogy is not taken in vain. The attempt is to establish Japan as a peer to the the West in geopolitical as well as cultural terms, to say that Japan as a nation-state is equal to the U.S. or to any European nation. "'I hope,' Miyake remarked toward the end of the Tokyo shows, 'that my contemporaries and I will be the last to have to go to Paris'" (Cocks, May 19, 1986, 94). Miyake's statement is both poignant and imbued with Japan's capitalist, first-world, imperialist histories. The Tokyo collections and the fashion "summit" restage Japan's status as a racially marked late-developer whose development must be measured largely according to Western standards, yet they also perform Japan as aspiring cultural peer and imperialist rival of Western nation-states.

ORIENTALIZING GAZES

"Japan," like any identity, takes shape relationally, amidst historically specific, power-laden discourses, and the Orientalisms that racially mark Japan and Asia can be deployed, twisted, and redeployed in multiple and contradictory ways. Fabrications of Japan vis-à-vis its Others are strikingly instantiated in three different sites: the first, Wim Wenders's film on Yohji Yamamoto that images the Orientalizing gaze of the West in masculine, high-modernist terms; the second and third, the women's and men's editions of a Japanese high-fashion magazine that articulate complex forms of Japanese autoexoticism, counter-Orientalisms, and the Orientalizing of Southeast Asia. In these disparate sites, we see multiple, sometimes contradictory articulations of Japanese identity.

Avant-garde Orientals

Wim Wenders's film, *A Notebook on Cities and Clothes* (1989), commissioned by the Centre Pompidou in Paris, is a documentary based on the work of designer

Yohji Yamamoto. Ostensibly a disquisition on postmodern identities, fashion, and creativity, it also transposes and recirculates familiar Orientalist tropes.

The film begins with the screen full of static snow. Credits roll, and the author/narrator's voice intones a meditation on identity:

YOU'RE LIVING HOWEVER YOU CAN.
YOU ARE WHOEVER YOU ARE
"IDENTITY" . . .
of a person,
of a thing,
of a place.
"Identity."
The word itself gives me shivers.
It rings of calm, comfort, contentedness.
What is it, identity?
   . . .
How do you recognize identity?
We are creating an image of ourselves,
We are attempting to resemble this image . . .
Is that what we call identity?
The accord
between the image we have created
of ourselves
and . . . ourselves?
Just who is that, "ourselves"?
We live in the cities.
The cities live in us. . . .
time passes.
We move from one city to another,
from one country to another.
We change languages,
we change habits,
we change opinions,
we change clothes,
we change everything.
Everything changes. And fast.
Images above all . . .

The film cuts to a shot of a Tokyo freeway from the interior of a car. We see the freeway, but we also see a hand on the left holding a video screen/viewfinder where a video of the freeway plays. Wenders, clearly alluding to Benjamin (1969) and Baudrillard (1983), speaks of the differences between mechanical

73

reproduction in photography and digital imaging in video. In photography, "the original was a negative, but with an electronic image, there is no more negative, no more positive, everything is copy." In such a world, "what is in vogue, but fashion itself?"

We cut to a shot of Yamamoto in Paris, shot from above ground, apparently at or near his boutique in Les Halles, close to the Centre Pompidou. At this early point, he articulates the dilemmas surrounding Japanese identity, for in Japan he defined himself as a Tokyo person, not a Japanese. Later, he comments on how this self-conception was forced to change upon his arrival in Paris. Yamamoto did not intend that his clothes appeal to people based on nationality, nor did he expect to be constantly subjected to racial categorizing. But "when I came to Paris, I . . . was pushed to realize I am a Japanese. I was told, "You are representing *mode japonaise*," and, despite his protests, that label continued to be pinned to his work. It was, he says, a major realization. Echoing Issey Miyake's complex claims for universality, Yamamoto finds that racial essentializing is always already part of the story when Japanese travel to the West.

Similarly, Yamamoto articulates the complexities of Japan's geopolitical positioning given the legacies of World War II, when he invokes the death of his father, who was drafted and died in China. His father's buddies were in Siberian camps. Yamamoto relates his reaction to their letters:

> I realize that the war is still raging inside me; there is no 'postwar' for me. What they wanted to achieve I am doing for them. It's a role I feel compelled to play. . . . When I think of my life, the first thing that comes to mind is that I'm not fighting alone; that it's the continuation of something else.

Here Yamamoto gestures toward Japan's imperialist project in World War II and uncritically invokes his own implication in that project. He further suggests that vis-à-vis the West, the goal is precisely to achieve equality or parity, extending the war into the realms of business and aesthetics, winning on Western ground as the racially marked rival.

Wenders, on the other hand, manages throughout to maintain the position of Master Subject through thematizing authorship and high-modernist assumptions of individual, masculine creative genius. He talks to Yamamoto about the dangers of becoming imprisoned in one's style, condemned forever to imitate oneself. Yamamoto replies that "the moment [he] learned to accept his own style. . . suddenly the prison. . . opened up to a great freedom. . . ." Wenders proclaims, "That for me is an author. Someone who has something to say in the first place, who then knows how to express himself with his own voice, and who can finally find the strength in himself and the insolence necessary to become the guardian of his prison, and not to stay its prisoner." The reinscription of modernist tropes of man as creator deity, the source of originary genius and the owner of a unique vision and voice, with an arrogant belief in himself, strongly emerges here. Tellingly, this sequence is followed by a reference to Yamamoto's love for a photograph of Jean-Paul Sartre by Henri Cartier-Bresson. Here all the men—Yamamoto, Sartre, Cartier-Bresson, and especially, Wenders—are linked in a patriline of genius.

However, within this patriline, not everyone is equally masculine. Gendered hierarchies first emerge with Wenders's discussion of the differences between film and video. Cinema is associated with the masculine auteur. Wenders intones that filmmaking is a high modernist Art form created in the nineteenth century, suited to the expression of the "grand themes" of "love and hate, war and peace." Film and video differ in that the classic 35-mm. camera requires constant reloading, while the video camera operates on real time, making it better suited to passively recording images and thus to recording the (women's) domain of fashion. In cinema, the director is auteur, and Wenders finds Yamamoto to be an auteur in another medium. Just as Wenders himself works in the two languages of cinema and video, Yamamoto must work in two languages, balancing the ephemerality of fashion with his affinity for the past. Here Wenders stresses similarities between his work and Yamamoto's. However, a subtle hierarchy begins to emerge. Again highlighting similarities between Yamamoto and himself, he includes a segment demonstrating the ways both filmmaker and designer work with form and image. Yamamoto describes the creative process, which for him begins with the fabric, the touch, and then to considerations of form. Yamamoto does not conceive the process to be one of *making* something, but of *waiting* for something to come. Wenders then cuts to a shot of his camera, and makes his Orientalizing gesture through feminizing both the camera and Yamamoto. "You have to wind her by hand," says he of the camera, and "she knows about waiting, too." The video camera is similarly feminized; in the car, "she was just there." Juxtaposing Yamamoto's waiting with the female camera waiting for Wender's touch to wind her, makes an equivalence between the feminized Yamamoto and the feminized camera, recirculating Orientalist tropes of Asia and Asian men as passive, feminized, "waiting."[20] In both cases, Wenders maintains his position as Master Subject; Yamamoto is almost, but not quite, an equal.

Further inscriptions of the director as masculine auteur emerge at the conclusion, when Wenders shows us the aftermath of the Paris collections.

75

Yamamoto's staff sits, raptly watching a video of the day's runway show. Wenders extols their virtues, speaking of Yamamoto's "tender and delicate language. His company . . . reminded me of a monastery. They were his translators . . . whose care and fervor assured that the integrity of Yohji's work remained intact." Wenders labels the staff "the guardian angels of an author." He makes explicit the parallels between Yamamoto's work as a designer and his own work as a director, likening the design staff to "a kind of film crew, that Yohji was a director of a never-ending film never shown on screen." Wenders extends the parallels, comparing the consumer's confrontation with the mirror image with a "private screen. . .so that you can better recognize and readily accept your body. . .your appearance, your history, in short yourself—that is the story of the continuing screenplay of the friendly film by Yohji Yamamoto." Yamamoto's staff act as guardian angels, in the same way that Wenders's crew plays the angel to his own version of masculine creator deity.

Here Orientalism laces Wenders's characterizations. Though Yamamoto is a fellow creator, a fellow author, he is clearly not equally masculine. Wenders labels Yamamoto's artistic language "tender and delicate," recirculating typical Orientalist tropes of the East as feminine, aestheticized, fragile. Yamamoto's "tenderness" is exhibited in the film through his particular understanding of women; presumably this is because Yamamoto himself possesses feminine qualities. Indeed, Yamamoto says that were he not a designer, he would be a kept man (*himo*) who stays home and takes care of the woman—a position that feminizes Yamamoto while preserving his heterosexual status. Further, Wenders's reference to a monastery alludes to characterizations of Yamamoto and Kawakubo's work as "monkish," both in Japan and abroad, and simultaneously recirculates stereotypes of Japanese asceticism, spirituality, and asexuality.

However, the film's most striking Orientalist feature is a recurring visual motif. Wenders frequently depicts Yamamoto through the small viewfinder/TV screen of the video camera; this screen is usually tilted, at an angle, and off to one side. Always, a hand—Wenders's hand, presumably—holds the camera aloft. Here, Yamamoto is miniaturized, marginalized, and manipulated by the Auteur. This relation of Orientalist dominance recurs in many ways. At one juncture, we hear Yamamoto talking about and apparently leafing through a book of photographs, entitled *Men of the 20th Century*, a book Wenders also owns and loves. (Again, modernity is troped as masculine.) In the large screen, we see hands leafing through the pages of a book; we presume these are

Yamamoto's hands. At the top-right corner of the screen is the small video screen, with another scene of hands leafing through pages. Suddenly, we realize that the hands in the small screen are gesturing according to Yamamoto's speech rhythms, and the pages are turned the Japanese way, from right to left. Apparently, the small screen is Yamamoto, while the large screen shows us the hands of the creator/auteur Wenders, who is simulating Yamamoto's page-turning. He has appropriated Yamamoto's gestures, reducing Yamamoto's image to the small screen of the less privileged medium of video.

Other moments are rife with Orientalist motifs. As Yamamoto describes his company as an inverted pyramid where he stands not at the apex but rather at its base, a hand holds the video screen of Yamamoto against a picture book opened to a woodblock print of Mount Fuji. "Yamamoto," Wenders informs us, "means at the foot of the mountain." At other moments, we see the hand hold the miniaturized Yamamoto against backdrops of woodblocks depicting feudal battles, as Yamamoto discusses men's clothing. The miniaturized Yamamoto again appears over photos of prewar Japanese women, photos of men in samurai costume, and once, as the left hand of the auteur holds a toy fighter plane, manipulating it to simulate flight. Presumably these are meant to signify the martial, perhaps the kamikaze. In all cases, Yamamoto embodies Orientalist stereotypes, both new and old: the miniaturized, high-tech Oriental shown against the background of older Orientalist figures. And ultimately, it is Wenders's hand of God that orchestrates the action.

Other segments heighten the Orientalist tone. One sequence shows Yamamoto signing his name—his signature is the trademark for his brand name—on a plaque outside the door of his new boutique. Attempting to get it right, he appears to redo his signature to the point of absurdity. What are we to make of this sequence? Are we to assume, as Western viewers, that the Japanese are inept at signature, the sign of individuality? The segment is tellingly placed between the highly serious, political sequence showing Yamamoto's serious avowal that for him, there is no end of the war, and the depiction of Yamamoto in miniature against the Mt. Fuji background. The Orientalist hegemony of Wenders's gaze reasserts itself by rendering absurd Yamamoto's serious statements about geopolitics that claim a parity with the West. After trivializing Yamamoto's attempt to appropriate Western individuality through the signature, Wenders can then depict Yamamoto in stereotyped miniaturized form against the most hackneyed Orientalist image: Mt. Fuji. Thus Wenders maintains his dominance and the dominance of the Western viewer.

A Notebook on Cities and Clothes is a purported homage to Yamamoto's work, and on one level, it is indeed highly valorized. However, Bhabha's mimicry applies here. The homage recirculates universalist notions of "creative genius" based on male bonding among auteurs, but race intrudes as the difference that fractures and destabilizes the universalist gesture in that homage. Never quite as masculine, never allowed full accession to genius, Yamamoto is contained by Wenders's deployment of neocolonial, avant-garde Orientalisms. This enshrining of Yamamoto's work occurs within an Orientalist context that provides a platform and a screen for the reassertion of Wenders's own high-modernist, masculine, Master Subject status and his notions of authorial genius and creativity. Though some of these qualities can be granted to Yamamoto, in the end, there is no question of who is on top.

The Orient Within: *Kyoto Etrangère*

In the face of a West that continues to Orientalize, what of Japanese identity formation from a Japanese position? Perhaps nowhere are these contradictions more complexly articulated than in the world of Japanese fashion magazines. Here, profound ambivalence, simultaneous and alternating gestures of parity/inferiority/superiority to the West occur in tandem with ambivalent dominance toward the rest of the world .

Striking to a Western reader of Japanese fashion magazines is an unproblematized enshrining of things Western, particularly in those journals catering to youthful, hip, urban audiences. The enshrinement takes many forms. Western models abound on these pages, particularly in high-fashion journals such as *Ryūkō Tsūshin (Fashion News)*, *Hai Fasshon (High Fashion)*, and Japanese versions of international magazines, like *W, Marie-Claire*, or *Elle*. Indeed, sometimes there is scarcely a Japanese face to be seen. The prestige of Western luxury designer goods—Hermès, Gucci, Louis Vuitton, Celine—continues unabated. Magazines for young men and young women are often detailed guides to consumption, describing trends in various Western countries in lapidarian detail: the street-by-street, gallery-by-gallery tour through Soho or Venice Beach in *Popeye* and *Brutus*, the shop-by-shop tour of Honolulu or Paris in *Hanako*, the consumer guide for "office ladies." Things Western still embody the fashionable.

Yet, in a world of the 1980s and early 1990s in which Japan was an undisputed world capitalist presence with a strong currency and considerable buying power, this presentation of Western goods had another side. Fashion magazines enshrine Western consumer items and Western ideals of beauty, but they also present the world to Japanese consumers as commodities available for consumption. The world displayed in the glossy pages invites appropriation and participation through engaging consumer desire. The enshrinement of things Western coexists with a drive toward appropriation, where the world is at the disposal of the now powerful, much sought after Japanese consumer—a consumer both desired and feared in the West. These senses of simultaneous distance and participation in world currents of style, of inferiority and of dominance, circulate in the metadiscourses of fashion.

The contradictory twists animating Japanese identity formation in its relation to Europe and America were strikingly visible in the July 1990 issue of *Ryūkō Tsūshin*, a large-format, high fashion magazine for women. The nostalgic construction of the "neo-japonesque" and "exotic Japan" Marilyn Ivy describes[21] emerges strongly here, as the issue skillfully, compellingly, and seductively interpellates the reader as consumer-subject, mobilizing alluring appeals for the recovery of a lost Japanese-ness that can be attained through travel, garments, restaurants, objects: that is, through consumption.[22]

Ryūkō Tsūshin first invokes this essentially Japanese identity via the surprise of the cover. Though most of its cover models are Western, this time we see the face of a young Japanese woman staring at us from a sepia-toned photograph. She wears garments reminiscent of prewar schoolgirl uniforms, recalling a past era of innocence; her unrelenting gaze directly engages us. Opening the pages, we begin our encounter with Japan through Kyoto. A *sumi* painting of mountains covered with forest is illuminated as a red globe—rising sun? harvest moon?—rises in the distance. Above the picture floats the English title, "Kyoto, snob resort," followed by the caption: "With a 'snob', 'étrange' feeling, you can go out into Kyoto, a town enveloped with an Oriental atmosphere." Through its mix of scripts and languages, the phrase exoticizes Kyoto as repository of essential Japanese-ness and locates the reader as an upper middle-class cosmopolite—or someone with those pretensions. Kyoto is rendered in the Western alphabet; "snob," "étrange," and "Oriental" in the syllabary reserved for foreign words (*katakana*), while the rest of the sentence utilizes the standard mixture of Sino-Japanese characters (*kanji*) and the Japanese syllabary (*hiragana*). The piece imagines a trip to Kyoto for a cosmopolitan Japanese who adopts the shifting gaze of a sometimes French, sometimes British, or American foreigner. The journey to Kyoto becomes more than mere tourism; it is a Proustian quest to recapture lost time and a lost identity, a time/space of essentialized Japanese-ness. The constitutive paradox of the piece lies in a double move that

79

Ying Hu, in another context, has called the vis-à-vis: on the one hand, exposure to the foreign has thrown into question that identity; on the other, Japan is itself (re)constituted through appropriating the West.

The figure of woman as privileged metonym for nation compels commentary. The inextricability of gender and nation has elicited commentary from numerous quarters.[23] Ivy (1995) describes two Japanese advertising campaigns promoting domestic tourism in which young women are prominently featured. In these campaigns, ad executives cast women as consummate consumer-subjects, seducible by consumer desire and available to seduce men into the pleasures of consumption. Given the tropings of women as emblematic of the inauthentic—"frivolous, easily manipulated, narcissistic, seductive" (43)—Ivy argues that the campaign's narrative trajectory became one of authenticating this inauthenticity through domestic travel. Indeed, I would argue that it is precisely the *domestic* that must be highlighted in *Kyoto étrangère*. Through their participation in transnational circuits of commodities and capital, women as consummate consumer-subjects fracture totalized cultural identities through the fissures of the foreign into the national body. Consequently, it is they who must also figure the reconstitution of domestic identity; they who must stitch together its fragments. Kyoto as metonym for essentialized tradition is itself associated with femininity, as in the feminine, graceful lilt of the Kyoto dialect, or the Kyoto beauty as an iconic figure of woman. What, then, could more aptly narrativize the quest for renewed authenticity than a young woman's journey to Kyoto?

Indeed, Kyoto becomes a metonym for authentic tradition and renewal for the postmodern Japanese. The section begins with a nostalgic, hazy pictorial spread, where unfolding before us is the journey of a solitary young Japanese woman to sites of tradition in Kyoto: tea houses, famous mountains, famous traditional restaurants. The first shot in a blue photographic wash shows the model looking dreamily off into space, seated in front of a thatched roof tea house. Captioned *Kyoto etoranjĕru*, *Kyoto étrangère*, the piece is subtitled, "Fascinated by *ekizochikku* (exotic) town, Kyoto." The introductory text addresses the cosmopolitan reader:

> While (we) are Japanese with black hair and black eyes, we've become too accustomed to collections of foreign brand names, to the latest Italian restaurant, to modern interiors, and we've come to experience objects in the Japanese style as exotic. If you are such a person, won't you come and visit Kyoto? To remember what you've forgotten. To encounter things you never knew. And to find a balance between beautiful Japanese things and beautiful Western things" (18).

The voice positions the reader as a cosmopolitan Japanese who has adopted a Western gaze and for whom Japanese-ness becomes exoticized and located in particular places and in particular objects emblematic of Japanese tradition. The icons of authentic difference are those that might attract a Westerner, and captions to subsequent photographs in the spread define for the Westernized Japanese reader terms like bamboo blinds, incense, *tatami* mats, even "black hair" (a poetic usage of the term in classical verse) or fix on some metonym of tradition, such as Arashiyama, the famous mountain near Kyoto.

This shifting between and blending of Eastern and Western in a nostalgic version of the present suffuses the piece. A sense of authentic Japanese-ness as the undifferentiated past is imparted by a nostalgic aura concretely encoded in clothing, editorial voice, and photographic techniques. As she appears in identifiably Japanese scenes of the traditional—a thatch-roofed tea house, on a mountain path, holding a lantern, near a shrine—the model wears clothing difficult to place in space or time. Whatever their thoroughly cosmopolitan origins, the garments allude to the past: the poetic styles of Italian designers Dolce e Gabbana and Romeo Gigli are reminiscent of ballet tutus or Pierrot costume; in the context of Kyoto, they also conjure associations to *ju-ni hitoe*, the multilayered kimono of the Heian court. This past is blurry, generalized: the neo-retro styles of Kensho Abe look vaguely 40s, Kazuko Yoneda's demure dress recycles turn-of-the-century motifs, Alpha Cubic's good-girl sweater could be any sweater from anytime after the war, London designer Betty Jackson's print dress is pure 50s retro. All keep us in some undifferentiated space of nostalgia. The photography heightens these effects. A cyan or bluish wash irregularly alternates with sepia tints reminiscent of old photographs, where the effects of distance in place and time are achieved through hazy softness and faded color. The location of the editorial voice is equally blurry. As it defines for a "postmodern" Japanese the icons of "authentic Japanese" identity—brocade, lanterns, black hair—it speaks distantly, anonymously, authoritatively, a voice from nowhere, from no particular time. The floating, omniscient voice invoked within the frame of the picture dominates a second voice, the hard copy that gives us the mundane details we consumers need to know: who designed the garment, where to get it, how much it costs. The practical information on consumption in the present is located *outside* the frame, leaving undisturbed the hazy nostalgia of the clothing, the authoritative voice, the atmosphere of the photograph. Japanese-ness as nostalgic essence is encoded through these material practices, producing a blurry, elegiac past—a past you, too can find, if you journey to Kyoto.

The journey continues in a more discursive mode in following sections, giving us multiple perspectives on Kyoto from a variety of observers. Its narrative line takes us on a journey from outside to inside. Beginning with a section called "Kyoto from Outside" (the title is in English), we see Kyoto through the perspectives of Pierre Loti, author of *Madame Chrysanthème* (the prototype for *Madame Butterfly*), Paul Claudel, and Roland Barthes, followed by David Hockney's witty photocollage of Ryōanji temple, musician David Sylvian's fragmented photographs, and finally, the films of Kenji Mizoguchi (a Tokyoite by birth), that depict the Gion district and the lives of geisha. A second section takes us closer to Kyoto, offering us the thoughts of two Japanese born elsewhere who are now Kyoto residents. One, an artist/designer of jewelry, is an icon of cosmopolitanism; he works with Tiffany and regularly travels an international circuit. The other embodies the invention of tradition. He is a television actor who also owns a coffeehouse and occasionally offers ricksha rides, literally *enacting* tradition for tourists in this picturesque neighborhood. These men offer us two ways of combining our presumed cosmopolitanism with Kyoto traditionalism: traveling the world while living in Kyoto or "acting" traditional. The following section, "Inside Looking," offers us the perspectives of a Kyoto resident who amusingly debunks and explains stereotypes of Kyoto, especially the politesse and reserve (some would say coldness) of its people. Photographs highlight unusual views of Kyoto—views of the street from the inside of a temple, a small gargoyle one might miss if one walked by too quickly. Featured in the margins are further interviews with Kyoto natives that a tourist might encounter in her travels: shop proprietors, hotel managers. Their presence signifies "authentic Kyoto" not only through what they say, but in the lilt of the Kyoto dialect.

The problematic of identity articulated in *Kyoto Etrangère*—how to achieve the balance between Japanese and Western things—is resolved in the final section of the spread, "Shopping Around Kyoto." The quest for the essence of Japanese-ness finds its culmination in Kyoto boutiques and restaurants, which offer us the animated, lovable objects that embody Japanese identity, both traditional and cosmopolitan. We have only to consume them zestfully in order to become truly Japanese. This involves the literal *incorporation* of place and of identity through the body: wearing the lovable garment, ingesting the *nouvelle japonaise* cuisine, touching the traditional object. "Shopping Around Kyoto" (again, in English) offers us a tour where we can shop and eat our way through Kyoto. Postmodern cosmopolitanism and authentic Japanese-ness are offered to the reader/consumer as equally important aspects of Japanese identity, for most of the featured shops combine Japanese and Western elements in a new synthesis that simultaneously maintains and destabilizes the East/West binary. The haziness of time and place in the first photographic spread, the anonymous, authoritative voice from nowhere, have disappeared. We are now fully in the present, with vibrantly colored photographs, a lively editorial voice, and seductive shots of beautifully presented objects. A description of a store where one can purchase traditional fans (a complement, we are told, to even the most modern interior decor) is juxtaposed to a jazz bar, "My One and Only Love," that combines a high-tech environment with offerings that include sixty varieties of bourbon and unusual traditional seasonal *tsukemono*, Japanese pickles. The final page of the spread is especially eloquent, showing us an an elegant cafe which serves tea and Westernized versions of a famous Kyoto confection, *yatsuhashi*, and, in our final take-home message, a shop selling antique porcelain. "Don't think about displaying them like precious objects," we are told. "[We] want you to use them every day on your dinner table, maybe for your special home-cooking." (47) Even if you don't, the magazines continues, the objects are so "lovable" that they make *you* want to make *them* part of your everyday life. The dreaminess of *Kyoto étrangère* has evaporated into a crisp, lively, totally present world where objects offer themselves up to the reader just as the woman's figure was offered up to our gaze in the fashion spread. Objects become lovable, animated, eager to be part of our lives, in a vivid demonstration of commodity fetishism; indeed, the personification of objects heightens in the use of a suffix usually used for groups of *people*, not groups of objects (*monotachi*). The editorial voice in the piece directly addresses us; it is chatty now, rather than formal and authoritative. Hard copy and distant authority are recombined and transposed into an informal register, giving us both the buying information we need and evoking the vibrant atmosphere we will enter when we visit the shop. This time, we are located in the present and the future, not in a hazy past. The voice constructs our subject-position and provokes our desire through its lively depiction of the ways we can purchase our Japanese identities. Perhaps, it suggests, we will splurge for a whole set of porcelain, or perhaps we'll indulge in a different style of buying, adding one piece at a time. Our individuality is thoroughly constituted through consumption; we are distinguishable by the *way we buy*. "Shopping Around Kyoto" shows us that authentically Japanese identity can combine the cosmopolitan and the traditional; Japaneseness can be part of our lives through the lovable objects that beckon from the photographs, awaiting only our consuming touch.

Thus, "Kyoto Snob Resort" eloquently catches up the contradictions of nostalgic identity formation in a regime of commodity aesthetics and commodity fetishism. It creates a postmodern, transnational space inhabited by the denizens of economically powerful Japan. Here, the construction of Japanese-ness occurs only through relations with the West; the nostalgic moves of *Kyoto Etrangère* unsettle and re-code these binaries. The garments with their nostalgic air, the mixing of scripts, the photographic effects blurring past and present become part of the creation of a new tradition, in a balance of Japanese and Western things. The discourse of loss and the mourning for what Marilyn Ivy terms the vanishing, endures. But so does a kind of ironic reappropriation of a Western gaze, the claiming of a cosmopolitan identity, and the construction of a postmodern world in which Dolce e Gabbana, Romeo Gigli, and Betty Jackson take their place alongside bamboo blinds and tatami mats. This is premised on the reduction of both to elements of consumption, as consumer capitalism in advanced industrial societies gives us the capacity to consume both Kyoto and European clothing. Indeed, for the interpellated Japanese subject, snob is not an insult or an epithet; it is an ideal for which to strive, an index of postwar Japanese affluence.

At another level, the clothing, the atmosphere, the cosmopolitan gesture, claim for Japan certain elements of identity and mobilize fragments of desire, producing an autoexoticism and incorporation of Western elements and a Western gaze that beats the West at its own game and subverts, as it reinscribes, Orientalist tropes. It marks a moment in historical, geopolitical relations, where autoexoticism and the appropriation of the West in a refigured, essential Japan indexes Japan's accession to the position of powerful nation-state. It marks a moment of confidence, where the mourning for an essentially Japanese past, the contradictions of Japan's status as an advanced capitalist nation and as a racially marked rival to the West are resolved, temporarily, through cheerful, confident consumption. The article suggests that racial marking can in effect be counterbalanced, even effaced, through upper-middle-class purchasing power: Kyoto as snob resort. The problematic of identity as posed here is linked not only to a moment in the development of late capitalism, or to the development of the postmodern, with its implication of the equivalent decentering of all subjects and the elision of historically specific relations of power. The slippery, multiple positionings of the Japanese in the magazine spread take up the slippery positionings of the Japanese nation-state in the late 1980s and early 1990s, when economic dominance, growing confidence, enshrinement/denigration of the West, and questions of race occur within a historical context of

Japanese imperial aggression and defeat in World War II, Western penetration and the Occupation of postwar Japan. The construction of a Japanese identity and the appropriation/domestication/enshrinement of Western objects must be seen within this sedimented political history; what is involved here is far more complex and specific than the autochthonous emergence of a postmodern, consumer, information society in late capitalism.

Orient Oriented: Neo-Colonialism and The Male Tourist

If *Ryūkō Tsūshin*'s nostalgic blend of East and West constructed Japan's first-world identity through the figure of woman, the same month's counterpart article in *Ryūkō Tsūshin* for men figures Japan as male. Masculinized Japan here dominates a feminized, sexualized Southeast Asia, overlaying the gender binary onto the domestic/foreign binary. *Kyoto Etrangère* adopts the subject position of woman in relationship to the West, that is, in a position of inferiority where the tropes of the Orient as feminine are recirculated. It also constructs single women as exemplary consumer-subjects, who are thereby endowed with the capacity to consume and hence rediscover their essential Japaneseness. The men's magazine creates Southeast Asia as the feminine, exotic Orient submissive to Japan's masculine dominance. A history of Japanese military aggression, colonization, and ongoing forms of exploitation, such as the notorious Japanese and Western sex tours of Thailand, Korea, and the Philippines, form the subtext here. In both the men's and women's issues of *Ryūkō Tsūshin*, woman figures the essential purity of national identity that is endangered by outside intrusion. In the men's issue, the article and accompanying photos pivot around axes of tradition/ modernity, Westernization/exoticism, and pastoral/urban difference. Throughout, woman anchors the discourses on national identities, first standing for danger and corruption, then offering a point of entry into the culture, and finally serving as exemplar of the purity of essentialized Thai-ness soon to be despoiled by the inevitable encroachment of modernity and Westernization.

The title piece, "Oriental Oriented," opens with a large, two-page spread. The first features a photo, presumably of a Bangkok skyline. On the left is a caption in small print:

Haven't we been seeing Southeast Asia through Westerners' eyes? It may be all right for them (i.e., Westerners; the masculine pronoun is used) to reflect on themselves, to take a new look at Asia and see it a kind of spiritual authority and all that. But it's a mistake for Japan to take that approach and swallow it whole. We took a data-gathering trip to Bali and Thailand, not just out of Orientalism, but as part of inhabitants of the same era in Asia. (29)

Here, the men's magazine differentiates itself from the Orientalism of the West and posits a time-space of Asian identity that Japan shares with Thailand. The putative goal is to avoid Western-style Orientalism, but the passage articulates the contradictions of Japanese identity: an ambivalent oscillation between equality and superiority, between Asian solidarity with Thailand and Bali and a desire for equality with the West as a First-World power that colonizes other Asian nations.

Despite the writer's intentions, unequal geopolitical positionings cannot be erased. Their arrival at the airport prompts a guilty avowal of the awkwardness of Japan's relation to Southeast Asia. The author notes Japanese commentary on Southeast Asian poverty and Japanese wealth, intimating that the latter is achieved at the expense of the former. While admitting the persuasiveness of this view, he marks the irony of thereby reinscribing Japanese superiority and fixing Southeast Asia in a position of inferiority. Instead, he wants to look at Thailand in a *furatto* (flat) perspective, as presumed equals. Accordingly, he and his all-male crew dine with fashion designers, the owner of Bangkok's only fashion school, and a translator, at a nouvelle Thai restaurant full of "snob" Thai and Westerners.

Japan's position within a gendered political economy emerges clearly the following day. The men happen upon a Japanese student, who utters a cautionary tale for the unwary Japanese man. Lured by a sexy Thai girl into a strip club, he is presented with an exorbitant bill and threatened with violence unless he pays. His quick tongue saves him, but the author reports the student's experience, both for his readers and because his female guide (who becomes a confidante and an object of desire) asks him to do so. Women here represent the exotic but dangerous lure of Thailand. Unremarked, however, are the relations of extraction that allow Japanese men to travel to Thailand precisely as consumers in the sex industry.

Predictably, the author alternates between professions of surprise at Thai modernity and guilt-laden realizations that his very surprise reveals his own assumptions of Japanese superiority. From the seductions of the red-light district and a visit to Chinatown, the crew ends the evening in a disco called NASA. The space theme and the MTV videos prompt authorial musing, as he notes that trends come as quickly to Thailand as they do to Japan. He then reflects that since Bangkok is a huge metropolis, new information would be disseminated in "real time." In a move redolent with liberal guilt, he avows in spirited fashion that this world of discos and MTV is indeed part of contemporary Thailand and that those who insist on seeking "exotic Thailand" are misguided. "Thailand's future should be decided by Thais," he avers (34).

The refrains of East/West, tradition/modernity, pulse through the next sections. The men make trips to a weekend market where international goods are available, a Thai restaurant that offers a pan-Asian menu, and the house of a famous expatriate Westerner in Bangkok, where the interior embodies an East/West synthesis. A visit to the floating market calls up associations with the soft-porn flick *Emanuelle*—an association heightened by a condom that comes floating down the river. The author's comment reveals his own assumptions about Thai exoticism: "After all, people here are living their lives. That's right, it's natural that such a thing would come floating along" (37). In a related remark, the author notices TV antennas amidst the exotic scenery, and comments, "The residents around here are living in the same 1989" (37). These attempts to de-exoticize the landscape succeed in reinscribing the author's implicit condescension.

Later tradition and modernity shift into the registers of the pastoral and the urban. Bangkok stands for a blend of the exotic and the cosmopolitan, but vis-à-vis the Thai provinces, it embodies the corruption of the big city. Taking leave of Bangkok, the crew flies to Chiang Mai and to the village on the border of Burma where their guide was born. Text and photos amplify impressions of pastoral exoticism: people swimming and playing in the river against a backdrop of traditional architecture, monks sitting and drinking Fanta, wooden puppets, and outdoor merchants selling animal skins. Their return to the Bangkok airport ends the piece, as the author describes an interaction with a waitress. She responds to their stares with embarrassment and shy self-consciousness, prompting an authorial diatribe against Japanese women who have forgotten their femininity. Nostalgically, he invokes a prelapsarian past through the figure of the waitress, who stands for the purity of Thai identity before the encroachment of Westernization. "But with such rapid Westernization and urbanization, perhaps everything, like the waitress's self-consciousness, will disappear. Thinking of the prospect, [I feel] a little melancholy, but that can't be helped. Because the fate of Thailand belongs to the Thais. Still, I just want them to be able to avoid the strains that Japan experienced, if only in small measure. (41)"

Here, the author voices capitalist and imperialist nostalgia for the purity of a past before capitalist (Japanese and Western) intrusion. As Renato Rosaldo (1989) and other analysts have noted, nostalgia enshrines a golden age before a destruction wrought precisely by the one who mourns the destruction—in this case, by Japanese capital. Exposure to Japanization, Westernization, urbanization, and other worldly forces will despoil this Thai flower's shy purity and turn her into a tough, threatening hussy—like the prostitutes who lured the hapless Japanese student or like contemporary Japanese women. By mourning the fate of Thailand through his projection of the waitress's fate, the journalist also mourns what he clearly perceives to be the ravages of modernization and the loss of identity undergone in Japan.

The gendered nature of this mourning is striking. As in the *Kyoto Etrangère* piece, essentialized national identity is figured through woman. Japan's relationship to Thailand is cast in gendered terms as one of male dominance, in which Japanese men penetrate through the gaze directed at the waitress and through friendship and intimacy with their female guide.[24] The protective regret the author feels vis-à-vis the waitress and the increasing romanticism/eroticism of his relationship with the guide are informed by the neocolonial relationship of foreign men to Thailand through the sex industry.[25] Ultimately, for the author getting to know Thailand is like becoming intimate with a woman; indeed, the two processes are virtually coextensive. Here, then, Japan adopts the position of endangered seducee, prostitute's john, masculine gazer, protective older brother, and prospective lover to feminized, exoticized Thailand.

Similar ambivalences clearly emerge through the photography and design that, like the text, oscillate between figuring Thailand as an equal and assuming Japanese economic, cultural, and political superiority. Shots thematize the exotic/Western, traditional/modern, rural/urban binaries: photos of teeming urban streets and the train station portrayed in harsh, grainy daylight are followed by exotic shots of the floating market, dolls and puppets; temples on one page alternate with a photo of the very chic receptionist at the design school; women selling slabs of meat and packages of produce appear in dark photos illumined only by the golden halo of exoticism, while the opposing page features another crowded street scene complete with prominently displayed Sony advertisements. A red border used for design continuity throughout the piece encodes exoticism through graphic design. The bright, deep red, when paired with the caption "Orient Oriented," conjures associations with Chinese red and tropes of decadence and foreignness. Pictorially and visually, Thailand is constructed as exotic Other, reinforcing the exoticizing authorial voice.

The second section shifts focus from place to people. In a bright-red panel that heads this section, graphic black characters inscribe the rationale for the piece: "In order to come in contact with the new Bangkok facing its future as a mass consumer society, we decided to meet the talented people who would highlight the 'now'" (42). Pictured on subsequent pages are the three subjects of the interviews: a clothing designer; his brother, an interior designer; and the owner of the only Thai design school. The presumed fledgling stage of Thai development in these fields emerges as the theme of this article, despite the professed intentions of the authors to the contrary. For example, significant Japanese influence is always noted: the designer read Japanese comic books in childhood, while the head of the school won a Japanese design competition and spent several months in Tokyo during his youth. The interviewees contrast Japan with Thailand. On the one hand, they say, the upper echelons are as hip and as well-informed as anyone in Tokyo; on the other, the relatively high degree of class stratification means that the average level of Thai style needs what they call a "level up." Nostalgic regret for the loss of traditional Thai identity is inextricable from the need to jettison traditional (*toradishonaru*) Thailand—at least for the moment—in order to create so-called "New Thailand."

However, perhaps the most striking assertion of Thai underdevelopment occurs through photography. Each of the three interviewees are shot in a striking interior: a stylish black chair against white background, an ultramodern desk against rounded bookshelves, the graphic black and white of the design school. Yet in each case, the lighting is simultaneously harsh and dim, as though the electricity had been inadequate; as a consequence, each photo has a retro feel that contrasts sharply to the beautiful haziness of *Kyoto étrangère*. It is as though these men do not in fact inhabit the same "real time." Moreover, the photos highlight small elements of what could be read as underdeveloped building construction: a light switch, for example, or exposed pipes that have been painted white. Wittingly or not, such practices reinscribe an implicit condescension toward Thailand's "developing" status in the world of design. These Thai men are cast as fellow Asians, brothers to the Japanese author. Yet they remain little brothers, in a position to learn from Japan's example. Japan stands as masculine penetrator of Thailand as woman, and as benevolent elder sibling to Thai men.

89

If Thailand is exoticized and rendered inferior in gendered terms, a second spread entitled "Bali, Hi" constructs Bali as another kind of Orient—this time, a tropical paradise and site of spiritual renewal, mysticism, and unspoiled nature. Bali becomes a playground available to the purchasing power of Japanese and Western tourists alike; as an unpopulated natural paradise, it becomes a stage setting for idealized masculine leisure consumption: male pleasure as resort activity. The men's fashion spread opens with a shot of Club Med Bali at night. Lights glow from within the rooms, while greenish lights illuminate pool and foliage, palm trees fringing the indigo sky. Green is the operative color, signifying nature, paradise, the tropics, in contrast to the exotic, Oriental red used for Thailand. Lettered in green we find the opening caption:

> Seeking a rest for spirit and body, we fly to the south. A paradise far from our urban lives spreads out before us. We want to move toward a vacation where we can spend our time as we please. Not the typical Japanese vacation, pressed by time and driven by a tour schedule. Let us introduce you to this summer's resort fashions that match up with Club Med Bali's exotic charms, offering us the pleasures of dressing with style (46).

The photographic spread features a young white couple in their twenties; he has thick, wavy blond hair, while the woman is brunette and encodes a Mediterranean or Latin exoticism. The photos feature the couple in various settings at Club Med Bali: eating, kissing, staring at us from among palm fronds, lounging at the pool, dancing, riding a bike, posing at the beach. The man is clearly the protagonist, and occasionally he is portrayed alone: in the gym, floating in the water in a flowered shirt, lounging in a rattan chair. The consumerist message figures masculinity through crisp, capitalist realism, rather than the oblique poetic romanticism of *Kyoto étrangère*. Here, the photos are fully in the present, a tourist brochure for Club Med. Showing the clothing in various Club Med settings highlights the resort's diverse offerings. The borders between travelogue, advertisement and fashion journalism are further transgressed in the only insert written in the copywriter's voice. It is set against the background of the man floating in the pool, as the copy extols the virtues of the active, sports-oriented vacation for men available at the resort. Again, for men the keynote is activity in the present—Japanese masculinity articulated through athletics and leisure activity—not the hazy nostalgic fantasy presented in its women's counterpart.

This interpellation of the masculine consumer articulates with the article's figurations of race. The use of white models positions Japanese readers in contradictory ways. On the one hand, it reinscribes white ideals of attractiveness and reinforces the allure of racial mimicry. This impression is strong, given the fact that neither model seemed to be familiar to Western readers; one suspects that neither would be as successful in the U.S. or Europe as they are in Japan, continuing a neocolonial practice that offers lucrative Japanese careers to dubious Western "talent" who can capitalize on their exotic cachet. On the other, the use of white models makes a racial substitution in a gesture of parity, signifying the cosmopolitanism and the equality with the West the Japanese have presumably attained through consumption. Such cosmopolitanism will only heighten, the spread implies, through their journey to Club Med Bali, where Japanese can leave behind the stereotypical, group-oriented, schedule-driven vacation for a more European, fancy-free independence. The piece both enshrines a Euro-American ideal and suggests that Japan has caught up with the West, so that Japanese readers can join ranks with Westerners in positions of neocolonial dominance over Bali as consumers of its natural paradise.

Here, the great equalizer between Japan and the West is capital, and the fashion magazine collapses various forms of difference into commodified opportunities for consumption. Places, objects, clothing, and experiences offer themselves on the glossy pages as equally available to our consuming touch. A transitional spread heightens these impressions, eliding fashion photograph and advertisement. The male model featured in "Bali, Hi" appears against green foliage and red hibiscus. The photos have no captions and would be indistinguishable from the rest of the spread except for the absence of captions and the discreet company trademark in the bottom-left corner. The following article, "Club Med Bali," further blurs reportage and advertisement in a description of Club Med and its facilities. The two-page piece describes typical days at Club Med and gives us information on prices, packages, and facilities. The copious photos feature no Japanese as guests; rather, we see scenery, the white models, or shots where all the guests are white. Balinese are conspicuous by their absence, save for the one or two smiling employees who stand behind serving tables. Here at Club Med Bali, race doesn't matter, the photos seem to say. Japanese can take their place among the tourist-consumers of the world untouched by racial discomfort vis-à-vis white Westerners and unbothered by the brown natives, who appear only to serve the needs of First-World consumers.

The final section combines information, travelogue, and advertising in an article entitled "Bali Marathon." Sponsored by the Japanese Nittoh corporation, the marathon is figured as part of the sporting, active vacation whose virtues were extolled in Club Med Bali, wedding male athleticism to stereotypes of Bali as mysterious, exotic, spiritual and close to nature. The writer's voice imagines the reader running in such a setting, complete with a map of the course and an account of sights and sounds runners will encounter. In a typical Orientalizing/tropicalizing move, Bali becomes a means for the tired, jaded Japanese man to renew himself physically and spiritually, promising him a disciplined body and replenished masculine energy. Bali in the guise of a (precapitalist) natural paradise is offered to the capitalist Japanese as a consumer object.

Here we see the continuing construction of differentiated Asian Orientalisms that write the contradictions of Japanese identity. Both Asian and advanced capitalist/imperialist, Japan can construct Thailand and Bali as related yet disparate Others. Here, the graphic design motifs are instructive. The use of red in the Thai section paints Thailand as hot, exotic, cosmopolitan, and ultimately alien, while the green of Bali figures the natural, the unspoiled, the tropical. Both are sites for masculine pleasure. In Thailand, a group of men travels—as in a sex tour—to discover contemporary Thailand, redolent of feminine sexuality, exotic splendor, and high-tech, urban leisure. In Bali, men are heterosexually coupled in a wholesome, athletic vacation—swimming, working out, running marathons, or relaxing outdoors by the sea or at the pool. In each, Asian-ness is differently thematized, foregrounding the contradictions of Japan's status as a racially marked capitalist power. Japan constructs solidarity with an Asian Thailand, but cannot help but dominate it—as male seducer or as older brother. With Bali, the shared Asian-ness recedes in preference to a gesture for parity with Europe and the U.S.; here, the use of white models and the travelogue on Club Med Bali writes Euro-style as both object of emulation and the subject-position of the Japanese reader. Bali becomes an undifferentiated site of renewal, a trope of the tropics. Balinese people do not appear to disturb this vision of untrammeled exotic beauty, except as nameless features of the resort landscape. Here, racial anxieties are both thematized and allayed. The potentially threatening natives exist, but as non-people, naturalized fixtures of the landscape. Of course the threat can never be entirely contained, for their very presence, however marginalized, is the return of the repressed, the excess that eludes containment. Vis-à-vis the West, the message is that consumption and economic power can perhaps offset racial marking, for Japanese can ostensibly travel to Bali in a position equivalent to a Westerner's. Yet equality can never be fully achieved. Anxieties return through the white models, who reinscribe Euro-American hegemony even as that hegemony is claimed as Japan's shared prerogative. Anxieties are embodied in the shadowy figures of the natives, who cannot be entirely erased in the attempts to consume Bali as depopulated tropical paradise. Both the white models and the Balinese stand as uneasy reminders of the forces of neocolonial economic expansion, the colonization of consciousness, the simultaneous ambivalence toward racial marking and its utter inescapability.

FABRICATING "JAPAN"

In these disparate sites, the fashion industry weaves the complexities of Japanese subject formation during a period of Japanese economic confidence and power. Despite this burgeoning economic power, however, Japan remains a relatively marginalized force in the fashion industry: almost a peer, but not quite. Old Orientalisms are transposed into new, historically specific figurations, as the Japanese now appear under the sign of high-tech experimentalism, innovators of fabric and shape who redeploy culturally specific costume conventions or as cutting-edge creators who play the feminized almost-equal to the European Master Subject. Not quite/not white.

Given this racialized geopolitical context, the autoexoticism and reappropriations of Orientalism in *Kyoto étrangère* acquire new significance. Commodity fetishism here becomes a solution to Japanese anxieties over loss of identity and its contradictory position as a racially marked capitalist nation-state. Confident consumption becomes a way to overcome racial marking and to resolve anxieties about loss of innocence, purity, essential Japanese-ness, and tradition. Perhaps one could say that this confidence always and only occludes loss. But here, race is the difference that makes a difference. In the face of Orientalizing discourses deployed from Western sites, *Kyoto étrangère* redeploys these Orientalisms for its own ends, appropriating a Western position as it also draws upon nativist discourses of cultural uniqueness, *Nihonjin-ron*. "Kyoto, snob resort" advances the proposition that Japan, too, has entered the first ranks of advanced capitalist nationhood. Kyoto as snob resort signifies a recovery of pride—that Kyoto, too, is worthy of our consuming attention, even as the appellation "snob resort" enshrines upper-middle-class hegemony. So confident is this Japan that it can ironically view itself from the gaze of the West and redeploy Western Orientalisms, a Japan so powerful that through consumption it can blend the best of East and West in a figuration of the "truly Japanese."[26]

Japan's accession to the ranks of first-world consumer constructs its version of the Orient as a site of (pre)capitalist nostalgia, whether it is a trip to Kyoto, a vacation that ensures masculine prowess and dominance, or clothing that blends East and West in a new Oriental synthesis. Fashion fabricates the commodity fetishisms that invite such consumption, while simultaneously fostering a capitalist nostalgia for a purer, precapitalist past reigned by use value. Yohji Yamamoto, for instance, articulates his vision of a time when function ruled people's lives. "They [the Japanese] think they can consume everything. . . . They think they can buy everything. That is very sad. So I am very happy to go back to that time when people cannot buy anything, when people were forced to live with very simple things around them" (*Notebook on Cities and Clothes*). Yamamoto's yearning for a precapitalist past is in part the product of the very industry that provides his own livelihood. He is thoroughly enmeshed—as we all are—in the reproduction of such a system and longs for a history that he has participated in destroying. Similarly, Thailand and Bali function as differentiated sites of nostalgia: in the Thai case, for a time of innocence and tradition before modernization and Westernization, as the site for staging regret for the loss of precapitalist Japan; Bali, for an untrammeled nature before urbanization and as consumable site of spiritual renewal. The fashion magazine suggests that both Thailand and Bali remind the Japanese of what they have lost, but the loss is not irrevocable. Through consumption, Japanese can (re)experience their lost innocence without jeopardizing the comforts of advanced capitalism that ensured its originary loss. Japan's neocolonial economic dominance assures access to spiritual renewal.

Yet such seeming certainties are never certain. Japan is constructed through constitutive contradiction, through the constitutive lack at its core—for identities are always constructed in relations of difference.[27] To suppress this contradiction requires always already ambivalent peformances of national identity that assert nationhood as unique and timeless essence. Essence fabrication must therefore be continuous, repeated in multiple sites, in multiple registers. In the fashion world, as elsewhere, "Japan" assumes a form against the West, as it both emulates and challenges Western hegemonies in the process reinscribing and contesting Orientalist discourses. Pan-Asian solidarities are riven with contradiction, as Southeast Asia becomes a locus for Japanese consumption enabled by neocolonial relations of dominance. These complex contradictions figure "Japan" at an historical moment of Japanese economic strength and a concern with Asian history and Asian exoticism that accompanied the appearance of a new postwar generation for whom earlier Japanese history was indeed exotic.

A key message circulated among these sites is that race matters. Race figures the space of difference between Japanese colonial projects, Japanese capitalism, and those projects in the West, racially marking those interimperial rivalries.[28] Race figures the space of contradiction when Japanese expansionist projects colonize other Asian nations, despite invocations of Asian solidarities. Invocations of East and West and essentialized Japanese culture, the neocolonialism and capitalist dominance of the Japanese nation-state, occur within a field that is always already racialized. Racial tropes are in turn imbricated with gender, as woman embodies essentialized national identity, vulnerable to the masculine penetration of Westernization and urbanization. She writes the figure of inferiority, whether it is Yohji Yamamoto in the miniaturized viewfinder, the blushing Thai waitress at the Bangkok airport—or Madama Butterfly. Enmeshments of gender, race, and geopolitics permeate the Orientalisms I have described as they circulate and recirculate in disparate and contradictory ways in the discourses of fashion, writing new, historically specific stories in all-too-familiar ways, fabricating and refabricating the contradictions of Japanese identity.

ENDNOTES

1. In a reversal of the usual accusations of Japanese copying, boutique owner Alan Bilzerian (quoted in Cocks 1986: 93) commented, "Every single fashion designer has copied their skirts, shapes, wraps." In his words, Japanese designers "have inspired the entire world . . ." Jean Drusedow, then curator at the Metropolitan Museum of Art's Costume Institute, noted in an interview with me the "enormous" impact of Japanese fashion in the 1980s, seen industry-wide in the looser cuts of clothing in fashion of all prices and all ranges of exclusivity. Barbara Weiser summarized for me the the influence of Japanese design on mainstream American fashion:

   The odd thing is that . . . outside urban places they don't know the influence the Japanese designers have had on the clothing that they all wear. That is, there are certain kinds of cuts and certain fits that have now become— whether it's oversized clothing or . . . elastic-waist pants, or square tops— these forms have been swept up by American manufacturers and trickle down to everything including, let's say, sweat clothes. But the people don't know that's where it comes from (1989).

2. Production, on the other hand, is often the province of Third-World women. For the avant-garde Japanese designers who have "made it" internationally, however, this tends to be slightly less true, as most of their clothing is sewn in Japan (the high-fashion lines), or in France and Italy (the "bridge" lines). In the latter cases, one wonders who, precisely, those garment workers might be—whether they are from formerly colonized countries, for example. Textiles are often made in Japan or by specially commissioned artisanal producers abroad. Miyake has used fabrics from Indian artisans, for instance; Yamamoto has worked with Thai producers.

3. The importance of fashion, garments, and textiles can be seen in the fact that, in the manufacturing sector alone, the garment/ textile industry is a major employer worldwide, even more extensive if one includes the world of fashion as such: journalists, models, advertisers, retailers, wholesalers, distributors, shippers. But in addition to keen economic competition, there is also the matter of cultural authority. Here, Japan is assuming a place at the forefront of the discursive field called design, meeting point of high technology and aesthetics. Fashion, graphic design, photography, industrial design, furniture, and architecture, among other forms, index Japanese participation in a world culture of functional objects provoking aesthetic pleasure, thus readily exemplifying the workings of commodity aesthetics.

4. See, for example, Carol Gluck, *Japan's Modern Myths*; Marilyn Ivy, *Discourses of the Vanishing*; Stefan Tanaka, *Japan's Orient*; Naoki Sakai, "Modernity and Its Critique: The Problem of Universalism and Particularism."

5. In a move common among Japanese designers, Tayama inverts the usual Japanese word order for person's names, and puts his given name first, Western-style, rendered in the Roman alphabet.

6. Of Margiela, a French employee of a Japanese design firm wryly said to me, "It's like being a Korean in Japan."

7. Onward Kashiyama is a considerable force in the fashion industry. They also own Dolce e Gabbana and Luciano Soprani boutiques in Italy, J. Press in the U.S., Paul Smith boutiques in France and Hong Kong, and U.S. distribution for Helmut Lang, Marcel Marongiu, and Todd Oldham's bridge line, Times Seven. In 1995 they signed American designer Michael Kors to design an international bridge-sportswear collection, ICB (*Women's Wear Daily*, February 7, 1995).

8. This strategy of claiming the universal is always problematic in its denial of positionality. For example, Asian American actors are never, at least at this historical moment, not "Asian American." This need not be read as limitation or ghettoization; rather, the problem lies in whiteness passing as the unmarked. For marked categories of persons, denying the marking can sometimes be a denial of the strategic necessity for deploying those marked identities in particular political struggles.

9. Haute couture, luxury made-to-order clothing, is contrasted to ready-to-wear, clothing in standard sizes. Haute couture is shown in a special series of collections in Paris. Though it loses money for all the design houses, it is considered a playground and a laboratory for the designers, who can indulge their fantasies with the most luxurious fabric and trimmings, with handmade, top-of-the-line workmanship. Women who buy these garments go to Paris for special fittings, rather than buying the clothing in a store.

10. Here, Miyake has been an innovator; he speaks of the collaborative effort required to create a collection, and has given much credit to fabric designer Makiko Minagawa and to younger members of his Miyake Design Studio, occasionally helping them to launch their own lines.

11. Harold Koda links this aesthetic to the Zen notions of *sabi* and *wabi*.

12. He was instrumental in helping to mount an exhibition of Indian textile design at the Musée des Arts Décoratifs in Paris in 1985 and also created garments from some of these Indian textiles.

13. Fortuny was a Venetian designer who worked from the turn of the century until the 1950s. He is known for his Grecian-inspired pleated gowns, particularly a style entitled Delphos. "This is a simple column of many narrow, irregular, vertical pleats permanently set in the silk by a secret process" (Stegemeyer 68). These garments are now museum pieces and collector's items.

14. Thanks to Sharon Traweek for this insight.

15. Qualities associated with Zen aesthetics: imperfection, understatedness, loneliness, quietness.

16. Partially because of her more conservative and tailored designs (designated for a market similar to, in the U.S., the classicism of a Bill Blass or Oscar de la Renta), and partially, one suspects, due to joint financial ventures with Fairchild (a Mori son publishes *W Japan*, the Japanese branch of the Fairchild publication), Hanae Mori tends to fare better in *WWD*, and her designs are featured with relative frequency.

17. That same year, an inquiry at the flagship Saks Fifth Avenue in Manhattan as to whether they carried the work of Japanese designers merited a sniff of condescension and an emphatic "No!" Perhaps it is a measure of increasing recognition that in 1994 this same store proudly advertised their exclusive on Issey Miyake's perfume and his new diffusion line, Pleats Please.

18. Oddly, in the fashion world, this emerges time and again as the highest compliment a designer can be accorded. It appears to mean that the garments are timeless: either so classic that they are not subject to the vicissitudes of this year's "in" look, or so avant-garde that they never go out of style because they are never quite in style; i.e., they will always look unusual and cutting-edge. Since the fashion industry is based on incessant and ceaseless seasonal change, enforced among the top designers and among retailers through the seasonal collections (for the designers who show both men's and women's lines, this means at least four yearly collections of ready-to-wear, with haute couture representing another additional round), this may reflect a barely submerged desire to be

97

out of the hectic business of preparing collections. Clearly, it also expresses the desire to be recognized as a kind of craftsperson/artist.

Miyake is one of the designers who is rethinking the incessant changes of fashion. His Permanente collection is based on styles from years past, and he claims his goal to be the kind of clothing in which new items can be mixed and matched with items from past collections.

19. Ichiō fasshon to iu sekai de shigoto o shite imasu ga, seijiteki na nagare nado ni taishite mo kō atte hoshī to iu negai wa arimasu. Ni jū seiki kōhan to iu gendai, samazama na kangaekata, ikikata ga aru wake desu ga, sono naka no ichibubun no hitotachi ga tsuyoi to iu koto dake de keizaiteki na shisutemu ya seijiteki pāwā ni yotte, ta no bunka nari shisō nari seikatsu, tsumari ikikata o hitei shitari okashitari suru koto wa ikenai n ja nai ka to omou. Samazama na bunka ga kyōson shite ikeru sekai o tsukutte ikanakereba ikenai to omoimasu. Nihon no fasshon ni shite mo hakujin shikō ga hijō ni tsuyokute, jū kyū seiki no matsu ni dekita hakujin bunka ga nani yori mo utsukushiku pāwāfuru de aru to iu kangaekata wa okashī. Utsukushisa to iu mono wa nihonjin no naka ni mo, chūgokujin no naka ni mo, kuroi hada no hitotachi no naka ni mo sorezore ni aru mono de, kimerareta puropōshon ga utsukushī to iu no wa, henken ni suginai koto desu. Utsukushisa to iu mono wa, keni zukerarerubeki mono de wa arimasen kara (1986).

20. See, e.g., the article on *M. Butterfly* in this volume.

21. Ivy (1995) deals insightfully with two remarkably similar ad campaigns for the Japanese National Railway, entitled "Discover Japan" and "Exotic Japan." Drawing upon the discourses of psychoanalysis and the postmodern, among others, her compelling analysis provokes meditations on nostalgia, modernity, and (re)figurations of national-cultural identity. Though the themes of the *Ryūkō Tsūshin* article in many ways echo the "Exotic Japan" campaign in particular, my interest is in highlighting the workings of Orientalism and the difference that race makes.

22. Laura Brousseau was instrumental in helping me think through the narrative trajectory and the material techniques deployed in this article.

23. See, e.g., Mani 1987; Parker, et al., eds. 1992, Silverberg 1993, Kondo, this volume.

24. For example, her narratives are privileged, and at points the author invokes the guide as his audience, explicitly commenting that she had become more of a partner than a guide. Their farewell is laced with nostalgic desire; the author mentions her distinctive phrases, her characteristic gestures in passages reminiscent of "bittersweet" partings from summer lovers.

25. Two sections explicitly thematize this relationship: the vignette concerning the Japanese student in the strip club, and the guide's tales of sexual harassment from tourists from around the world—especially Italians and Japanese.

26. Such a stance redeploys nativist discourses of Japanese uniqueness as it accedes to the discourse of the nation-state, in the dialectic of universalism/particularism Sakai cogently critiques. Transnationalism represented by the cosmopolitanism of the

consumer-subject of *Kyoto étrangère* only magnifies these concerns with the essentially national.

27. See, e.g., Homi Bhabha, *Nation and Narration*, and Andrew Parker, et al., eds. *Nationalisms and Sexualities*.

28. The classic work here is John Dower's *War Without Mercy: Race and Power in the Pacific War*.

CONSUMING

GENDER, RACE, AND NATION

PART TWO

PARIS 1990

March. Time for the fall/winter women's ready-to-wear collections. A bewildering world, late capitalism at its most seductive and its most repellent. I am standing in the Cour Carrée of the Louvre along with hundreds of other members of the fashion pack. The designers seem to measure their stature by how long they can make their audiences wait, and this one is at least an hour late. Never have I seen a gathering of such intimidatingly stylish people. It's not simply what they're wearing and the aplomb or arrogance with which they carry themselves, but the fact that everyone is checking out everyone else. Who's who, who's wearing what, assessed by an audience that knows exactly which designer, what year, the exact price points. We are, I suppose, performing for each other. The sourness of intense class distinction and status jockeying pervades the air.

Inside, more politics—this time, of seating. Are you in the front row? Further back? At the foot of the runway or somewhere along the side? Do you get a seat at all? Buyers—without whom the fashion designers could not survive—always complain that they are given low seating priority. The choice spots go to powerful fashion journalists, the editors of Vogue, Elle, The New York Times, The

International Herald Tribune, *among others, celebrities (including other designers, sometimes), and wealthy clients. Seating can reflect the way a particular
journalist writes about a particular designer; those who "appreciate" the work
have better seats, while those who pan a collection can be moved toward the
back—in extreme cases, even banned. For those like me, who operate at a far less
exalted level, seating still matters. The best seats and most cordial treatment
come from Comme des Garçons, and no doubt this is one reason I have written
about them so extensively. Yet seating can be forgotten at a truly outstanding
show. Occasionally, even standing, one can forget the cramped quarters, the sore
feet, the crowds. When the lights go up and the models parade down the runway,
color, form, and movement can create captivating visions of beauty.*

*Afterwards, there is for the buyers and the assiduous fashion journalist the
nitty-gritty work of going to the showrooms and viewing the clothes on the rack.
Here one can see other color and fabric choices. Here the orders are placed. Assistants bring drinks and food for guests; occasionally there is a self-service table.
Rail-thin models, often clad in black catsuits or leotards, stand ready to try on
a particular garment if buyers want to see it draped and moving on a body.
Videos of the collection play; assistants attentively follow buyers as they place
their orders. It is an exhausting, busy time, for the decisions made here are com-
mercially critical for designer and retailer alike.*

*And competition is fierce. This is no less true for Japanese designers, who keep
close tabs on the competition, down to the smallest detail. I attended one collection with two representatives from a rival; they discovered that the programs had
an error which had been painted over with white-out—and chortled with glee at
the unseemly mistake. When I visited for interviews, each press liaison asked me
where I had been, to whom I had spoken, what I thought of the collections. In
one case, I informally mentioned to one representative that I had liked another
designer's collection; it was the kiss of death for fieldwork rapport. After that, I
could say nothing right. A fashion editor who was with us took sympathetic note
and winked at me knowingly. Small incidents, yet they eloquently point to the
continuous jockeying for critical and commercial success in an industry
renowned for its economic vicissitudes. The seeming frivolity of aesthetic spectacle and play are, for those in the industry, a deadly serious business, where reputations, jobs, capital, and perhaps a company's very existence are at stake.
Nowhere do the contradictions of our consumer capitalist lives seem more readily visible.*

4.

the limits of the avant-garde? gender and race on the runway

THE WORK OF the Japanese avant-garde and the general arena of fashion provide a unique lens through which to view a central political/intellectual dilemma of our late twentieth century-worlds: the possibilities, not for pristine resistance or opposition, as though such a thing were possible, but for what Linda Hutcheon (1989) calls "complicitous critique" within a discursive field defined by commodity capitalism and mass culture. The work of the avant-garde designers enacts oppositional gestures to convention: contesting the boundaries between fashion and art, challenging the conventions about what counts as clothing, rethinking the relationship between form and function and the relationship between garments and gendered, raced bodies, refiguring the beautiful, enlarging possibilities for enacting gender, and subverting the gender binary. But what can their contestations and oppositional practices mean in a domain suffused, indeed constituted, by commodification? A domain whose very existence is defined by the endless production of desire in consumers, planned obsolescence, the global assembly line, and the reinscription of class distinctions?

Focusing on these questions in the arena of fashion forms part of my larger political and intellectual project as a woman of color in the academy. For many people on the margins, style is not merely superficial decoration but an arena for the production of potentially oppositional identities. Sometimes the body is the most available surface for inscribing resistance. Studying fashion thus becomes an intervention that seeks to widen the spaces in the academy for what counts as legitimate academic inquiry and for what counts as political. Popular or mass culture is still viewed with considerable suspicion in some circles, and fashion, in particular, still indexes the frivolous. On the plane of gender, philosopher Iris Young articulates the dilemma (1990), what one might call a patriarchal double bind: that fashion both defines woman as object, requiring our interest in the aesthetic production of ourselves as gendered subjects in order to be fully woman, while at the same time condemning fashion as a trivial occupation for silly girls. Such a stance presupposes some inviolable moral space beyond fashion, thereby ignoring the ways we all create our identities through clothing and gesture, and masking the fact that there is no outside the fashion industry. The notion of fashion as frivolous also indexes a particular positioning vis-à-vis "the masses": Fashion is suspect because convention associates it with consumption not production, peace not war, women not men, pleasure not pain, aesthetics not politics, embodied subjects marked by and constituted through gender, race, class, culture, and history, not the disembodied Master Subject.[1] A scrutiny of fashion requires a reexamination of these hierarchized binaries, forcing a serious confrontation with pleasure, desire and aesthetic beauty as well as with disciplines, coercions, and oppressions—or, restated more felicitously, with the aesthetic pleasures, desires, and political possibilities that can open up within particular regimes of power.

What are those possibilities? Walter Benjamin long ago articulated the problematic that still haunts us in our very different historical moment, in his Arcades Project. Unlike more pessimistic members of the Frankfurt School, Benjamin found contestatory potential in the utopian dream-images and the desires articulated in mass culture, including fashion. In his version of dialectical thinking, mass culture could contain the seeds of historical awakenings that might spur socially transformative change (cf. Buck-Morss 1989). On the level of fashion and the individual subject, Carolyn Steedman makes a related point in her *Landscape for a Good Woman*, when she writes of her mother's desire for a Dior New Look dress, a "proper envy" of the upper classes that constituted a political critique of class structure. For Steedman's mother, fashion enabled the moment of critique, and Steedman calls for a structure of political thought and action that could take seriously her "proper envy." Benjamin articulated this constitutive contradiction: fashion's utopian dream wish that held critical and transformative possibility, coupled with its reinscription of capitalist logics, its commodity fetishism, and its dissimulation of ruling class interests, where the desires for revolutionary and perhaps violent change could be channeled into the fetishizing of fashion's latest trend. This chapter explores some ramifications of this constitutive contradiction. Animating the analysis is the supposition that any utopian gestures in fashion always occur within, and inevitably reinforce—even as at other levels they might contest—our contemporary capitalist regime of truth.

However, when we consider questions of contestation, disparate and perhaps contradictory fields of power must be considered. Fashion immediately suggests its imbrication in reproducing the forces of capitalism, making it at first glance unlikely to support any contestatory claims. Yet the fashion world is globally dispersed, profoundly implicated in capitalist *and* colonial/neocolonial relations, and it is perhaps the key site in urban societies for the production and performance of identities as gendered, raced, sexualized, class bodies. Consequently, fashion's wish images and fantasies must also be analyzed as they are worked through gender, sexuality, and race, perhaps at some levels contesting, contradicting, yet remaining inextricable from class reproduction and capitalist recuperation. After appraising the insights of European social theorists on the subject of fashion, this essay examines questions of contestation through an analysis of several Comme des Garçons runway shows over a ten-year period, asking, in effect, what difference a *non-Western* fashion avant-garde might make in terms of fashion's contestatory potential.

CONTESTATORY FASHION?

Fashion has provided the ground for articulating far-reaching arguments about the nature of our present society and historical moment, including processes of signification, subject formation, forces of domination and inequality, and the possibilities for political transformation. Using fashion as their point of entry, several Continental thinkers have theorized critical aspects of social formation and cultural politics.

Any mention of fashion in academic circles immediately evokes Roland Barthes's *The Fashion System*, an exercise in early high semiotics and an attempt to demonstrate the privileged status of linguistic models for social analysis. Barthes takes as his object of study the discourses of fashion as they circulate in fashion magazines[2] in service of his larger project: to further studies in semiology, the science of signs, applying Saussurean linguistic models to extralinguistic domains. In *The Fashion System* he attempts to capture the structure and the code of fashion and, on one level, he successfully argues that fashion discourses constitute a signifying matrix. In analyzing "how vestimentary meaning is produced" (59), Barthes attempts mightily to apply Saussurean categories to the corpus of fashion discourses he has amassed: delineating *langue* from *parole*, finding the elementary signifying unit ("the *vesteme*") of what he calls "the vestimentary system," distinguishing syntagm from paradigm, establishing the system of meaningful differences and their variants that constitute the vestimentary code. Though fashion is convincingly presented as a meaningful discourse through this semiological approach, Barthes begins to show the strains of applying Saussurean concepts when he is forced to confront the literal materiality of clothing. He distinguishes an *object* of signification (e.g., a sweater), a *support* of signification (e.g., a collar), and a *variant* (e.g., the type of collar: boatneck, closed, etc.). The support of signification is the excess that cannot be accounted for in the vestimentary sign.

Here, we see the inadequacy of Saussurean formulations that figure language as an abstract system of differences, i.e., of negative relations. The materiality of the garment in this instance must be conceived as prior to signification and cannot be accounted for within a purely negative system of differences. Barthes's appropriation of the Saussurean paradigm cannot account for this materiality within its own terms, revealing the limits of a Saussurean semiological project. Pierre Bourdieu (1975, 23) rightly notes Barthes's rigid formalism and his forced transposition of linguistic models to extralinguistic domains, further arguing that Barthes's mode of analysis simply uncritically reproduces common-sense assumptions in an academic register. For Bourdieu, Barthes remains part of the celebratory apparatus that creates the phenomenon of fashion; for him, a truly critical approach would reveal and problematize the underlying mechanisms of capitalist production and class reproduction (26). Further, in terms of the understanding of fashion itself, Barthes's rigid, structured semiological grid is of minimal usefulness, for the operations of signification Barthes describes could be attributed with equal persuasiveness to any extralinguistic signifying system. That he chose fashion as his object seems merely incidental.

In contrast, for Jean Baudrillard (1976), fashion is the central logic of our "consumer society," "the most superficial game and the most profound social form—the inexorable investment of all domains by the code"[3] (*"le jeu le plus superficiel et . . . la forme sociale la plus profonde—l'investissement inexorable de tous les domaines par le code"*) (Baudrillard 131). In *L'échange symbolique et la mort*, Baudrillard is in a transitional phase of his thinking. He has problematized the Marxist categories of production and consumption which were foundational in his earlier work and is on the way to articulating fully the notions of simulation and the hyperreal that animate his later theorizing. At this point, Baudrillard associates production with a phase of history defined by the Industrial Revolution (77). In its place, he argues, we have entered a new regime of simulation, a world where the referential and the real dissolve in an enchanting play of floating signs that refer only to each other. Fashion embodies the processes of simulation and the rule of the code. Rather than the "real" itself, Baudrillard argues that fashion creates a world of representations or models of the real. Fashion becomes the *"jouissance de l'arbitraire,"* at once exceeding the purely economic domain even as it remains the highest expression of the workings of commodity capitalism (142). According to Baudrillard, fashion invites censure not because of its sexual element—indeed, he argues that fashion paradoxically desexualizes subjects into mannequins—but because it interrupts the economic principle of utility, the puritanical valorization of use and function. Fashion's power is precisely that of the "pure sign that signifies nothing" (*"signe pur qui ne signifie rien"*) (144).

For Baudrillard, fashion is a totalizing logic permeating what he calls at this point "modernity" and will later call "postmodernity." Consequently, there is no way to subvert fashion, "for there is no reference with which to place it in contradiction (its reference is itself)" (*"parce qu'elle n'a pas de référentiel avec lequel la mettre en contradiction (son référentiel, c'est elle-même)"*) (151). Reacting against fashion simply reproduces the principles of its code; fashion cannot be transcended. Instead, the project must involve "a deconstruction of the form of the sign of fashion and of the very principle of signification, just as the alternative to political economy can only be in the deconstruction of the commodity form and the very principle of production" (*"une déconstruction de la forme du signe de mode, et du principe même de la signification, comme l'alternative à l'économie politique ne peut être que dans la déconstruction de la forme/marchandise et du principe même de la production"*) (151).

Baudrillard's characterization of fashion displays his penchant for hyperbole, particularly in his insistence on fashion as the enchantment and *jouissance* of the code, a fairyland of floating signs; this emphasis on simulation and models will spin off in ever more grandiose formulations in later work.[4] Nonetheless, he does argue convincingly that fashion is an exemplary instance—*the* exemplary instance—of the logic of contemporary society, a logic that cannot be transcended. Baudrillard's formulations are useful and prescient, articulating what will become a standard premise of a poststructuralist politics: that there can be no outside space of transcendence and that a political project must depend in part upon problematizing the foundational assumptions constituting the tacit, unspoken—hence unquestioned—rules of the game.

In *Distinction* (1984) Pierre Bourdieu combines a Durkheimian preoccupation with systems of classification with a Marxist concern for systematic inequality and class struggle. In this study of taste and consumption, he seeks to give "a scientific answer to the old questions of Kant's critique of judgment, by seeking in the structure of social classes the basis of the systems of classification which structure perception of the world and designate the objects of aesthetic enjoyment" (xiii). Bourdieu's project is to demystify the claims of high culture, showing how the supposedly transcendent domains of refined taste are constituted through a system of class distinction, permeated by the logic of cultural and symbolic capital. Fashion, music, political orientation, leisure, lifestyle, tastes in food, types of dwelling, and interior decoration become sites where class distinctions are articulated and reproduced. Basing his project on a comprehensive survey of over 1,200 respondents, Bourdieu convincingly analyzes the functioning of taste and its relation to social class. He utilizes the standard methodologies of social science to impressive effect, persuasively mapping this relationship through discursive analysis supplemented with charts, photographs, statistical tables, interviews, excerpts from journals, and advertisements.

However, the seemingly comprehensive nature of the inquiry cannot mask the limits of its conceptual foundationalisms. Despite occasional protestations to the contrary, Bourdieu in the end appears to subscribe to a class-based objectivism that takes consciousness and meaning as ultimately derivative. Indeed, structure, culture, science, production, consumption, among other categories, remain unproblematized, rather than terms that must themselves be subject to interrogation. The Durkheimian legacy couples a classificatory imperative with an emphasis on social *science*, creating a matrix of closed categories that ultimately misses the fluidity of the social battles Bourdieu so richly describes in his vignettes. The lived nature of the classificatory *struggle* never sufficiently emerges from the totalizing grid of classification. Here, for example, is the revealing description of the presuppositions that inform *Distinction*:

> Thus, the spaces defined by preferences in food, clothing, or cosmetics are organized according to the *same fundamental structure*, that of the social space determined by volume and composition of capital. Fully to construct the space of life-styles within which cultural practices are defined, one would first have to establish, for each class and class fraction, that is, *for each of the configurations of capital, the generative formula of the habitus* which retranslates the necessities and facilities characteristic of that class of (relatively) homogeneous conditions of existence into a particular lifestyle. . . . By superimposing these homologous spaces one would obtain a *rigorous representation* of the space of lifestyles, making it possible to characterize each of the *distinctive features* (e.g., wearing a cap or playing the piano) in the two respects in which it is *objectively defined*. (208–9, emphasis mine)

Bourdieu clearly assumes that he can exhaustively, objectively specify class and class fractions, precisely linking them with specific displays of taste. Yet one wonders whether his respondents' choices can be so neatly read off this presumed foundational structure. The fixity and "objectivity" of his categories are meant to signify rigor. Ironically, however, despite Bourdieu's criticism of Barthes's rigidity, the totalizing reach of his own rationalizing grid seems equally rigid, exposing the limits of this classificatory imperative.

In *Distinction* Bourdieu's appraisal of fashion exhibits similar conceptual difficulties. At one level, his analysis does the important work of enabling us to understand the ways the clothing we wear, indeed, the very production of bodies, is inseparable from class relations. Distinguishing "being" from "seeming" (200), he argues that the working classes value function and labor, while the clerical and managerial classes place a greater emphasis on appearance. Accordingly, in choosing clothing or cosmetics, the working classes are presumably concerned with practicality, value, durability, and function; conforming to normative fashionable bodies and gendered ideals of attractiveness are of peripheral concern. In the middle classes, for whom performance evaluations on the job may in fact be related to appearance, preoccupations with cosmetics, diet, and proper clothing heighten markedly. Indeed, Bourdieu makes even more precise and far-reaching claims: "The interest the different classes have in self-presentation, the attention they devote to it, their awareness of the profits it gives and the investment of time, effort, sacrifice, and care which they actually put into it are proportionate to the chances of material or symbolic profit they can reasonably expect from it" (202). According to Bourdieu, the upper classes demonstrate the greatest satisfaction with their appearance and their bodies, as the literal embodiments of hegemonic ideals, conquering nature through the moral/aesthetic value they call *"tenue"*—that which is not vulgar (206). Once again, the correlations are presented as being seamlessly—and suspiciously—tight. The outlines of the analysis are convincing, but one wonders what Bourdieu might do with someone like Carolyn Steedman's mother, whose working-class positioning combined with an uneasy, contradictory identification with the upper classes and a political critique of class structure that was paradoxically nurtured by her very identificatory desire and her resulting envy of the upper classes. That is, while Bourdieu's reproductive model is compelling in its general contours, empirical realities are likely to be more open-ended, contradictory, and complicated. And it is precisely the fissures and contradictions in such a narrative of reproduction that might reveal contestatory possibility.

Bourdieu's work on the fashion industry as such is therefore useful, indeed indispensable, at one level, but its totalizing closure and class foundationalism prove once again to limit the analysis. In a work that precedes *Distinction*, entitled *"Le couturier et sa griffe,"* "The couturier and his signature" (1975), Bourdieu takes as his object the domain of haute couture (luxurious made-to-order clothing, rather than high fashion ready-to-wear).[5] He characterizes the dynamics of the field of haute couture through its two poles: the established couturiers, who represent luxury, aristocracy, and elegance, versus the challengers, who emphasize their difference from established convention through the invocation of modernity, artistry, and the subversion of perfection. He perceptively describes the challengers' task as "vigorously breaking with certain conventions (introducing, for example, mixtures of colors or materials that had been excluded up to that point), but within the limits of convention and without calling into question the rules of the game or the game itself." (*"Le jeu des nouveaux entrants consiste à peu près toujours à rompre avec certaines des conventions en vigueur (en introduisant par exemple des mélanges de couleurs ou de matières jusque-là exclus), mais dans les limites des convenances et sans mettre en question la règle du jeu et le jeu lui-même"*) (12). In the same passage, Bourdieu goes on to note that the newer couturiers often emphasize "liberty, fantasy, newness (often identified with youth)" (*"la liberté, la fantaisie, la nouveauté* (*souvent identifiées à la jeunesse*)," while older, established houses shun anything too unconventional, instead opting for understatement, elegance, and refinement. Because the newcomers to the field cannot hope for the same kind of haute-bourgeois prestige accorded the established houses, they must discredit as unfashionable or outmoded anything owing its prestige to age, to history, and to the existence of the bourgeoisie/aristocracy who are its primary customers (15). An emphasis on modernity, the future, or on revolutionary visions is thus always already part of the challengers' stories; so are the invocations of street style and youth. Art, finally, holds a special place for challenger and established designer alike. Given that fashion is designated a decorative and therefore lesser art, Bourdieu notes that designers often gesture toward their own artistic endeavors and their links to the artistic world (16).[6]

Through this delineation of fashion, Bourdieu probes the more general operations of what he calls a field: art, fashion, sports, academia, politics. In fact, one could argue that Bourdieu has little interest in fashion as such. Rather, he shows the ways these challenges to convention through battles for legitimacy never really threaten the existence of a dominant class or subvert the rules of the game (27). What is missing, Bourdieu argues, is the possibility for agnosticism about the game itself, an agnosticism he finds essential to an "objective apprehension of the struggle" (28). This objective apprehension would reveal fashion's implication in the reproduction of class. Bourdieu notes that the appearance of new couturiers, such as the influential modernist Courrèges, signals the emergence of a new managerial class that espouses values such as dynamism, function, modernity, and freedom. In this class, women as well as men may hold managerial positions. Bourdieu notes that the new couturiers have adapted to the shift in gender roles, pointing to this phenomenon as one of the ways the "effects of recent transformations of the dominant class make themselves directly felt in the field of haute couture" ("*les effets des transformations récentes de la classe dominante se font le plus directement sentir dans le champ de la haute couture*") (33). Fashion and other fields (art, the academy, politics) in fact become arenas for the reproduction of class and for the imposition of the symbolic violence of legitimation, "gentle violence that can only be exercised with the complicity of its victims and because of this fact give the appearance of liberatory action to an arbitrary imposition of arbitrary needs" ("*violence douce qui ne peut s'exercer qu'avec la complicité de ses victimes et qui peut de ce fait donner à l'imposition arbitraire de besoins arbitraires les apparences d'une action libératrice*") (35). Bourdieu ends his article with a clear message. Fashion is simply another battlefield in the timeless, eternal class struggle: "The dialectic of distinction and of pretension is the principle of this sort of race pursued among the classes, which implies the recognition of the same goals: it is the motor of this competition that is none other than the gentle, continuous, interminable form of the class struggle." "*La dialectique de la distinction et de la prétention est le principe de cette sorte de course poursuite entre les classes qui implique la reconnaissance des mêmes buts: elle est le moteur de cette concurrence qui n'est que la forme douce, continue et interminable de la lutte des classes*" (36).

In this essay Bourdieu convincingly demonstrates that fashion and other domains of taste are inseparable from class distinction. His analysis of the operations of haute couture are unfailingly insightful and can apply with equal elegance to the field of ready-to-wear. For example, Bourdieu's description of the strategies available for newcomers to challenge the fashion establishment aptly characterizes the work of Comme des Garçons and other so-called avant-gardistes.[7] Their invocations of modernity, street style, the subversion of convention, and artistry are predictable, even as related claims have been made by French challengers to the established couturiers. Yet, though at one level indispensable and incontrovertible, the reproductive model of class cannot exhaust the political and interpretive possibilities presented in the fashion world.

Bourdieu's treatment of gender is especially telling in this regard. In the end, for Bourdieu the historical emergence of a new class and new possibilities for women's employment signify simply another shift in the ways the dominant classes can reproduce themselves. Bourdieu's analysis is compelling; at the level of class, the new managers—whether male or female—can find their interests and their class bodies articulated in the work of the new couturiers. Yet might the entry of more women into the labor force in the new managerial classes and elsewhere produce other kinds of shifts that cannot be reduced fully to class reproduction? What of gendered power relations and the gendered constructions of families and workplaces? Bourdieu's final invocation of the symbolic violence of the eternal class struggle in the end is oddly ahistorical, for historical developments are reduced to mere instantiations of class reproduction. Again, he leaves no room for contestation, for ambiguity, for meanings that resist closure, for the disruptions other forces such as gender and race might offer to this totalizing narrative, or for the ways class formation and class identities are themselves gendered and raced. Though Bourdieu might provide us with provocative insights and a useful framework for understanding the world of high fashion, we must take care to note the ways that his narrative of class reproduction might be interrupted by other forces, especially in the work of non-European, non-white Others.

A final analyst of fashion provides a critique that reveals fissures in Bourdieu's classificatory grid, yet ultimately remains within a liberal humanist, power-evasive theoretical frame. Gilles Lipovetsky criticizes Bourdieu and takes Baudrillard's emphasis on the totalizing logic of fashion into historical terrain in *L'empire de l'éphémère* (translated as *The Empire of Fashion*). Taking his cue from Baudrillard, he sees seduction and the ephemeral as central organizing principles of social life. Lipovetsky's historical approach enables him to argue against Bourdieu that fashion is far more than a site of class struggle, for when seen in terms of the *longue durée*, it has constituted a democratizing influence and a sign of modernity. For example, the sumptuary regulations of aristocratic societies enforced fixed social hierarchies, while modern fashion introduces the possibility of mobility and change. The old class order is disrupted by a valorization of youthfulness; the age hierarchy supersedes the class hierarchy. Indeed, for Lipovetsky fashion is a democratizing influence that promotes individualization and the formation of consumer-subjects who hold the democratic values of tolerance, pluralism, and openness to transformation. Like Bourdieu, Lipovetsky subscribes to a conceptual scheme that problematically separates culture from structure. Against Bourdieu's analysis of class *structure*, he stresses the centrality of modern *cultural* values and significations, in particular that of the New, which permeates fashion and forms the basis of modern democratic society.

Lipovetsky makes a convincing case for analyzing the emergence of fashion historically, arguing that its appearance was coextensive with modernity. However, his appraisal of fashion as a domain fostering democratic values uncritically reinscribes liberal humanist presuppositions about the subject and about power. For example, he celebrates the notion of the individual (the always already whole subject), who chooses and who is conditioned to accept the New. There is too little acknowledgment of the ways the emergence of the liberal humanist choosing subject is above all a consumer-subject, inextricable from the growth of capitalism and the formation of bourgeois possessive individualism. Lipovetsky's embracing of this choosing subject inevitably erases those histories of power and domination. Indeed, Bourdieu shows that the valorization of the New among the couturiers and the managerial classes is simply part of the struggle for legitimacy among the dominant classes, a struggle that never seriously jeopardizes class hierarchy itself. And because

Lipovetsky accepts as foundational divisions such as public/private, he fails to account for the ways public social forces intersect in, and construct, the private. Consequently, he cannot effectively come to terms with Bourdieu's class analysis. For example, Lipovetsky argues that in a society permeated by the logic of fashion, individuals no longer buy with an eye toward social recognition or social competition, but keep uppermost the purely private values of functionality and individual well-being. Yet as Bourdieu eloquently argued, these seemingly private values can in fact be produced and reproduced through "public" discourses and are far from innocent of class distinction. Lipovetsky ultimately becomes a liberal humanist cheerleader for fashion.

In different ways, these theorists of fashion offer insights into the fashion world. Barthes argues for fashion as a signifying system. Despite its class foundationalism and totalizing classificatory imperative, Bourdieu's insightful work on fashion provides a political and conceptual frame for understanding the dynamics of the avant-garde in fashion and the inextricability of taste from class reproduction. Lipovetsky and Baudrillard mark the pervasiveness of the logic of fashion in our regime of capitalist (post)modernity, while Lipovetsky's fissuring of Bourdieu's narrative of relentless class reproduction leads to a critical reappraisal of Bourdieu's description of the fashion world. Finally, Baudrillard articulates the possibilities for always already complicitous critique in a commoditized world defined by fashion.

Still, these insights are mediated through a highly problematic, Eurocentric gaze. What happens to their Western narratives of signification—the *jouissance* of the code, class reproduction, and the formation of individualist bourgeois subjects—when we consider other axes of power, such as gender, race, sexuality, and (neo)colonialism? Without a broader consideration of these issues, can we adequately address the possibilities for contestation in this elitist, highly problematic domain? The following section explores these issues, arguing that in the early 1980s Japanese avant-garde designers created a sensation in the fashion world, presenting what seemed to be a shockingly different version of gender and fundamentally problematizing what counts as clothing. Bourdieu's model of the field of fashion, and particularly his treatment of the role of avant-gardes, enable us to appraise avant-garde experimentation within our regime of commodity capitalism. After setting the shock of Japanese fashion into historical context, our inquiry focuses on the stagings of gender, sexuality and race in Comme des Garçons runway shows. The wish-images showcased on the Comme des Garçons runway, the fact that the designers are Japanese—not

European, not white, and in particular shifting relations of power vis-à-vis the West—inevitably position this work differently. The nature and the degree of difference are the issues. These considerations in turn bear implications for European theories of fashion, and in particular, for Bourdieu's model of class reproduction. For what happens when we think seriously about gender, race, and Orientalism along with the workings of class and commodity capitalism Bourdieu and others so acutely describe?

STARTING FROM ZERO

Let us return, then, to the early 1980s and the initial shock of Japanese fashion. Why the uproar? What was so radically different? The October 23, 1982 edition of the *Toronto Star* and its UPI correspondent situate us historically, in this report on the collections shown in the fall for the following spring. The headline trumpets:

Oo-la-la! Sexy French fashions fall back on derrières
PARIS (UPI-Special)—Sexy fashion is back—and behind.

The liberation of women from being sex objects has gone out the window in this week's 1983 Paris spring-summer and ready-to-wear shows for international store buyers and press.

Tight skirts with a Marilyn Monroe wiggle, skirts slit up front-back-sides, tops like wired brassieres, bareback sweaters, strapless gowns, tight waists, necklines cut to the point of no return, bare navels, see-through dresses . . .

The revolutionary turn to sensuous styles means 1983 will be the year of the derrière.

The French press calls the look 'la starlette.' And it could be fun for some women but a put-down for others with an anti-sexist outlook (A3).

The article sets the dominant tone of fashion for the year, and ends with the appearance of the Japanese designers. This was the second Paris show for Rei Kawakubo and Comme des Garçons.

However, the most-talked-about show was not one by a Paris creator, but by one of six visiting Japanese designers invited in an unusual gesture by the French to show their wares.

Rei Kawakubo of the Comme des Garçons firm stunned the audience by draping gray tatters full of holes on mannequins with hair drooping in all directions and blobs of lipstick on one eyebrow or cheek.

117

They looked like street fighters in a slum, victims of a nuclear war or females beaten up by men in the final insult to women of the Paris 'sex object' fashion parade.

But Kawakubo said she had in mind an anti-fashion 'natural look' with pre-washed and stretched fabrics, unset hair and lipstick any place a liberated woman felt like putting it" (A3).

The contestation here lies in particular figurations of gender and, less obviously, race. For what lay behind this anti-fashion, natural look, the drooping hair and gray tatters? As analysts have argued (Chapter 2, this volume), Kawakubo, along with Yamamoto and Miyake, share certain aesthetic points of departure that can be read as an aesthetic oppositional to reigning European and especially French clothing conventions. These points of departure must be understood in terms of the different ways clothing articulates gendered, raced bodies. Comparisons to the contemporaneous work of classic French designer Yves St.-Laurent and the more avant-garde Claude Montana and Thierry Mugler are revealing. All three articulate the body and clothing in terms of an exquisite, precise fit based on cutting and tailoring. Theirs are crisply articulated, disciplined bodies, curving and normatively feminine bodies in a Western sense. This aesthetic point of departure depends on cutting and tailoring fabric to conform closely to, even creating, an idealized notion of feminine curves. These are bodies shaped by a Western disciplinary regime, premised on the ideal of a tall, long-legged woman with an hourglass shape.

The challenge represented by the work of Rei Kawakubo, Issey Miyake, and Yohji Yamamoto lies precisely in the potential radical refiguration of clothing's articulation of bodies. Perhaps this refiguration reached its most uncompromised expression in the Comme des Garçons lines of the early eighties. Kawakubo talks of the sensuality of the clothing coming not from the way a person looks, but from the feel of the clothing. Her stated goal is to create a sense of *jiyū*, freedom, in her designs. One way this freedom is enacted is through the input of the wearer; that is, many of the early designs based on wrapping can adapt to individual bodies, and the garments can be worn a variety of ways, changing with the wearer. For me, this is one of the strengths of the Japanese design from this period: that it usually looks as good on Asian bodies as it does on other raced bodies. Kawakubo's clothing does not shy away from making Japanese bodies look Japanese rather than some inadequate imitation of Western ideals; many different kinds of bodies can wear her clothing well. Indeed, the work of Comme des Garçons offers wearers multiple possibilities for adjust-

Elasticized cotton dress. Spring/Summer 1983
Photographed by Peter Lindbergh. Courtesy Comme des Garçons

ing garments to the shape of the individual wearer. For example, a line in the mid-80s, the "elastic" collection—based on shirring and gathers—created holes in different places in a garment and gathered the fabric around the holes. Wearers could choose where they wanted to put their heads or their arms. Play and the pleasure of the unexpected animate this clothing, and this play can articulate a different vision of gender and race.

In addition to deploying culturally specific aesthetics and refiguring the relation of clothing to bodies, Kawakubo and others have been engaged in rethinking the decorative "prettiness" of fashion. In an exhibit at the Fashion Institute of Technology called "Three Women," that focused on the radical challenges presented by the clothing of Madeleine Vionnet, Claire MacCardell, and Kawakubo (representing the '20s, the '50s, and the '80s, respectively), curator Harold Koda told me that for all three designers, decoration was adjunct to function, so that, for example, a bow would be of a piece with a collar. In Kawakubo's case, the finishing on a garment will often serve as decoration. In a modernist sense, for her form follows function. But the garments she designs often go beyond the modernist aesthetic, challenging us to examine our assumptions about what counts as function—collars are attached to nothing, jackets appear with four arms, what looks like a coat is a collar and lapel, but a void gapes where the garment's shoulders, front and back should be. Such a coat surely offers next to no functional protection from the elements. One could argue that Kawakubo is deconstructing garments—literally, by exposing their constituent parts, and figuratively, by making the so-called functional non-functional and decorative, while making the functional decorative. In the process, she subverts our notions of decoration and function.

This aesthetic disruption, leading us to confront our assumptions about what counts as clothing, constituted the challenge of Japanese fashion. In an analysis of the reception of the work of David Henry Hwang, Angela Pao (1992) argued that *M. Butterfly*'s subversive potential should be appraised in terms of "the undeniable challenge it presented to the spectators' socially and culturally determined narrations of experience and their allied competence as theater goers" (14). I would argue that in the fashion world, the work of Kawakubo, Yamamoto, and Miyake, among others, forced a similar reappraisal of cultural competencies and interpretive practices that construct clothing conventions. This radical questioning participates, in a different medium, in the anti-foundationalist critiques of received categories that so defined the 1970s and 1980s. I see in the work of the avant-garde Japanese designers, especially in the early

1980s, a parallel in another medium to the world of social theory, a laying bare of the equivalent of fashion's narrative conventions. As I have argued elsewhere in this volume, the reception of their work in the European and U.S. fashion worlds cannot be separated from discourses of race and nation. Their avant-garde challenge is always already raced.

At another level, however, Bourdieu's analysis of the fashion world provides us with significant insights into the degree of potential intervention. Though perhaps the Japanese disrupted convention and challenged the reigning interpretive apparatus of fashion, they could not do so in a manner that completely called into question the world of fashion itself; after all, their goal was acceptance in the West and the world of international fashion, and acceptance means marketability and at least some degree of critical approbation. We will see that the initial shock was inevitably recuperated, appropriated, and further commodified as one might expect in the culture industries, even as the influence of Japanese fashion spread in the 1980s and even as Kawakubo, Yamamoto, and Miyake are still known for—and are marketed in terms of—their experimental and avant-garde aesthetic moves. Indeed, as Bourdieu pointed out, challengers to fashion hegemonies often stress modernity (in this case, new fabrics dependent upon high-tech research and development), and a future orientation—starting from zero.

The particular niche occupied by the avant-garde is one that is designed to appeal to the artist/iconoclast; consequently, the invocation of art recurs repeatedly in these circles. Indeed, Bourdieu has argued that fashion's secondary status as a decorative or applied art further fosters this compensatory invocation. For example, Kawakubo and Yamamoto have originated artistic image books distributed to the press and to customers, which commission work from some of the art and fashion world's best known photographers (e.g., the Starn Twins, Peter Lindbergh, Bruce Weber, Timothy Greenfield-Sanders). The images are often abstract and enigmatic, or playful visual rhymes that may have nothing explicitly to do with clothing. Rather, they enact and express an "artistic vision." Kawakubo is known for the aesthetic and design control she exercises over her boutiques, and indeed, the main boutique on Aoyama-dōri in Tokyo is a virtual art gallery; the work of a featured artist is displayed near the entrance to the boutique. Within the last five years, these have included American artist Jim Dine, French artist/designer Line Vautrin, and Cindy Sherman, whose photographs for Comme des Garçons were also featured on their large format, direct-mail postcards. In addition to clothing, Kawakubo sporadically designs a line of furniture that draws on both minimalist and, more recently, postmodern aesthetic traditions. Yamamoto finds other means of artistic expression through music—acoustic guitar and vocals that allude to James Taylor and Neil Young. Miyake, in particular, has had his designs showcased in museums and among the three is best known for the creation of artistic, otherworldly museum pieces.

Yet art and fashion are also industries, and aesthetics cannot be divorced from commerce, for these designers also head large capitalist organizations with hundreds of employees. All have subsidiary lines that are less expensive, less radical, and thus more commercial. For Miyake, these include Plantation, a more casual line, and Permanente, which recycles classic Miyake designs in slightly modified form. Miyake also licenses widely, so that one can buy Issey Miyake handkerchiefs, futon covers, umbrellas, luggage, and fragrance. Yamamoto's "Y's" features classic tailored shapes;[8] Kawakubo's ancillary lines include Tricot, Shirt, Robe de Chambre for nightwear, Homme Deux, men's business suits, perfume, and the recent "Comme des Garçons Comme des Garçons" bridge (intermediately priced) line manufactured in Italy. Any capitalist firm must sell to remain in business, and though the aesthetically minded find it problematic, being understandable—i.e., marketable—is considered a virtue in the fashion industry.[9] The commercial lines may also whet consumer desire for the high fashion items. In aesthetic terms, then, any avant-garde gesture is tempered by the fact that: (1) it may be less contestatory because it must eventually be sold, and no collection can consist entirely of "image pieces"; and (2) aesthetic experimentation in one line may be supported by the economic success of more commercial lines.

In short, the aesthetic principles informing Japanese avant-garde work are always already raced, based on different clothing/body relationships that arise in part from different cultural conventions. These different cultural conventions and practices constitute an implicit critique of Eurocentrism. In the moment of their appearance in the West, the work of the Japanese designers presented a challenge to Western clothing conventions and the cultural competencies and interpretive practices that reigned in the Paris-Milan-New York-London fashion circuit. And these occurred on the planes of gender and race.

This said, Bourdieu points out the common strategies required of challengers to the established couturiers: they must promote themselves as subverting the old order without wholly problematizing the field of fashion itself. Indeed, they cannot do so without calling into question their own *raison d'être*—after all, their ultimate goal is not to deconstruct the field, but to succeed in it. Similarly, Baudrillard argues that the only significant intervention possible in the commoditized regime of fashion is to throw into question its foundational logic, which again no designer can completely afford to do. Do we say, given these inevitably compromised and complicit interventions, that all contestatory potential is therefore vitiated?

FABRICATING GENDER

I have argued that one of the key interventions made in the clothing of "the Japanese avant-garde" designers lies in their figurations of gender. Inevitably, however, these interventions are animated by multiple, constitutive contradictions.

First, the high-fashion industry and by extension the work of Kawakubo, Yamamoto, and Miyake at one level participate enthusiastically in the relentless reproduction of the gender binary. The industry itself is predicated on the division of markets between men's and women's clothing (though of course there can be crossover in the practices of consumption), reflected in the showing of the collections (men's and women's collections are shown separately, according to entirely different schedules), in the organization of retailing (departments or boutiques specialize in either men's or women's clothes), and in fashion journalism (women's magazines and trade papers are often separate from the men's, e.g., *Women's Wear Daily* and *Daily News Record*, *Ryūkō Tsūshin* and *Ryūkō Tsūshin Homme*).[10]

Even within the binary organizational strictures of the fashion industry, the work of avant-garde designers in Japan offers a different way of crafting gender, based on the presumed relationship between clothing and bodies. Certainly, especially in the 1980s, Miyake, Yamamoto, and Kawakubo made strong statements about a different aesthetic of shape, where the garments do not follow the body's outlines, but define a space around the body. This inevitably refigures the clothing-body relationship and the construction of gender based on womanly curves or masculine linearity. For example, Kawakubo claims she begins with an abstract shape, and her concern is first for the clothing itself. In an interview with me, Kawakubo spoke of her point of departure as a "concept," not pattern or tailoring techniques. She further emphasized the spontaneity of her sources of inspiration: "It's not on the basis of the pattern. The sensation of having experienced the feel of the material. . . . It's purely the sensation of the moment. Right now, I like warm things or heavy things. . . . It's just that sensation." This conceptual and tactile aesthetic takes on marked contrast to the "body conscious" fashion of the West:

123

> I don't understand the term "body-conscious" very well. . . . I enter the process from interest in the shape of the clothing and from the feeling of volume you get from the clothing, which is probably a little different from the pleasure Western women take in showing the shapes of their bodies. It bothers Japanese women, doesn't it, . . . to reveal their bodies. I myself understand that feeling very well, so I take that into account, adding more material, or whatever. It feels like one would get bored with 'body-conscious' clothing (1987, 92).[11]

Here Kawakubo links different principles of clothing construction to differences in gender construction, sexuality, race, and nationality; Western "body-conscious" clothing depends upon Western figurations of gender and sexual display, while Kawakubo's clothing and aesthetic sensibility articulate a sensuality enjoyed by Japanese women. Kawakubo thus discursively constructs racialized gender differences as a principle shaping her work.

Yamamoto and Kawakubo have spoken specifically of a blurring of gender categories, where the wearer they envision is not bound by familiar gender conventions. Even the name of Kawakubo's company, Comme des Garçons ("like the boys")[12] gestures toward these gender contestations, enshrining a kind of boyish (manisshu, "mannish," as it is sometimes called in the Japanese press),[13] troublemaking image. Paradoxically, early on this was articulated in a highly Western mode: before it became known in the West, Comme des Garçons clothing was often photographed in ways that were very garçonne, illustrative of the company name: hat tilted to the side, a cigarette dangling from the mouths of the very French-looking models.[14]

It is precisely this ambiguous gender imagery that has puzzled many a Western observer. A male editor at a well-known fashion magazine told me of his bewilderment in the face of the "shapeless" clothing designed by the Japanese, which fails to reveal a woman's body. He said that he would never want *his* girlfriend to wear Japanese fashions; rather, his taste ran to the form-fitting styles of Azzedine Alaia, whose clothing has curves, even if there is no one in them, and Thierry Mugler, famous for his parodically sadomasochistic, femme-fatale designs.

Amanda Stinchecum, a commentator on Japanese aesthetics, has this to say about Kawakubo's work and its challenge to conventional gendered images:[15]

> As a woman, she is aware of the expectations of not only men, but women as well, that women look and act pretty, and that this prettiness conform to accepted norms. The lips should be red, the eyelids blue, the waist narrow, the hips curved, and so on. To be appealing, clothing, too, is supposed to meet certain expectations: symmetry, neatness, sexiness (suggesting if not revealing—

Kawakubo's clothes do neither). Her designs express both a reaction against these expectations, and an interest in pure form. . . . Kawakubo's clothes are the most extreme because she, more than the others, refuses to meet the expectations we have of clothing and of women (76).

Kawakubo concurs, restating emphatically to me, "I've never once thought about a woman's 'beauty.'" ("*Yappari, onna no utsukushisa ni kangaeta koto ga nai.*") In some interviews, Kawakubo expresses the expectation that her ideal consumer would be someone like herself: an independent career woman (1987, 90).[16] A Comme des Garçons representative explained, "The goal for all women should be to make her own living and to support herself, to be self-sufficient. That is the philosophy of her clothes. They are working for modern women. Women who do not need to assure their happiness by looking sexy to men, by emphasizing their figures, but who attract them with their minds" (Coleridge 1988, 89). Indeed, to me Kawakubo insisted fiercely on that independence: "I don't have the slightest conception of depending on someone, of saying, 'Help me.'" She elaborates elsewhere that she does not design with a particular kind of person in mind; rather, the concern is with the feeling the clothing imparts: "To put it in extreme terms, I want to value the feeling of freedom that comes when someone wears the clothes, something psychological and spiritual rather than the actual feel and fit of the clothing" (1988).[17] The refrain of newness, of freedom emerges strongly in Kawakubo's discourse. At one level, such statements could be taken as typical strategies mounted by new designers, for Bourdieu perceptively argues that the necessity to assert marketable difference often takes the form of dynamism, modernity, and subverting convention.

Moreover, the reference to independent women as consumers is surely a marker of the accession of women to the professional and managerial classes in advanced capitalist societies. Kawakubo, Miyake, and Yamamoto clearly design with professional and creative women in mind. The late designer Tokio Kumagai links clothing to these dramatic social changes:

> Men and women are crossing over. There's no longer a notion that because you're a man, you have to do this, or because you're a woman you have to do this. . . . Even husbands wake up in the middle of the night to take care of the kids; even wives are working, earning money, so from the point of view of everyday life, differences are disappearing. The obstructive view that because you are a woman you have to wear a slim skirt no longer exists (142, translation mine).

Bourdieu might simply see these developments as expanding the reach of the professional and managerial classes, this time in a female guise. Certainly this

125

is at one level unassailable. Yet can we say that considerations of gender and race might nuance a narrative of class reproduction?

To address such questions will require a closer examination of how this difference is embodied and enacted in the designer's own creative vision. How, if at all, has it shifted over the years? I want here to make an argument that the initial, extremely radical shock has been gradually modified, though not necessarily in a linear progression. Comme des Garçons is establishment now, although it is still considered experimental and avant-garde; indeed, experimentation has been institutionalized as the distinctive feature and the trademark of the work of Kawakubo, Miyake, and Yamamoto. Their aesthetic moves have been incorporated into mainstream fashion. After the 1991 fall/winter collection, a Comme des Garçons employee commented to me that that even a well-known conservative fashion reporter seemed at last to have understood the clothing and gave the collection excellent reviews. "We're wondering whether someone slipped something into her drink," she said wryly.

A closer examination of four women's collections—early, middle, late periods, if you will—allow us to consider more specifically the nature of the gender contestations Comme des Garçons clothing might foster. Inevitably, such an analysis is partial and located; I include, for example, those collections I actually attended in Paris and Tokyo. Because I was interested primarily in decoding the aesthetic/capitalist logic by which the collections operate over time, the focus remains on the women's collections. A thorough analysis of gender production must also take into account the contemporaneous men's collections and, ultimately, processes of consumption and resignification.[18] I will argue that through changes observable in the women's collections, we can see gradual modifications in the radical silhouettes as well as critically important aesthetic continuities and the possibilities for continuing opposition and difference. Though partial, these stagings of wish-images will also be suggestive, allowing us more concretely to examine provisionally questions of gender contestation and recuperation, foregrounding the contradictions animating Kawakubo's work and by extension the work of all avant-gardes in the fashion industry.

PERFORMING GENDER

126

The focus of my analysis here is the presentation of Comme des Garçons high-fashion ready-to-wear in the Paris runway shows, which must be set within the context of Comme des Garçons's history and more generally, within the land-scape of the Paris collections, or *défilés*.

Comme des Garçons had been in existence for over ten years by the time they showed in Paris. The firm was established in 1973, and Kawakubo opened her first boutique in the fashionable Minami Aoyama section of Tokyo in 1976. She added a men's line in 1978, and in 1981 presented her first women's collection in Paris—not in one of the large tents at the Louvre, where established designers show, but in the Hotel Intercontinental. This early 1981 collection forms a reference point for Western analysts, even though Kawakubo had been designing clothing for a decade or more. This is one telling indicator of racial marking: for racialized, non-Western subjects, existence commences from the time of introduction to the West.

The *défilé* is a very particular event, and an equally particular yet revealing object of study. It is a climactic moment in a designer's work on a collection, an opening night for the world's fashion critics and buyers. It presents designers with an opportunity to showcase their clothing and to stage their aesthetic and corporate image, for shows ideally unify the meanings of individual clothing pieces in ways difficult to achieve were the garments simply hanging in a showroom. The collections allow designers the opportunity to thematize the significant difference(s) that will ideally bolster their reputation as creators and stimulate consumer desire. In fact, the ways things are shown on the runway are not necessarily exactly the ways they will be sold, and designers usually showcase a few image pieces that embody the spirit of the house or the collection; these are not expected to sell on a large scale. Fashion shows are thought to enact creative visions, and they have the feeling of festival, of reunion with colleagues, of performance.

What made the early Comme des Garçons shows so radical? Holly Brubach, style editor for *The New York Times*, once classified designers in terms of two approaches to fashion. One, exemplified in the work of the Japanese and most of the British avant-garde designers, makes an intellectual and aesthetic challenge, calling attention to the troubles in the world. The other views fashion as simply one of life's exquisite pleasures, where clothing is meant "for eating lunch at a French restaurant where the walls are painted some flattering shade of pink" (92). I myself had not appreciated the degree of this difference until I went to Paris in 1990 to see the collections and attended shows mounted by establishment high-fashion designers such as Hanae Mori, the only Japanese designer of haute couture. Like her peers at Chanel, Ungaro, and St. Laurent, Mori is known for upper-class, classically feminine looks. Her clothing tends to be tailored, soigné, close to the body. The *défilé* performs this version of femininity. At the Mori ready-to-wear show, carefully coiffed and painted models sashayed out in high heels to the latest Top-40 hits—that year, Paula Abdul and Soul II Soul. Tossing their hair, they flirted with the audience and the video cameras at the end of the runway in an almost parodically feminine style. This conventional gender performance characterizes many fashion shows. Staging, then, is crucial. The models' makeup and gestures, the way they walk, the music, the lighting, all shape representations of gender. With this in mind, let us turn our attention to four Comme des Garçons women's collections shown over a period of eleven years.

Fall/Winter 1984–5

This collection extended themes from the first Paris showings in 1981, but still presented a dramatic alternative to the exaggerated padded shoulders and the sexy styles that characterized the fashion of the period.

Staging of this and other early Comme des Garçons shows was considered highly unconventional at the time. The antifashion tone to this Comme des Garçons *défilé* begins with the music: initially, there is none, a feature that attracted much commentary in the fashion press. Generally, shows begin when the lights go down and the music starts; when the lights rise, the models emerge. The 1984–5 show is brightly lit from the outset, and the models stride out to silence. When music does begin—at an unpredictable moment—it is relentless percussion, rather than the usual Top-40 or latest house hits.[19] The models walk briskly, energetically, wearing heavy, flat shoes and sandals. There is no flirting or simpering here: the women are unsmiling, sullen, sober, sometimes defiant, and they seem oblivious, even hostile, to the onlooker's gaze. The women wear little makeup, and hair is arranged to appear messy, standing out from the head. Occasionally, the models wear tricornered hats, like soldiers from the Revolutionary War, or crushed caps reminiscent of a medieval burgher, heightening the impression of gender transgression or cross-gender impersonation—except, perhaps, for the long hair that protrudes from underneath the hats. Indeed, the models look unkempt, rather than conventionally pretty or elegant. Unlike celebrations of conventional femininity in most fashion shows, the atmosphere here indicates that the world is a troubled place, and that fashion is not outside or above that trouble. Women are not meant to be pretty, but tough and defiant. These are women with a major attitude.

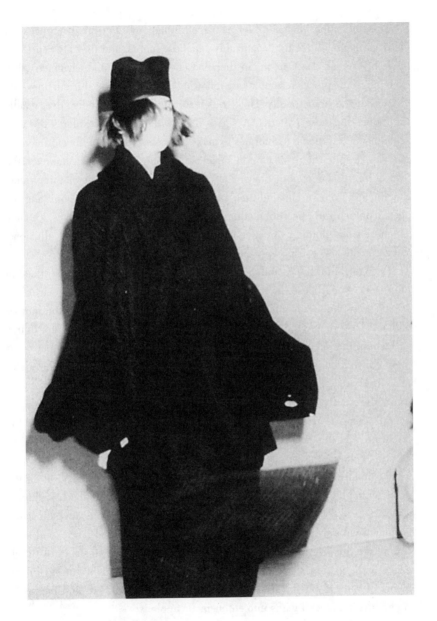

Comme des Garçons Collection
Autumn/Winter 1984–5, Courtesy Comme des Garçons

This collection was known for its use of indigo and *sumi*-ink dye processes; many garments allude to recognizably Japanese motifs, and they are representative of Comme des Garçons in their looseness, volume, and asymmetry. For example, some pieces resemble large, flowing caftans that are shirred, unevenly cut, or hang asymmetrically. The series featuring *aizome*, or indigo dye, recalls traditional Japanese patterns. A series dyed with *sumi* ink explores the gray scale, using traditional techniques to make garments that push the cutting edge of style. Despite the invocation of Japanese techniques and dyes, however, the overall impression is of displacement in space and time, for the clothing refers to garments from various cultures and various historical periods, unifying the ages: monkish garb, peasant clothing, medieval attire, academic robes, kimono, Japanese work clothing, street style and bag ladies. In making these allusions, the garments also escape easy encompassment into any single category.

Recognizable shapes and motifs occur in this collection and are reprised in later work. Long, loose, layered, asymmetrical pieces dominate this particular season. Kawakubo has often designed jumpers; a typical shape is the jumper with one bare shoulder, held up by a single asymmetrical piece or strap. In this collection, the shape is wide and loose; in later collections, the jumper is far more conventionally elegant and close to the body. Another Kawakubo trademark is layering, appearing here in long knit dresses made from loose, sometimes differently colored, layers. The effect this time is bulky, though the overall shape is relatively close to the body. Staging elements heighten the importance of this segment: lights go down and relentless, atonal music commences, echoing the percussion in the beginning segments.

By this time, Comme des Garçons's work is sufficiently well-known for the designer to play with her own image. In this case, the innovation occurs with the appearance of color. A series of pale wheat, beige and ivory knits, including slim asymmetrical sweaters, pants created from draped and folded fabric, and loose caftan-like dresses and coats, garners applause. A later series stages its difference: the lights dim, then rise, as models silently stride onto the runway in garments of warmly hued burnt orange, gold, salmon pink, rust, and burgundy. Again, the audience breaks into enthusiastic applause.

By 1984, Comme des Garçons and Yohji Yamamoto had attained international prominence. The aesthetic conventions of this collection—wrapping, tortured shirring, voluminous layers and folds, the absolute rejection of symmetry—had become familiar themes in their work and disseminated outward. Chunky, flat shoes and voluminous shapes were beginning to take hold in other designers' collections. The loose, black clothing first shown on the runways by the Japanese could be seen on the streets, even worn by the fashion pack in the Cour Carrée of the Louvre, where the major collections are shown. Bernadine Morris of *The New York Times*, reporting on this 1984 show, wrote: "While the Japanese clothes provide an original approach to the art of dressing, they no longer inspire panic. The world still seems safe for Western dress" (C10). The invocations of panic and safety for Western dress demonstrate in what threatening and revolutionary terms Japanese designers were initially perceived. This collection should impart a sense of why "the Japanese" and Comme des Garçons caused such a sensation and inspired such strong international reactions.

Still, at this point the gender images and subversions of staging conventions were clearly occurring within a highly comprehensible frame. The long, loose, primarily black or navy garments were by now no longer surprising; rather, they presented an alternative to "sexy" styles that could, in 1984, be subsumed within the realm of the intelligible. Indeed, one could argue that by this time there had been some modification in the garments themselves; for example, Kawakubo showed some narrow shapes that fit the body closely, even though the body is wrapped in multiple layers or swathed in fabric. Shirring and smocking in these pieces simultaneously obscure and reveal "feminine curves." Moreover, though Comme des Garçons had used innovative staging devices and gender performances—sullen models in a silent parade, for example—the convention of the fashion show itself is clearly still fully in place. In short, the work of Comme des Garçons contested certain fashion conventions, presenting particular wish-images for gender that highlighted independence, rejection of stereotypical femininity, dynamism, movement, and loose, architectural shapes that had a unisex look, problematizing conventional notions of sexiness. Yet these contestations occurred fully within a frame of intelligibility that does not—cannot—fundamentally call into question the rules of the game.

During the mid-80s, Kawakubo concentrated on slimmer silhouettes, saying she had grown tired of wrapping and enormous volume, and she often chose to play with Western tailoring in forms like the suit. However, in this movement toward tailoring, there was always a recognizable Comme des Garçons difference: for example, combining cutting and tailoring with draping. The distinctive Comme des Garçons aesthetic preoccupations with wrapping, asymmetry, and folding never disappear, but occur along with drafting techniques associated with Western clothing traditions.

To illustrate more recent strategies, I analyze here the two collections that I attended: the first in Paris, the second in Tokyo. They carry through recognizable Comme des Garçons drafting themes and aesthetic motifs, yet differ markedly from the 1984–5 collection in staging, silhouette, and figurations of gender.

Fall/Winter 1990

I attended this show in Paris and subsequently paid a visit to the Paris showroom, where Comme des Garçons representative Jody Quon provided technical and aesthetic commentary.

Staging and music set the tone for this gender performance. The theme for the collection is "modern sweetness," a message carried out in the selection of urbane pop/jazz by female vocalists: Dionne Warwick, Eartha Kitt, Sarah Vaughan, Astrud Gilberto, among others.[20]

The music accompanies a gender performance that emphasizes the gamine; the women here are energetic, but retain a touch of sweetness and naiveté. The model who opens and closes the show displays a gangly, slightly embarrassed awkwardness. On the one hand, this injects a note of artlessness refreshing in the face of the supermodel sophistication typical of many fashion shows, but such charm remains recognizably, even stereotypically, feminine. The jaunty, fast-paced music provides accompaniment as the models walk out briskly (again, no sashaying here); most smile engagingly at the audience. Makeup appears conventionally feminine; hairstyles tend toward the short and gamine, while longer hair is tied up in irregular, spiky strands. Sometimes, the models wear whimsical caps shaped like a Hershey's kiss.

This collection features a number of themes connected to drafting and to fabrication. One was the L-shape; many garments display an L-shaped piece that dangles from the garment like an extra appendage. A second is the use of strings. In Paris and New York, this is the year of the anorak: a parka gathered at the waist, sometimes hooded, and closed at the hem by a string. Comme des Garçons not only plays with the anorak shape, but uses string closures for skirts and pants as well as jackets. A third theme is nonwoven fabric, including synthetics that resembled insulation batting, for example, or tubular nylon jersey woven into updated versions of fishermen's sweaters.

In this collection Kawakubo deconstructs Western clothing conventions. She cites Western garments—anorak, jacket, jumper, schoolgirl dress, middy blouse—so that each retains distinctive features that make it recognizable, yet each is thrown off balance. For example, anorak shapes are cut with voluminous amounts of fabric; one displays a ballooning L-shaped appendage, like a huge extra sleeve or pouch, dangling from the back. Baseball jackets appear with the typical knit collar, but the sleeves are closed with string, and the jacket is cut so that the back is split and gathered, making an inverted "V" that extends above the waist. Sometimes the fabrication is unusual, another characteristic Comme des Garçons move: for example, long versions of baseball jackets made of nylon tricot over bonded fabric—a 2 × 1 polyester where two threads to one are knitted together. Generally, such material appears *inside* the garment, as interfacing. Kawakubo also appropriates schoolgirl uniforms and girlish dresses in the form of Peter Pan collars and middy blouses. These look demure, yet feature unusual drafting techniques that create an off-kilter, sometimes even tortured, impression. For example, a dress with a Peter Pan collar is asymmetrically skewed and has a large pouch-like protrusion of extra fabric in the front; the middy blouses display characteristic shirring, asymmetries, and unexpected appendages of fabric.

Among Kawakubo's strong points are her jackets, where innovations appear in both fabrication and drafting. A major series features jackets and trousers of soft, synthetic fabric reminiscent of insulation batting, in shades of celadon, gold, rust, and gray. A jacket I own from this collection has a shawl collar that can be worn conventionally, displaying an open slit at the base of the neck. Alternatively, the head fits through the opening, making the "collar" a decorative piece that floats horizontally across the collarbone. Some jackets and trousers feature L-shaped pieces that hang like extra arms or droopy pockets. Transparent blouses appear with banks of ruffles cascading down the model's *back* instead of the bodice. Another jacket series pairs brightly colored plaids with solids. These garments are formed from pieces of fabric sewn together, so that they can expand or contract depending on the shape of the wearer's body.

Sometimes, the drafting innovations are scarcely visible. The Noir, or evening, collection exemplifies the economy of expression for which the Japanese are famous. For example, armholes are cut as slits on the bias of the fabric, rather than cutting a round hole in the fabric or setting in a sleeve. A fairly straightforward pair of pull-on slacks and a tube skirt have an L-shaped waistband, visible only to the wearer. Occasionally, the drafting is more apparent. One series combines rust and blue stripes in a series of tops and garments that are both shorts and skirts. Stripes reveal the direction of the grain of the fabric, so the ensemble inevitably reveals the complexities of its construction in its vertical, slanted, and horizontal stripes. Quon's commen-

133

tary is eloquent here: "There is tension in all the garments, yet they are made for comfort."

The Noir, or evening series, as well as the show's finale, accent soft fabrics and feminine, gamine images. The long dresses in Noir use velvets of polyester/rayon/chambray; two colors are woven together and the fabric cut as close to the surface as possible in order to produce an iridescent effect and a soft, luxurious surface texture. The dresses are long, relatively simple shapes; some feature scarves, capelets, and trains, others have armholes in a halter or racerback style, or open under the arms, like a kimono. The finale is unprecedented for Comme des Garçons: a bride, who traditionally ends the shows of the established couturiers. She appears in a wedding gown with short sleeves, a fitted bodice, and a skirt made of multiple layers of fabric in the material reminiscent of insulation batting. Her veil is a white cap with a huge visor.

As the bride clearly shows, the clothing itself combines with staging to produce recognizable gender performances. Baseball jackets, parkas, pants, capris, and culottes produce a young, sweetly boyish effect when worn by the short-haired, gamine models. The schoolgirl look defines another important series: however deconstructed and unusual, this is a gender image of naiveté and innocence. Here, the hair, pulled up in topknots that end in spiky tendrils, adds an air of youth with an edge of unruliness. Suits and jackets are more sophisticated, yet the staging—the smiling, gamine models, the jaunty, urbane music—imparts the impression of "modern sweetness" otherwise absent from the garments themselves. Finally, one can only note the ironic, yet unmistakable gender recuperation in the finale, marked by the appearance of a bride—no matter how unusual her garment. Gamine, at once girlish and boyish, heterosexually coupled, the women in this Comme des Garçons show may be brisk, energetic, and cheery, wearing clothes that cite and deconstruct Western clothing conventions, but they are indisputably feminine.

Spring/Summer 1991

This collection was seen as a real departure for the company, the first really "pretty" show in Comme des Garçons history. Kawakubo used "feminine" fabrics, including diaphanous chiffon, jerseys, taffetas, hand-crocheted lace, and a range of colors, from soft pastels and chiffon hand-dyed with *sumi* ink to brilliant reds. Wrapping and folding were carried to new heights with this collection. One theme was a rolled hem, in which hems were not cut and stitched; rather, the fabric was folded over on itself, imparting a softer look. Each chiffon piece was constructed of multiple layers, or chiffon was layered over lace or stretch fabrics. The drafting theme for this collection was the circle. Accordingly, the Noir section featured Grecian-inspired ball gowns with circular sleeves, and taffeta gowns with layers of circularly draped material, first stiffly protruding in front, like a pouch, then in the finale to the collection, dipping low in the back. Characteristic Comme des Garçons preoccupations with asymmetry—blouses and dresses with one sleeve, scarves dangling to one side, notches cut under the arms at odd angles—recur here.

The theme of this collection is "mature elegance," a marked staging contrast to the young, jaunty collection preceding it. Again, music is telling: the show begins with quiet, ambient sounds of birds chirping, a shimmery New Age score followed by soft solo piano reminiscent of Satie. The models walk out slowly, in stately fashion, mostly unsmiling; their (usually long) hair is pinned up loosely and powdered to give it a subdued, gray cast. Faces, too, are powdered to a matte finish. Retro elegance is a theme: the hairstyles evoke the turn-of-the-century, while the accessories—hats with veils, cloches, large flowers pinned to the head—recall the 1920s and 1940s. According to Kawakubo, the atmosphere of the collection is meant to symbolize beauty in a troubled world.

This collection approaches conventional Western clothing, but we also see striking continuity in the Comme des Garçons aesthetic/corporate image of avant-garde artistry. Kawakubo claims to have become tired of volume, wanting to work with slimmer (and more commercial, more accessible) shapes and different materials. Nonetheless, she retains the distinctive features that enable Comme des Garçons to set itself apart from the mainstream. For example, the rolled hems are at first glance barely discernible, but they give the garments an unfinished softness and constitute a patterning innovation. The use of folding emerges even in very simple-looking garments: a double-layered chiffon T-shirt I have from the collection is a single, continuous piece with two sleeves and a hole for the neck at either end. To wear the T-shirt, one must fold it up inside itself. Such distinctive features are both drafting innovations and effective commercial strategies that distinguish a Comme des Garçons product.

Themes from previous collections recur, yet are refigured in distinctive ways. For example, the show begins with a series of garments dyed with *sumi* ink, reminiscent of the *sumi*-dyed garments in the 1984/5 show. This time, however, the fabric is chiffon, and the gender presentation is ladylike, feminine, stately. Models appear in flowing chiffon jumpsuits and dresses, some

135

Comme des Garçons Collection
Spring/Summer 1991, Courtesy Comme des Garçons

with diaphanous vests that float as the women walk slowly down the runway. Layers occur in many guises: a long, diaphanous dress with an open bodice that reveals the breasts is worn over another transparent dress, so that the breasts are covered, yet visible through the fabric. Some chiffon dresses end in a triple hem. One characteristic print for this collection is a stained-glass pattern that appears on dresses and jumpsuits; many of these are worn underneath transparent chiffon. Another distinctive feature is a series of coats, jumpsuits, and dresses made of lace in a daisy pattern; these are often shown with a translucent chiffon overgarment.

The drafting theme, the circle, appears primarily in two forms. One is a circular sleeve made of a continuous piece of fabric joined in the back. It appears most strikingly in a series of long jersey dresses with a Grecian air. All are of pale gray or white, with slightly flared skirts and a train; sometimes the train resembles a scarf tied at the waist, draping to the floor from the hip, while another trails from the waist at the back of the garment. Smocking positions the skirt asymmetrically on the hips. A second circle motif is a pouch. As waltzes set the tone, the Noir or evening collection culminates in two brilliantly red ballgowns. One is a jumper style in which the stiff fabric creates a huge, circular pouch in front, revealing a diaphanous red blouse underneath. The finale is a short ballgown of bonded fabric rising to the knees in front, dipping almost to the floor in back. The circle motif here appears in a back that curves low, displaying bare skin almost to the waist.

What of the gender images presented here? Mature elegance is indeed an apt characterization. The stately manner of the models' walks, their hair and makeup, the contemplative music, the historical resonances to the turn of the twentieth century, the '20s and the '40s, the soft, recognizable femininity of the fabrics (lace, chiffon, taffeta, jersey), the gentle colors (gray, white, apricot, pale green), the soft prints (stained glass and mineral patterns) all seemed recognizably feminine, elegant, pretty. The brilliant reds and characteristic navy and black also appeared; these, too, were used in garments that often emphasized softness and revealed the body even as they often retained a characteristic Comme des Garçons sense of complex, tense construction. I found this collection moving when I viewed it in person, precisely because the combination of conventional femininity and the subversion of clothing conventions throws the viewer off balance. One's expectations are at first defined by the conventionality of the clothing silhouettes and the feminine gender performances, but these are undercut by the fabric and drafting innovations. Con-

137

ventionality, then, creates a ground for the figure of striking innovation. The
tension between reinscription and subversion of convention seems to be a productive one in this instance. Still, as in the previous collection, there is no
doubt that the performances of gender here remain firmly within recognizable
gender binaries.

Spring/Summer 1995, "Transcending Gender"

These binaries are opened out and problematized four years later in the
Comme des Garçons collection for Spring/Summer 1995, which explicitly thematizes gender transgression. Labelled "Transcending Gender," it features a
combination of elements considered masculine with the conventionally feminine, pairing man-tailored suits and stiff fabrics with ruffles, skirts, and
diaphanous materials. It is the first collection we treat here that explicitly goes
beyond the feminine/masculine binary to problematize conventional definitions of gender and sexuality.

The leimotif of the collection is a skirt or dress worn over slacks, topped
with a man-tailored jacket and finished with flat, mannish shoes. The collection begins with androgynous model Kristin McMenamy striding out in a gray
suit jacket and white shirt, and a skirt worn over a pair of narrow slacks. Her
white "men's" shoes pick up the dazzling white of the shirt and offer stark contrast to the gray slacks; their flatness emphasizes her businesslike walk. This
first series offers variations on the serious business suit, worn by various super-
models with slicked down hair, spit curls, and bright red lips. Like latter-day
Marlene Dietrichs, they walk, serious and unsmiling, down the runway.

The basic motif of dress or skirt over pants occurs in multiple variations.
One series features diaphanous skirts that float over shiny, stiff pants, peeking
out from a man-tailored jacket; another, all white, highlights asymmetrically,
irregularly ruffled or scallopped dresses over white trousers, topped by morning
coats or jackets. A later series is based on variations of white shirts, often with
tortured ruffles or ties, that are dress length and worn over pants. The subsequent series is based on variations of short evening or cocktail dresses, all char-
acteristically asymmetrical, worn over narrow slacks. Some are short ballgowns,
white with black tulle underskirts, recalling in shape both the bridal dress of
fall/winter 1990 and the red ballgowns of spring/summer 1991. Characteristic
Comme des Garçons jumpers and dresses appear, but this time over straight-
leg trousers. A cocoa-colored strapless gown is paired with crisp, white slacks.

The Noir collection garners applause, shouts of approval, and an explosion of flashes as photographers catch the images on camera. The garments are truly striking: slim, tailored redingotes or morning coats and stovepipe trousers in black and charcoal are combined with a frothy overskirt of white tulle; sometimes the skirt is long enough to make a train. It is as though one could be Cinderella and Prince Charming at once, in a tuxedo/morning coat *and* a full-length ballgown.

The collection highlights other characteristic Comme des Garçons themes. In a distinctive move returning to her work of the 1980s, Kawakubo sometimes plays with jackets, literally deconstructing them into their constituent elements. "Jackets" appear with no back, hanging from the neck like an apron, a vestigial sleeve dangling from the front; in a few instances the jacket is simply a pair of asymmetrically cut lapels that hang off the neck, worn over unusually high-waisted pants. It is as though Kawakubo is asking us to problematize what counts as a jacket. How many of its distinguishing features can be removed before it signifies something else?

A third visible theme is a return to volume in some of the pieces. Some pants and skirts are constructed to be so voluminously wide that they look several sizes too large for the wearer. Waistbands appear to be folded over and held up by a belt. Large-shouldered jackets appear, in an apparent parody of the broad-shouldered silhouettes of the 1980s. As always, the collection both possesses its distinctive features—the skirt over pants, the transcending gender theme—and carries through recognizable Comme des Garçons motifs: layering, asymmetry, volume, uneven shirring and hems, the backless jacket, deconstructed silhouettes, the voluminous ballgown silhouette for Noir.

Elements of staging carry through the ironic "Transcending Gender" theme. Most obvious is the use of models: a pair of male twins stride down the runways with the women, reinforcing the ambisexual look of the collection. At one juncture, they open a series featuring diaphanous tops, suit jackets with open backs, and long skirts; at another, tight jumpsuits; at yet another, jackets with peplums ruffled in the back. The men present no obvious break in continuity with the female models, save that they wear no lipstick. The musical aspect of staging plays ironic counterpoint to the clothing, serenading the audience with jazz versions of 1960s retro tunes: "Wives and Lovers," where we see jackets and vests vaguely reminiscent of aprons appearing first on the male models; "Come Together," accompanying a series of Nehru jackets; "The Look of Love," featuring cocktail dresses over pants, in an avant-garde Palm

Comme des Garçons Collection
Spring/Summer 1995, Courtesy Comme des Garçons

Comme des Garçons Collection
Spring/Summer 1995, Courtesy Comme des Garçons

Beach/Jackie O look. Other instrumentals have a synthesized, astral quality, culminating in the finale: a synthesized version of "Telstar" accompanying the final parade of all the models on stage. Perhaps the synthesized quality of the music could be said to highlight modernity and constructedness. Perhaps it alerts us to the notion of gender as itself synthetic or man-made.

What, then, of gender subversion? Certainly, the collection strikingly recombines conventionally gendered elements in new, unexpected syntheses that subvert gender binaries. The masculine silhouette is modified by touches of conventional femininity when the jackets appear with both skirt and pants; the gender binary is problematized from the opposite side when masculine trousers are added to feminine cocktail dresses. The use of male models highlights the potential appropriateness of the clothing for "both" sexes, while the combination of conventionally gendered elements highlight the constructedness of what is masculine and what is feminine. Moreover, the collection overtly introduces the issue of sexuality: the women in suits look relatively butch, if softened by lipstick and a skirt, while the men in skin-tight jumpsuits, diaphanous blouses, and jackets with ruffles on the back introduce a femme softness. Notably, gender transgressions were not spectacularized in ways that made them seem unnatural. Rather, the seriousness of the models' expressions, the businesslike walk, the seamless procession of both female and male models, made gender transgression seem unremarkable.

Though the explicit theme in this collection was "transcending gender," I have argued that even the most "feminine" Comme des Garçons collections contain elements of subversion in their usual avoidance of Western curves: nipped waist, décolleté, short, tight skirts. Nonetheless, the innovative and thought-provoking recombinations of gendered elements visible here do not occur in every collection. Indeed, "Transcending Gender" was followed in 1995 by "Sweeter than Sweet," which featured feminine motifs such as the use of pink—again, even though the silhouettes retain characteristic Comme des Garçons oddities and asymmetries. Gender reinscription thus followed gender "transcendence."

To understand this shift, we must understand the workings of capitalist logics in these collections and in any designer's work. Like others, Kawakubo operates according to this logic. Whatever the previous collection, the present collection must somehow both contrast dramatically with it and yet retain the distinctive features that mark it as the work of a particular designer. I would argue that the function of the fashion show is to stage these crucial differences and similarities between collections. The differences create a sense of novelty in order to stimulate consumer desire: we must have the latest. Hence, the themes, the music, sometimes the fabrication, of specific collections become a study in distinctive contrasts. For example, for a three-year period, including the two years I describe in this section, the themes were: (1) Fall/Winter 1990—"modern sweetness," featuring jaunty, girlish models, "manmade" fabrics like tubular nylon, and a lighthearted feeling in music and presentation; (2) Spring/Summer 1991—"mature elegance," a serious, ethereal, womanly collection, with transparent fabrics and a nostalgic air; (3) Fall/Winter 1992—"chic rebel," tough gender images that featured black lipstick, strong shapes, vinyl skirts, fishnet leggings, and loud, 1960s music, notably, Led Zeppelin. The distinctive difference necessarily reproduces the logic of fashion, the marketing tactic that keeps consumers buying.

Yet because Kawakubo's clothing and that of all the avant-garde designers is always off-kilter, never just the latest trend, it is also somewhat removed from the vicissitudes on the level of consumption that affect more conventional clothing. It will always be unconventional. In this way, the work of the avant-garde goes "beyond fashion," the industry's highest compliment; never completely in-fashion in the trendy sense, it is also rarely out-of-fashion. While inevitably reproducing a capitalist logic premised on the recombination of old elements in new syntheses to whet consumer appetites, the work of Kawakubo and others can in fact be worn for years. After all, the distinctive differences between collections cannot overshadow the necessity for the designer to possess certain trademark features that make it recognizably hers; Comme des Garçons garments are generally successful in imparting these trademark continuities. Though the construction of distinctive differences surely ignites consuming passions afresh with each collection, I am more skeptical about the differences between any two collections if one were to examine the garments free of their framing in the shows. For example, the "modern sweetness" collection featured numerous pieces that were far from young and sweet. Many are suitable for a professional wardrobe and in fact remain "in-style" for many years. A constitutive contradiction, then: Comme des Garçons, like other designers, depends on the novelty and contrast from collection to collection to create and feed consumer desire, yet it must also perform its distinctive, recognizable Comme des Garçons features from collection to collection. These continuities become their trademark. Finally, its clothing can also serve the wearer for many years, in some ways subverting the logic of incessant and rapid change that fuels the capitalist engine. Gender and aesthetic contestation, then, can be arresting, and it is always already contradictory, both reinscribing and contesting convention. These interventions in turn are inevitably compromised by their participation in the logic of commodity fetishism and the production of consumer-subjects.

COMPLICITOUS CRITIQUE

Finally, then, what can it mean to be a "chic rebel"? What can we say about the contestatory potential of Kawakubo and Comme des Garçons in providing an aesthetic/political/intellectual challenge in the field of fashion? And what sort of intervention could this be, given the elitism of high fashion and its inextricability from the forces of capitalist reproduction?

Bourdieu gives us the tools to understand the operations of this particular field. His analysis would suggest that the Japanese, like other challengers, would have to present their work as innovative, whether in fabrication, color, experimentation, modernity, youth, or street style. This strategy is itself dictated by the structure of the field and the designers they challenge: the "tradition" of elegance associated with the aristocracy and haute bourgeoisie. Here, Bourdieu captures the overall contours of the Comme des Garçons corporate image, marketing strategy, and critical reputation in the field. In this case, the emphasis on modernity, experimentation, and new directions takes on a distinctive cast: it is linked with race and nation, as I argued in Chapter Two, as the Japanese are troped in terms of a culturally specific aesthetic and an emphasis on experimentation. Extending Bourdieu's analysis of the modernist revolution of the 1960s in the work of designer Courrèges, in which he linked the appearance of such designers to changes in class structure, one could argue that the emergence of "the Japanese" simply indicates the addition of another first-world superpower to the roster of global capitalist consumers and corporate exploiters in the garment industry. Such an interpretation is indisputable at one level, as interimperial and capitalist rivalries are played out in the fashion arena. Furthermore, as Bourdieu indicated, challenges to convention within a field of fashion are inherently limited. Even if new colors or fabrics or shapes or drafting techniques might appear, the game of fashion itself can never be fully called into question, for ultimately the new or subversive strategies are attempts for designers to distinguish themselves from others in order to succeed at that game.

Indeed, this necessity to ever recreate the new often leads designers, whether established or avant-garde, to plunder the world for ideas. The exotic, whether in terms of the Orient (Martin and Koda), Africa, Latin America, or folkloric costume from Europe, recurs in the fashion world. So do enshrinements of a neocolonial WASP/European dominance, embodied most strikingly in the clothing and advertisements of Ralph Lauren and the success of companies such as Banana Republic. The politics of such moves are, of course, never considered, as relations of domination are rendered into high style. A recent Comme des Garçons controversy serves as a case in point. Their 1995 men's show featured models with shaved heads and striped, pajama-like clothing sometimes printed with identification numbers. The resonances with the Nazi death camps were unmistakable, and in the wake of protest from Jewish groups, Comme des Garçons removed those garments from their collection ("A Bad Fashion Statement," 8). Kawakubo herself claimed that the designs were supposed to resemble pajamas and averred that she had no intention of invoking the camps. Similar controversies had erupted the previous year when Chanel featured designs based on the Koran, and with Jean-Louis Scherrer's collection that seemed to recall Nazi uniforms ("Designer Won't Sell Pajamas," 3). Decontextualized from structures of power, oppressive historical events, sacred objects, and subjugated peoples can become simply appropriable aesthetic motifs.

Finally, contestatory gestures—refiguring clothing conventions, offering different possibilities for constructing gender—are inevitably mitigated through the fact that fashion is above all a capitalist enterprise based on making a profit, that it is premised on the production of desire in consumers, and that high fashion in particular, through its exorbitant cost, is centrally implicated in the production of social distinction. The breathtaking price tag is part of the object's preciosity, an index of social status, and it arouses and maintains desire. Issey Miyake put it well when he stated that the price is part of the design. Kawakubo herself says that she is very practical; she wanted to be able to make something and sell it. She is equally dedicated to the notion that her work is different and challenging, insofar as the entire line cannot be so different that it will not sell.

The consideration of these issues cannot be seen solely in terms of the work of the design firm itself, and here, the fashion show offers one very partial and particular point of entry into issues of contestation. Ideally, further inquiry should be extended to include the processes of production and consumption. Who is it, for example, who is sewing those clothes, and under what condi-

145

tions? At best, the answer is likely to be problematic, as it would be throughout the garment industry. On the other hand, it is on the plane of reception where possibilities for contestation often lie, and much of the celebratory literature on fashion and subculture from British cultural studies, feminists and people of color, stress the ways the creative recombining of clothing and gesture provide potential arenas for opposition—that is never beyond contradiction and at least partial recuperation.

Production processes were off limits to me at Comme des Garçons, as was most of the business end of the enterprise, but preliminary interviews with consumers of avant-garde fashion in both the U.S. and in Japan suggest that in both settings Comme des Garçons signifies the different. Playwright David Henry Hwang, who sometimes wears Comme des Garçons, comments that there is always something off-kilter about Comme des Garçons clothing that gives it a distinctive quality. This distinctiveness contributes to the construction of an inner circle of fashion cognoscenti who are able to recognize the aesthetic, class-bound meanings of Comme des Garçons and other avant-garde designers. In Japan and in the United States, consumers tend to be those who want something artsy and different about their clothing, and include many in the art, design, advertising and media fields (*gyōkai*, "the industry," as it is known in Japan). The prime difference between Japan and the U.S. is that the average Japanese consumer of Comme des Garçons and other Japanese designers is much younger. This is due in part to the strong yen and the correspondingly greater cost of the garments in the United States or Europe. It can also be attributed to the vast numbers of younger Japanese working people who live at home and have large disposable incomes. For them, Comme des Garçons is something one might wear in college or before getting married—when one might turn to Hanae Mori, for example. The twentysomething graphic designer daughter of Japanese friends owns pieces from Yohji Yamamoto's Y's and from Comme des Garçons; the latter she likes because "it's a little different" (*chotto chigau deshō*). In the marketplace of commodity capitalism, Comme des Garçons signifies the unusual, even as it confers name brand social status and enforces exclusion and elitism, marking the wearer as unconventional, perhaps artistic, iconoclastic. When specifying the class fractions to which Comme des Garçons most appeals, one could say that Rei Kawakubo is an artist's and designer's designer.

As compelling as these interpretations might be, one wonders whether the narratives of global capitalist systems and class reproduction exhaust the political and interpretive possibilities presented by the work of Comme des Garçons and others. What difference, I asked at the outset, do gender and race make in the reproductive model of class? Two recent interactions at an academic party alerted me to one axis along which the work of Japanese designers continues to assume importance. Upon learning about my book, a woman asked how the Japanese designers were affected by Paris, as though Parisian fashion were the sole standard and model which, surely, the Japanese must imitate. Later that evening, a colleague asked me about the production of Comme des Garçons garments. I replied that both Comme des Garçons and Yohji Yamamoto produce their "simple" garments—the less expensive and structurally less complicated bridge lines such as Comme des Garçons Shirt—in France and Italy. He evinced considerable surprise, averring that it was France and Italy that were known for the quality of their production. The existence of high-quality high-fashion production in Japan seemed astonishing, given Asia's association with cheap labor. In both cases, assumptions of racialized cultural superiority in the terrain of fashion buttress a European hegemony. Under such circumstances, the work of non-white, non-Western designers can reveal and challenge Eurocentrisms in the elitist domain of high fashion.

Along the same lines, gender and race come to bear in Western discourses about designer Rei Kawakubo herself. As a Japanese woman, she is unusual in the field of international fashion design for her strong and unconventional aesthetic vision and for the figurations of gender her clothing allows. Equally notable, she is president of her company. Other Asian women have been internationally successful, but through more conventionally feminine and elegant clothing and through more conventional personas. Kawakubo by contrast is known for her asceticism and seriousness. The stereotypes to which all Asian women are subject in the West also plague Kawakubo. In the Western press, one invariably finds allusions to her height ("petite") and her demeanor ("quiet," "timid"), even as her designs are bold and iconoclastic. Alternatively, dragon-lady stereotypes resurface (e.g., "iron lady"), particularly in relation to Kawakubo's control of the company and her leadership in projects such as the image book/magazine *Six*, and the design of her boutiques and furniture lines. Kawakubo is inevitably subject to stereotyping as an Asian woman, but her production and creation of challenging garments and her simultaneous management of the business, disrupt any assumption of fragility or submissiveness.

More important, Japanese avant-garde clothing offers to consumers different opportunities to construct gendered, raced bodies that do not seem like inferior imitations of normative Western bodies.[21] In a gesture of parity with the

147

West, Kawakubo uses few Asian models in her shows. This is an eloquent statement that she, like other Asian designers, must work on the terrain of *yōfuku*, Western clothing, at one level enshrining Western ideals. An aesthetic imperialism is replayed there. However, Kawakubo does not attempt to adopt Western clothing conventions wholesale or to make Japanese bodies look like Western bodies; indeed, her clothing—especially in the earlier collections—can adapt to the shape of the individual wearer. It offers to consumers possibilities for gender figuration that are largely absent from the work of designers from the Parisian cut-and-tailor mode. In short, the work of Comme des Garçons and other Japanese designers implicitly contests Eurocentric racial hegemony in the garment industry.

Comme des Garçons and the others among the Japanese avant-garde further provided a challenge to established reading and interpretive practices in the world of fashion, including fundamental issues like what counts as clothing and the very definition of fashion itself. Bourdieu suggests that all designers must at some level invoke art in order to compensate for fashion's more lowly status. Yet the subversion offered here may be more thoroughgoing than Bourdieu would lead us to believe, for the work of Comme des Garçons and others suggests productive possibilities for critique in the blurring of boundaries between fashion and art, fashion and sculpture, fashion and architecture. These border-crossings lead to questions about commodification in the artistic domain, where as in the fashion world, vanguardism always occurs within a capitalist regime that recuperates novelty and contestation as marketable difference. Such moves from a non-Western locale also allow fashion to make claims for intellectual, political, and aesthetic seriousness, including the rethinking of the field itself: for example, reconsidering the cultural and historical specificity of the art/craft boundary as in Japan, where conventions allow the designation of craftspeople as "living national treasures," a phenomenon not found in the U.S. Questioning the fashion/art boundary from the other direction calls to mind a whole host of artists, especially women artists, who use conventionally feminine materials and themes such as clothing in their artistic productions. I think here of the work of Judith Shea, whose metal sculptures are eerie fragments of clothed bodies—a tank suit, part of a pair of jeans—that disturbingly evoke the fragmentariness of the subject, or the powerful feminist work of Japanese artist Shōko Maemoto, who uses men's and women's clothing in installations bristling with savage irony. These women tell us through their work that mundane feminine preoccupations like clothing can also be the stuff of serious art and of serious political and intellectual critique.

Finally, what of gender contestation? I would argue that certainly the early collections of the 1980s and the "Transcending Gender" collection enacted possibilities for performances of gender, sexuality, and, less obviously, race that had not existed on the high-fashion runways. The early collections departed dramatically from the fitted, womanly silhouettes prevalent in high fashion to that point. The intervening years have seen occasional gender subversions, such as Jean-Paul Gaultier's eroticizing of male bodies with backless pants, transparent tops, and skirt/pants; Yamamoto has also put men in skirts. The "Transcending Gender" collection is notable in women's wear for its ironic, humorous, even parodic juxtaposition of conventionally gendered elements, and it provoked reflection on gender conventions. The use of male models for the women's collection clearly departs from standard practice, even from Comme des Garçons's own usual practice, drawing attention to the arbitrariness of the gender binary and to definitions of normative sexuality. Other houses have sometimes used male models in their women's collections, but in such cases, it is likely to be someone in flamboyant drag—RuPaul, for example. The marked difference in the Comme des Garçons show was the smooth continuity of male models with the female, the lack of disruption to the serious, yet gently ironic, tone. "Real men" and "real women" could wear these clothes on an everyday basis, the show seemed to say. Though the runway show is indeed a particular, delimited phenomenon, certainly this Comme des Garçons collection presented a vision of gender and sexuality that remains unusual, both on the runway and on the street. "Transcending Gender" dramatized this wish-image, a different form of cultural possibility despite, or rather enabled by, its enmeshment in capitalist structures of class reproduction.

Ultimately, the point is to try and understand the multiple and contradictory forces at work when we consider issues of contestation and reinscription. Fashion as a field is inevitably problematic, and as the logic of commodity capitalism, it permeates our lives: there is no outside fashion. It is also one of the key arenas for the formation of subjectivities, and as such, reproductive models of class—though crucial—cannot exhaust the complexities of subject formation. The emphasis on closure and totalization along the class axis forecloses the possibility of ruptures and interventions when other forces are considered. Indeed, excluding those other forces is a fundamentally Eurocentric move that elides its own positioning in a gendered, neocolonial world system. For example, in the context of the nineteenth century, Ann Stoler argues that the formation of European bourgeois subjectivity and sexuality in fact occurred through a gendered, racialized imperialist project that implicitly contrasted the European bourgeois subject with its colonized Others. Stoler's point is telling: the formation of European class relations and classed subjectivities *cannot be thought* without considering its simultaneous enmeshment in the forces of race, gender, and imperialism.

What difference do gender, race, and neocolonialism make in the work of Comme des Garçons? I have argued that their shows and the reception of their work indicates that important kinds of gender subversions and rethinking of clothing conventions occurred, especially in the early collections. The neo-colonial positionings and colonizations of consciousness represented by European and U.S. popular culture and standards of beauty were both reinscribed and contested in this work. These interventions were in turn inseparable from geopolitical and racial positionings and were understood at least partially in racial and national terms. Indeed, one could argue that the challenge Japanese fashion offered to figurations of gender was precisely a racial challenge. Over the years, the disruption Comme des Garçons and other avant-garde designers represented has become less surprising, as some of the moves have been incorporated into mainstream fashion. Still, one cannot say the clothing has lost its edge, as the "Transcending Gender" show indicated. Gender, race, sexuality, as well as class, shape the performances of identity enacted on the runway and the wish-images and visions of cultural possibility they represent.

In the end, the work of Comme des Garçons points us toward a proliferation of contradictions and questions, and perhaps a reconsideration of conventional categories such as resistance or accommodation, opposition or sell-out. Its contestatory gestures and radical moves should spur a rethinking of hierarchized binaries that would relegate to fashion and other conventionally feminine preoccupations a secondary place. Such conventional critiques of fashion and of "mass culture as woman" (Huyssen), exemplified in the work of analysts like Jameson and neo-Frankfurt School analyst Wolfgang Haug, are premised on an anxiety of contamination that threatens the purity of the intellectual's location above the masses. But the recuperations and contradictions in the avant-garde enterprise also suggest the inadequacy of recent celebratory moves enacted in scholarship by feminists (Young, Silverman) and people of color (Mercer), or, more insidiously, Lipovetsky's enshrinement of heroic, individualistic resistance through fashion, based on an always already masculine, liberal, individualist subject. The complex, contradictory nature of contestation and of any attempt at intervention must be held in mind. Avant-gardes may make limited interventions that are at one level contestatory, but heroic claims for revolution, novelty, and vanguardism must always be suspect—and, therefore, interrogated. Inevitably, novelty and revolution become recuperated as commodifiable difference. Nonetheless, as I argued in the context of a Japanese factory (1990), though one cannot cleave to easy definitions of accommodation, sell-out, and resistance, one cannot abandon attempts at intervention, no matter how problematic the site.

Ultimately, fashion seems a particularly compromised arena for hopes of radical contestation. But, as in academia—another elitist domain whose existence is partially premised on the reproduction of class—limited contestation within a field is possible, as the Comme des Garçons collections demonstrate. After all, meaning is never fully closed, and in those moments of instability, ambiguity, and contradiction may lie the potential for interventions that might destabilize a field, ultimately exposing and throwing into question its constitutive logic. Indeed, to leave conventions unchallenged is, I think, the more problematic stance. To do so would abdicate whole realms of pleasure, desire, self-creation, and potential opposition and critique. As Baudrillard argued, this would fail to disrupt the totalizing logic of fashion and commodity capitalism, the regime of truth within which we, inevitably, fabricate our lives. The work of the Japanese avant-garde designers, while seeming initially ex-orbitant to our political and intellectual concerns, may be suggestive, perhaps even instructive. Even as the designers mount a limited challenge on the terrains of clothing conventions, aesthetics, Orientalist figurations of race, and the representation of gender, they do so in a domain thoroughly constituted by the logic of the commodity, class elitisms, neocolonial dominance, and the global assembly line. None of us can escape fashion; no one among us lives beyond it. In considering questions of cultural politics, the dangers are many: the claims of an avant-garde that would deny its enmeshment in capitalist reproduction, celebrations of the popular that ignore the forces of massification, celebrations of the aesthetic that ignore politics, pessimistic views of the masses that view any attempt at contestation as always already vitiated. Our inquiry into high fashion suggests that narrowing our political scope to the aesthetic domain conventionally defined—remaining a chic rebel without engaging other organized efforts at mobilizing political subjectivities and effecting social transformation—is, to understate the case, a limited strategy. Yet to abdicate any site—particularly one, like fashion, that is so thoroughly emblematic of the workings of contemporary capitalism—is even more problematic. Our task as politically committed cultural workers is to seek out the conditions of possibility for efforts at transformation in multiple sites and to pursue those efforts, not as a heroic vanguard of resistance from some transcendent space outside discourse, politics, and the logic of late capitalism, but as subversion that is always and only subversion from within.

ENDNOTES

1. Thanks to Elizabeth Long for helping to clarify these issues.
2. Primarily *Elle* and *Le Jardin des Modes*.
3. The translations from Baudrillard in this section are mine.
4. For a cogent analysis of Baudrillard's work, see Douglas Kellner, *Jean Baudrillard: From Marxism to Postmodernism and Beyond*.
5. Cf. Chapter 2, "Orientalizing." Haute couture can be designed only by a select number of houses, whose ranks are controlled by the Chambre Syndicale de la Couture. Hanae Mori is the only Japanese among those ranks. Miyake and Kawakubo would likely disdain the idea of haute couture as elitist, passé or perhaps too limiting, while Yamamoto has offered what he has called "nouvelle couture"—fanciful designs in his ready-to-wear collection that evoke the made-to-order fantasies of haute couture. The son of a dressmaker, he speaks nostalgically of clothing made to order for a single customer.
6. Bourdieu goes on to describe the ways avant-garde artists sell not just their artistic work, but their lifestyles and their artistic comportment, something that could well be said of the avant-garde designers as well.
7. For three classic works on avant-garde contestation in the arts, see Renato Poggioli, *The Theory of the Avant-Garde*, Peter Bürger, *Theory of the Avant-Garde*, and Rosalind Krauss, *The Originality of the Avant-Garde and Other Modernist Myths*. For a general perspective on avant-garde aesthetics, see Paul Mann, *The Theory Death of the Avant-Garde*. The latter two works, in particular, point out with skepticism the avant-garde's inevitable and problematic claims for novelty and originality.
8. Yamamoto's mother was a dressmaker, and he himself is a graduate of Bunka Fukusō, the renowed fashion school which produced many of Japan's top designers, including Kenzo and Mitsuhiro Matsuda. Of the three avant-garde designers, Yamamoto is known as the most commercial and the most apt to use tailored silhouettes.
9. For example, in an interview Jeff Weinstein of *The Village Voice* deplored Comme des Garçons's decision to put out the "Shirt" line, speaking disparagingly of a "market-driven aesthetic," which he contrasted to the purer aesthetics of the Comme des Garçons women's line and Homme Plus.
10. The imperative to reproduce these dualisms was strikingly apparent in a 1989 exhibition at the Musée des Arts Décoratifs, commemorating the fortieth anniversary of Snoopy, the famous beagle from the Charles Schulz comic strips. A sister/consort, Belle, was invented for Snoopy, and the museum curators asked designers to create costumes

for Snoopy and Belle, which most of the designers did. Seeing hundreds of men's and women's fashions worn by two anthropomorphized stuffed animals demonstrated the pervasive stubbornness of the gender binary, even as the exhibit also produced a bemused irony in some, where the very absurdity of men's and women's clothing in this context could act to destabilize the categories.

11. Bodei konshasu tte yoku wakarimasen ne. Onna no hito no sen wa kirei da kara dasanakya mottainai to iu kanjikata mo konshasu deshō. Watashi nanka, dochira ka to ieba, fuku no shiruetto ni tsuite no kyōmi, fuku jitai no voryumu kan kara hairu no de, sukoshi chigau n desu, tabun, seiyō no josei wa sen o dasu no ga kairaku mitai na. . . Nihon no josei wa sen ga deteru to totemo ki ni suru deshō. Sō iu kanji ga yoku jibun de mo wakaru no de, soko o keisan shite bunryō o iretari shimasu. De mo bodei konshasu ni tsuite wa, chotto aki ga kiteru kanji desu ne.

12. The use of French, English, or Italian names is common, indeed the norm, among Japanese fashion companies, unless the name of the individual creator is used. Some examples include Monsieur Nicole, Rose is Rose, Oxford Quincy, Novespazio. Even when the creator's name serves as the name of the company, it is usually given in Western order, family name last, given name first, rather than the usual Japanese order, which reverses the terms. Consequently, we have Yohji Yamamoto, Issey Miyake, Hanae Mori, Atsuro Tayama for A.T., and so on. This I would read as a sediment of aesthetic colonization and the fact that Japanese designers are playing the fashion game on someone else's field, which is still defined in Paris, Milan, London, and New York. All the Japanese designers of international stature are eager to be accepted as "universal," which means, de facto, being accepted in Europe and the United States.

13. See, for example, an article in *An-an*, the quintessential young woman's fashion magazine. In a section called "Mannish," the caption extols the virtues of a monotone look in brown, that gives a "mannish look with a boyish image" (*An-An* 593. September 18, 1987, 77).

14. This early work is sometimes compared to that of Sonia Rykiel—whose casually elegant, very French designs now seem extremely conventional in comparison to Kawakubo's (Sudjič 79).

15. Further gender contestation occurred in the early collections, when makeup was eschewed or used to disrupt convention. Neither Kawakubo nor most of her staff wear any makeup, and in her early shows the models tended to wear makeup used in unconventional ways—pink on the corners of the eyes, color underneath the eyes. The greatest aesthetic disruptions in this regard took place in the early Paris collections, when makeup artists placed "blotches of color on their faces suggesting that the designer had battered women or the victims of Hiroshima in mind. Nothing of the sort" (Morris 1982, C10). It was, in fact, a move to subvert aesthetic conventions. Kawakubo said, "If you are to put color on the face, it need not be on the lips. It can be anywhere" (ibid.).

16. On the consumption side, there appears to be some truth to this image, at least according to a Brussels boutique owner who carries both Comme des Garçons and Yohji Yamamoto clothing. She says in response to a question about the kind of woman who

buys this clothing, "My clientele is composed for the most part of women who want to please themselves above all. These women are therefore physically and financially independent. In general they have strong personalities, feel good about themselves, and want to safeguard that spirit of independence." (Ma clientèle est composée en grande partie de femmes qui veulent se plaire avant tout à elle-mêmes. Ces femmes sont donc physiquement et financièrement indépendantes. Elles ont en général une forte personnalité, se sentent bien dans leur peau et veulent sauvegarder cet état d'esprit.) ("Les japonais: incompris ou admirés?": 97).

17. Kyokutan ni ieba, kigokorochi yori mo fuku o kita toki ni sono hito ga ukeru seishinteki na mono, fuku o kiru koto de kimochi ga furī ni natta to iu yō na koto o daiji ni shitai.

18. One crucial difference marks the staging of the Comme des Garçons men's collections. Unlike the women's, which uses professional models, the men's shows feature "real men" who are not models. For example, a joint Comme des Garçons/Yohji Yamamoto show in Tokyo in 1990 featured many musicians, including jazz luminaries Don Cherry and Charles Lloyd, Lounge Lizard John Lurie, Edgar Winter, Ottmar Liebert, among others, as well as film stars such as Dennis Hopper. The rationale for this practice has to do with the perceived necessity to acquaint men with the appeal of fashion; seeing "real men" who have other lives and who are not models should, according to this logic, make the clothing seem more approachable to other "real men." In practice, this allows a degree of role subversion absent from the women's collections; the men sometimes joke among themselves, ham it up, or otherwise show that they are indeed not professional mannequins.

19. For the 1991 spring/summer collections, for example, the big hit on the runways in Paris was house group Dee-Lite's "Power of Love"; in Tokyo it was Dee-Lite's "Groove is in the Heart," followed closely by Snap's "Oops Up" and Caron Wheeler's "Living in the Light."

20. For example, the first tune was a breathy rendition of "*L-O-V-E*" followed by Dionne Warwick's "You'll Never Get to Heaven."

21. In *A Notebook on Cities and Clothes*, Yamamoto shifts to European bodies as the model, while making adjustments for the domestic Japanese market.

TOKYO 1990

The excitement of the collections, the whirlwind schedule of show after show, the inevitable waiting, the politics of seating, the sense of anticipation. For me, a neophyte, everything seems thrilling; my senses strain to take it all in.

After only a few collections, though, the routine becomes all too familiar. Most of what I see is—how can I say this—"just clothes." Oxford Quincy looks like young high-school girls anywhere, Takeo Nishida's "madame" classics seem merely uninspired, Junko Shimada cites Chanel and Sonia Rykiel. . . The parade of "just clothes" continues day after day. In this milieu, the artistic innovations of a Kawakubo, a Miyake, a Yamamoto, are on another level of sophistication altogether. Memorable, too, are the domestic designers who do something unusual: Kyōko Higa's bright patterns, Innov's interesting constructions, Masaji Masatomo's indescribably intense colors, Kenshō Abe's play with form and shape.

At one show, the poignancy of Japanese fashion forcefully emerges. At the end of the program, a designer—Japanese, middle-aged, not much more than five *feet tall and a little stocky—comes out to take a bow, surrounded by six-foot tall, blonde models. The final bow always introduces a discrepancy between idealized model and the designer, but here the contrast is racialized and ineffably sad. I cannot help but wonder, for whom is this woman designing? What about all the Japanese women who will never be six feet tall and blonde? What kind of colonization of consciousness results in the production of "just clothes" for idealized white models? A memory flashes through my mind: the mural adorning the walls of Casa Zapata, the Chicano theme house at Stanford, where I was an undergraduate. A faceless blonde occupied the foreground, as the women of color arrayed behind her shed tears of blood. It was always a little hard for me to work up an appetite in its presence, but the mural's graphic, powerful message remains with me, indelible. These "just clothes," this show, these models, this designer . . . like gotas de sangre, the blood from psychic wounds.*

fabricating masculinity: gender, race, and nation in the transnational circuit

RECENT DISCOURSES OF the transnational or postnational mark a critical shift in the figuration of identities and of global geopolitical realities. Multinational capital, diasporas, migration, tourism, the Internet, the global dissemination of popular culture, and the global assembly line index these transformations and have increasingly compelled the attention of cultural critics. Such shifts lead us to rethink categories of identity such as "nation," loosing them from their foundational moorings without jettisoning the categories themselves, for the very appearance of foundational certainty gives them weight in the world. Indeed, nationalism and transnationalism can operate dialectically, as mutually interdependent discourses.

Concerns with the national and transnational have been refrains in Japan of late, taking the form in the 1980s of a preoccupation with Japanese identity and internationalization. Japan's historical positioning fostered assertions of a new Japanese confidence and a burgeoning nationalism commensurate with Japan's status as an economic superpower, a "Japan that can say no" (Ishihara 1991). In the Japanese case the popularity of so-called *kokusaika* (internationalization) ideology in the 1980s is arguably of a piece with the rise of neonationalism. Internationalization in fact results in the reinscription of what is called *Nihonjinron*, "the master narrative celebrating Japanese uniqueness" (Yoshimoto 22), in which an ineffable Japanese essence inaccessible to foreigners grounds claims to Japanese economic and political superiority.

In this essay I examine the complex interweavings of nationalism/transnationalism with the forces of class and especially gender, in two sites that at first glance seem strikingly disparate: a Comme des Garçons ad campaign for a domestic line of menswear, called "the Japanese Suit," and the literature on transnationalism/diaspora as exemplified in the work of two pivotal male theorists in the field, Paul Gilroy and Arjun Appadurai. Carefully attending to the specificity of each site, we will find gender and class to be always already implicated in the nation and the transnational, in which both the Japanese ads and the texts of social theory provide materials for fabricating class-bound masculinities. Holding together for a moment these two different sites may give us cause for productive reflection on the interconnections among the forces I describe, including perhaps unexpected resonances between the world of fashion and the world of academe.

CONSUMING SUBJECTS

Within our regime of commodity capitalism, it is hardly surprising to find powerful articulations of identity in a domain whose business is the figuration of idealized objects of desire: advertising. Designed specifically to promote identification and provoke object lust, consciously deploying techniques to pull on issues resonant for their audience, ads—particularly fashion ads—become privileged sites for the examination of subject formation.[1] In the Japanese Suit ad campaign, avant-garde design house Comme des Garçons strikingly articulates the contradictions in contemporary Japanese identity.

It is equally fitting that subject formation and the imbrications of masculinity with nationalism, race, and class would be so eloquently elaborated in a campaign for men's suits. Anne Hollander outlines their development in the West, primarily in Britain and France. She argues that the classic Greek nude provided the model for the idealized masculine figure enshrined in what we now know as the suit. Garments became sites where social transformations appeared in material form; for example, at the turn of the nineteenth century, men's garments and the masculine ideal shifted from "courtly refinement to natural simplicity" (90), as their form changed from aristocratic finery to a more sober silhouette incorporating motifs from multiple sources variously marked with respect to class, including the garments of the French *sans-culottes* and the wardrobe of English country gentlemen. Hollander vividly details the complexities of subject formation the suit reveals:

> The modern masculine image was thus virtually in place by 1820, and it has been only slightly modified since. The modern suit has provided so perfect a visualization of modern male pride that it has so far not needed replacement, and it has gradually provided the standard costume of civil leadership for the whole world. The masculine suit now suggests probity and restraint, prudence and detachment; but under these enlightened virtues also seethe its hunting, laboring, and revolutionary origins; and therefore the suit still remains sexually potent and more than a little menacing . . . one true mirror of modern male self-esteem (55).

Suits thus provide an exemplary site for our examination of the interweavings of aesthetics, politics, class, nation, sexuality, and masculinity.[2]

I first came across the ads for the Japanese suit as a relatively minor part of my study on Japanese fashion. "Homme Deux," the line of domestic menswear promoted in the Japanese suit campaign, is one of the many ancillary lines that bear the Comme des Garçons label. These are secondary in both ideological and financial terms to the high-fashion labels "Comme des Garçons" for women and "Homme Plus" for men. Looking through clippings at the Comme des Garçons office one muggy August afternoon in Tokyo, I came across a striking ad, bold black characters arrayed on a stark white background. Reading it, I was stunned—both seduced and compelled to read on.

> THE JAPANESE SUIT
> COMME DES GARCONS HOMME DEUX IS CLOTHING FOR THE JAPANESE BUSINESSMAN OF THE FUTURE.
> IT IS THE CLOTHING FOR THE SPIRITUAL ELITE, WHO LIVE AS PART OF A HARMONIOUS WHOLE, YET STILL POSSESS A CLEARLY DEFINED INDIVIDUALITY BASED ON INNER REFINEMENT.
> *WAKON YŌSAI* (JAPANESE SPIRIT AND WESTERN KNOWLEDGE)[3] expressed the Meiji[4] man's way of life. It means living by the Japanese spirit while flexibly assimilating Western civilization. Created in 1978, Comme des Garçons Homme is clothing designed to keep alive the Meiji spirit and aesthetic sensibility, carrying it into the present. This clothing appealed to the young who have no inferiority complex vis-à-vis the West.

The campaign intricately, boldly interweaves history, nationhood, and masculinity through its invocation of a *Japanese* aesthetic sensibility, a *Japanese* masculine body and Japan's present historical position in the world. This figuration of Japan ultimately culminates in the need for a particularly Japanese suit. These ads directly confront geopolitical histories of defeat and "inferiority" symbolized by the "demasculinization" and de-eroticizing of Japanese men. They eloquently write the complexity of Japan's positioning at a transitional historical moment: the dilemmas facing a First-World, capitalist power with an imperialist history and thinly veiled neoimperialist ambitions that is nonetheless racially marked and Orientalized.

Comme des Garçons mobilizes and amplifies the circulating discourses of Nihonjinron,[5] Orientalism, internationalism, and neonationalism that thrust into the foreground the constitutive contradictions animating Japanese identity. Given a history of penetration by the West and continuing racism in Japan-U.S. interactions, the problematic invocation of Nihonjinron simultaneously becomes an intervention in various Orientalisms that constitute and unravel the East/West binary, eloquent testimony to the salience of racial marking in the fields of global geopolitics. In so doing, the ads deploy strategies that are premised on the creation of consumer-subjects, the provocation of neoimperialist and nationalist nostalgias, the gendering of abjection as feminine, elitist class distinctions, and the reinscription of highly problematic or even dangerous essentialisms.

Yet given an Asian American subject position, the ad copy can also stir deep feelings about Japanese American/Asian American/Asian bodies, highlighting the importance of clothing as a medium for fashioning gendered, raced identities. In its skillful mobilization of history, politics, and the geopolitical histories of specific bodies, "The Japanese Suit" campaign serves as a point of entry into gender, race, nation, the transnational, in which the tensions between nationalism and transnationalism are materially embodied in its figuration of masculine subjects.

Homme Deux and "The Japanese Suit"

The Comme des Garçons Homme Deux line is aimed at a tough, competitive domestic market for business suits that would seem to be initially resistant to inroads from high-fashion companies. Homme Deux possesses several distinctive features. First, it combines a conservative look with elements that are unconventional in a Japanese work setting stereotypically known for its single-breasted navy blue suits and white shirts. To a Western eye, they are not recognizably high style. Aside from a slightly looser fit, a soft shoulder, and no back vents, they are not visibly different from any other tasteful, nicely tailored, rather conservative business suit. However, the lone photograph of a suit in the campaign, featured in an in-house brochure, shows a double-breasted jacket: a challenge to convention, since double-breasted jackets are not quite *comme il faut* in a Japanese corporate setting.[6] Second, Homme Deux is aimed at an older, more conservative market than is Homme Plus; alternatively, it can be worn by Homme Plus devotees of any age who might need to dress more conservatively at the workplace but who still want the Comme des Garçons cachet. Third, the Homme Deux advertising campaign is unprecedented in Comme des Garçons history both in terms of placement of the ads and the design of the ads themselves: the extensive use of text[7] and the adroit, aggressive use of the thematics of gender, race and nation. The campaigns clearly aim for name recognition and market share in this untapped market for high style.

How different is this campaign from the Comme des Garçons approach to its primary lines? For its high fashion lines, the firm rarely advertises in fashion magazines. If ads are placed at all, they might appear in *Artforum* or *BAM*, but almost never in *Vogue*. In 1988 Comme des Garçons developed an image book distributed to the fashion press and to customers, a practice shared by other artistic design houses such as Yohji Yamamoto and Romeo Gigli. Here, the emphasis on the allusive and the oblique is pushed to an extreme. "Art" rather than "mere advertising," the image books encode the message that Comme des Garçons is about more than just clothes.

In contrast, the Homme Deux campaign is striking in its direct approach. Comme des Garçons has targeted its market and advertises in the equivalents of *The Wall Street Journal*, *Business Week*, and *Fortune* (e.g., *Nihon Keizai Shimbun*, *Nikkei Business*). Even more fascinating, they have developed a strategy to direct advertising at women, capitalizing on the tendency of women to buy clothing for their husbands and sons. Ad copy shows well-known women as commentators on men's style, and these ads appear in the venerable *Katei Gahō*, a large-format glossy women's magazine that represents the epitome of upscale feminine respectability.

In choosing to enter the highly competitive domestic market for men's suits, Comme des Garçons is faced with the problem of convincing Japanese men to attend more carefully to the aesthetics of appearance at the workplace. Thus, the thematics of the campaign are crucial. Having strategically targeted the venues that will reach businessmen, what better way for Comme des Garçons to pique their interest than to link clothing choice to the resonant, weighty matters of nationalism, politics, history, and masculinity? Let us return to the rest of the ad:

> Since the Industrial Revolution of the 19th century, THE WORLD OF MEN'S CLOTHING possesses a history in which the world's economic and cultural leader sets world style. Isn't the timing right for Japan, now said to be a world economic power, to set forth its own distinctive style of menswear? Now. . . what might be the basis for this uniquely Japanese aesthetic awareness and Japanese way of living?
>
> THE AESTHETIC SENSE OF SHIBUI (tasteful, quiet elegance) is the answer. Like the stylish flair of a man wearing a pongee kimono. This sensibility is sustained by a fundamentally Japanese aesthetic awareness and feeling for life that downplays surface showiness, concealing and refining individuality deeply within. The notion of *bankara* (rustic, unconventional dress) that once thrived among the students of the old high school system, is one of these expressions of *shibui*.
>
> JAPAN is now moving and shaking IN THE WORLD. It is squarely facing numerous problems: the recession caused by the appreciation of the yen, the growth of domestic demand, the opening of markets, the limitation of exports. Perhaps there has never before been a time when we have felt so strongly that, through economics, we live as individuals within a larger world, in a Japan that is globally interconnected. What is needed in this new world are the sense of judgment and the decision-making power to clearly set forth your point of view by choosing wisely from the flood of available information.
>
> COMME DES GARÇONS HOMME DEUX is businesswear for this historical era. Clothing that is easy to wear, tastefully elegant, not restrictive to the body. As "preppie" clothing represented the Ivy Leaguer of the American East Coast, this is the new businesswear based on the aesthetic sensibility of Japan's business élite.

The suit here becomes a site for the play of geopolitical relations between Japan and the West. The ad copy calls on the suit as a material emblem of Japanese conformity and racial inferiority. Derisive jokes both within and outside Japan about Organization Men in their stodgy navy blue jackets pointedly satirize the restrictive conventions of the male business world. Historically, suits have resonated deeply with the feelings of discomfort some Japanese have felt vis-à-vis Europe and the United States. One recalls Natsume Soseki, the celebrated Meiji period author, who writes with considerable pathos of his sojourn in London. His feelings of inferiority were embodied in his sense of looking out-of-place and ill-at-ease in Western clothing. In a searing anecdote,

Soseki tells us that as he walked down the street in a frock coat and top hat, two working men derisively called out "a handsome Jap!"[8] Here, the attempt to fit into British society through adopting the proper outward accoutrements of Westernness—the frock coat and top hat—cannot disguise Soseki's racial markings.

Comme des Garçons skillfully plays upon this history of conformity, discomfort, and inferiority. Of course, the conditions for perceived inferiority have undergone major transformations since the Meiji period. The Japan of the 1980s was economically powerful, increasingly confident, and, in many quarters, increasingly exasperated at U.S. assertions of dominance in arenas such as the ongoing trade negotiations. The dilemma of the 1980s was not one of playing catch-up, since in many economic fields Japan had assumed a position of eminence, if not preeminence. Rather, it involved combatting racism and perceived unfairness, attempts to deal with the anger that American and European assumptions of superiority provoked. The ads write this dilemma: how should Japan address a complex situation of historical inferiority, shifting economic and geopolitical balances, domestic confidence, and U.S./European fear, racism, and condescension? In writing this problem they also propose the means for its resolution: the Japanese Suit.

The campaign's catchphrase *Nihon no sebiro* engages the complexities of the changing dynamic between Japan and the West. Foregoing the more contemporary word *sūtsu*, Comme des Garçons selected the nostalgic term *sebiro*, from the English "Savile Row," a testament to British hegemony as world power and world trendsetter in the late nineteenth century. But it is not just any *sebiro* Comme des Garçons invokes, it is a *Japanese sebiro*. Japan has appropriated and made its own a genre of clothing originally defined as quintessentially British. Clad in such a suit, no longer will Japanese men feel out-of-place or inferior. The ad copy allows readers and consumers to participate in a nostalgia for the glories of empire, both British and Japanese, giving implicit license to neoimperialist fantasies in which Japan displaces Britain. Indeed, say the ads, style is set by world powers, and Japan has finally joined those ranks, suggesting that Japan is Britain's proper heir.

Further, the ads deploy script styles and word choice as essentializing practices that write an ambivalent and complexly positioned Japanese identity. Take, for example, the use of loan words. It is no accident that they are primarily from English, given a constitutive history of occupation and penetration. The use of loan words indexes that relationship of historical inferiority and defeat. On the other hand, English terms have been appropriated in ways that render them Japanese. Significantly, *sebiro* is written in characters that mean "back" and "broad." More common for foreign loan words is the use of the *katakana* syllabary that marks the terms as foreign; the many other English loan words sprinkled throughout the ad are rendered in the usual *katakana*: *bizinesuea* ("business wear"), *toraddo* ("traditional or preppie"), *bodeishieipu* ("body shape"), *apīru* ("appeal"). And of course there is the Japanicized French of the company name itself, indexing the history of French dominance in the fashion world. The liberal use of loan words endows the piece with cosmopolitan cachet, as it both gestures toward the West as center and indexes the Japanese appropriation of the West.[9] Yet, the piece carefully retains the essence of Japanese identity in its invocation of *shibui* (adjective) or of *shibusa* (noun) in Japanese characters, allowing subtle understatement to remain the distinctive feature of Japanese culture and aesthetics. Thus, the use of script and effective choice of terms gives us a Japan flexible enough to assimilate and appropriate the West, in a resynthesized identity that asserts an essential Japaneseness based in the culture of *shibusa*, a term that itself possesses eloquent double meanings. Among younger people, *shibui* signifies "hip," "cool."[10] Consequently, *shibui* as the essence of Japanese identity temporarily resolves the tradition/modernity binary, evoking both a history of subtle aestheticism *and* the vibrantly contemporary.

The subject-position created here is at one level oppositional to certain kinds of Orientalist discourses. In combatting the Orientalist stereotype of the businessman as the corporate drone as well as domestic critiques of the conservatism and lack of creativity of the Organization Man, the campaign asserts a creative assimilation of the West that contests narratives of Western preeminence or Japanese imitativeness and, arguably, undermines the East/West binary. Indeed, the ad challenges stereotypes of Japanese conformity by invoking a particularly *Japanese* individuality imbued with *shibusa*. Both refined and hip, the businessman who will wear *Nihon no sebiro* is his own man. He is neither a conformist in a cheap navy blue suit and white shirt nor a wild radical incapable of getting along with others in society. His personality, his unique dispositions, are ineffably present but visible only in elegant, tasteful—yet contemporary—form. The foundation for this unique synthesis is located in the cultural essence of *shibusa*. Thus, at one level the ads take on Orientalist stereotypes, while at another level engaging a self-Orientalizing that reinscribes a nationalist essence based in racial difference.

The contradictions of Japanese identity at this transitional historical juncture thus permeate the text: racially marked and Orientalized on the one hand, a First-World power with neoimperialist ambitions on the other. The campaign highlights subtextually a history of various forms of domination by the West—the opening and penetration of Japan by Commodore Perry, defeat in World War II and the subsequent Occupation and foreign intrusion into the national body, the continuing dominance of American and European popular culture. The businessman is located within this history. The would-be consumer of *Nihon no sebiro* is a cosmopolitan man of erudition, as the frequent use of loan words would suggest. The ad also writes the potential consumer as the class equivalent of an Ivy Leaguer, possessing both the financial and cultural capital to be part of the business and government power elites in Japan. But he is also someone of a vintage who must remember the humiliations of the war and who yearns to be free of feelings of inferiority toward the West. The Japanese suit promises to fulfill this yearning, giving the consumer the material means by which he can assume leadership on a par with the men of Meiji and the confidence of today's cosmopolitan young people. The ad campaign writes a particular subject of desire, who can satisfy that desire and create a satisfying Japanese masculinity by purchasing a Japanese Suit.

The Homme Deux ads weave a compelling, skillfully constructed narrative that is, simultaneously, profoundly gendered. Japan's history of defeat and the Orientalizing and racializing of the body are implicitly associated with femininity. Feminized and Orientalized in his relations to the West, the businessman is given an opportunity to construct a fully masculine identity that would necessarily involve righting former geopolitical imbalances, embracing a masculinity based on strength, leadership, individuality, intelligence. This masculinity becomes the figure defined against the ground of a passive femininity defined as defeat, penetration, and subjection to domination. Becoming fully a man, then, will require dominance—a dominance attainable in a Japanese Suit.

Precisely this issue reveals the fissures in this stirring narrative. Invoking the Meiji period highlights a revolutionary moment of nation-building in Japan, a massive mobilization in response to Western challenges. But along with nation-state formation came imperialist ambitions, and the advertisements' focus on Meiji nation-building elides other imperial and colonial histories, including the Sino-Japanese and Russo-Japanese wars, the colonization of Korea and Taiwan, and the processes of militarization that brought Japan to the Pacific War. In the ads, parity is conceived only in terms of Japan's relation to the West. But the tacit message is that dominance can also evoke fantasies of Japanese empire as Japan takes over Britain's imperial mantle. The man who wears a Japanese suit then will truly stand as Britain's heir.

"Real" Men Consume Fashion

In making such bold appeals to gendered nationalisms, Comme des Garçons is attempting to address the daunting task of differentiating its product within a highly competitive market. The following sections analyze three other phases of the campaign, three related strategies the company pursues in order to capitalize on its high-fashion cachet for a diffident, conservative consumer who may consider fashion a trivial female concern.

One series involves testimonials from well-known critics, authors, and technological experts, who thematize the links between a satisfying Japanese male identity and the world of style. Not only is it permissible for men to care about clothing, but such care is synonymous with masculinity and worldly success. One critic tells a sad tale of going to America in the immediate post-World War II period, where he suffered discrimination as a Japanese. Defeat and poverty left him poorly dressed, and he suffered further humiliation for his out-of-date garments. The vignette ends with his acquisition of a fashionable American suit, which he wears home to Japan in a triumphant return. A second writes about managerial dress, emphasizing the ways clothing reflects corporate identity: the histories, personalities, and identities of both the companies and the managers. An art critic discusses East/West exchange in art, especially the popularity of Japonaiserie among the fin-de-siècle Impressionists and post-Impressionists. He suggests that the Japanese artists who had gone to Paris and returned to Japan at the turn of the century were fundamentally changed by the experience; they also brought Paris back with them. He ties this East/West exchange and the blurring of East/West distinctions to clothing and to the need for a suit reflecting this "blend culture." An engineer and computer specialist talks about technological innovations in the fashion industry, forecasting future developments. Fashion, these ads tell us, is for real men.

Muramatsu Yūgen, a writer/novelist, offers an especially telling vignette thematizing style as a marker of national, racial, and gender identities. In a quirky, humorous, breezy testimonial, he says:

> Now for a Japanese, the suit . . . well, this is alien territory. The Japanese were
> originally pros at wearing kimono, but in the span of just a hundred years, wear-

ing Western clothes has become our common sense. Should we comment on how quickly the Japanese can transform themselves? Find it amazing to change so much in the space of a hundred years? In any case, it's indisputable that a lifestyle of European haircuts, beef, and Western clothing has firmly taken hold since Meiji.

From that moment, the importation of a "Western sensibility" began. The men (of Meiji) who had been at fashion's cutting edge successfully adapted their bodies to the demands of Western clothing. In this era these men achieved the same success with their economic endeavors. Now, if you look at their photographs—men who had only a short history of acquaintance with Western dress—you immediately notice their surprisingly fresh, stylish way of wearing the clothes. It's a strange shock to see that these Japanese men whose inner spirit was far from tranquil, whose spirit led them to do things like commit *seppuku*, were far more stylish than the men of today, who wear Western fashions in a Western way.

Maybe there's an important hint here for the men who live in today's so-called fashion era. If you think about body type [of the Japanese], . . . I sense the possibility of a style that reaches a good compromise, in a suit that's a touch different from a Westerner's. The suit envelops the Japanese soul. (*Sebiro ga Nihonjin no tamashī o tsutsunde iru.*) This is the promise for the future, this is the secret ingredient of a Japanese suit that transforms a former minus into a plus, a world of the Japanese suit that transcends the original.

As in other vignettes, the preoccupation here is with preserving some sense of Japanese identity in the face of internationalization/globalization/transnationalism. Again the historical referent is the Meiji period, citing a moment of national mobilization and success in imperial endeavors. The play of inner and outer is thematized through intertwining racialized masculinities and nationalisms: the Meiji men who wore Western suits as though they weren't really Western suits looked better than present-day Japanese men, who are more thoroughly acquainted with Western dress, presumably because the Meiji men were preserving something Japanese in their bearing. It implies that the Meiji men were more *manly* because of their untamed, martial, truly Japanese spirit. Here, the invocation of *seppuku*, though comic and somewhat fearful, is eloquent. The stylish attractiveness of these men who lived by the samurai codes far surpasses that of today's domesticated—dare I say feminized?—imitators of Western style. Muramatsu thereby writes a gendered, raced body distinctive in its stature, skin color, physical movements, and gestures. This distinctiveness becomes the essence of Japanese identity. One could wear a Western suit while retaining such an essence, but even better would be a suit designed especially

167

to express the Japanese soul. The transcendent, inspirational ring of that phrase echoes historically with powerful nationalist sentiment, from the relatively innocuous to the right-wing and jingoistic. For example, it raises the specter of *Yamato damashī*, the Japanese spirit linked to *bushidō*, the way of the warrior, a key component of the ideologies and nationalisms of the Sino-Japanese War and World War II. The citation is, quite frankly, stunning in its baldness. This Japanese spirit animates the Japanese suit in a refigured world in which the Japanese have taken a foreign object, appropriated it and made it their own. Indeed, *Nihon no sebiro* surpasses in style, quality and appropriateness a "real" British suit tailored on Savile Row. Conversely, a suit is far more than frivolous adornment; it protects and expresses the Japanese soul. Style, gender, and nationalism are inextricably linked. If you buy The Japanese Suit, you too can become a Japanese Man imbued with an essence of Japanese masculinity, who wears the suit made for *his* distinctive spirit and *his* distinctive body, a man who is no longer a feminized, Orientalized, domesticated subject vis-à-vis the West. Far from being an exclusively feminine preoccupation, Comme des Garçons tells us that fashion can become the idealized expression of Japanese masculinity.

Ad(d)-ing History

A third phase of the campaign picks up these themes, invoking even more explicitly the parallels between the 1980s and the Meiji era. Contemporary commentary evoking the Golden Age of Meiji gives way here to a more direct deployment of gendered masculinity and nationalism in the persons of historical figures—many from the Meiji period—who played key roles in the internationalization of Japan. It features photographs of prominent writers and political figures, with accompanying text that ties their accomplishments to geopolitics and to style. This series narrates the need for a Japanese suit appropriate for this historical moment when Japan has taken its place as a world economic power. The suit here reflects personal character, national identity, and international prominence.[11] The vignettes mobilize a nostalgia for a Golden Age when Japan was able to respond to the threat of the West through the efforts of "great men." Rearticulating 1980s concerns with *kokusaika* (internationalization) and with the continued global success of Japanese business, these ads construct a Japanese masculinity that is successful in challenging Western hegemony, where masculinity means dominance in the worldly domains of the political and economic, implicitly defined against the passive, Orientalized femininity of Japan's opening to the West and its defeat in World War II.

One ad features a full-page photograph of Gotō Shinpei, a leading government administrator in the Meiji (1868–1912) and Taishō (1912–26) periods. The text reads:

> Born in the home of poor aristocrats in Mizusawa, Gotō Shinpei was an impoverished student, dressed in "ragged *hakama* and mismatched *geta*," the forerunner of "*bankara*" [the rustic, unconventional style of students of this era]. A practitioner of medicine, student in Germany, President of the Manchurian Railroad, Home Minister, a count, he lived through the Meiji era as one of its great politicians. In that period, *bankara* became *haikara* [stylish dandy], and he continued to create a persona that could take any garment and wear it with his refined, personalized sense of style. In another sense, isn't *bankara* perhaps like Japan's punk, the explosion of youthful energy? Gotō Shimpei was a person who throughout his life possessed the spirit of the avant-garde.

This is the most obvious case of a discursively produced history that asserts a dubious historical equivalence. It enshrines Gotō in a particular way: as someone who could be stylish in any situation—indeed, poverty is encoded as simple style in this text. Power, internationalism, and the force to shape history are linked to fashion; being a great politician and being in vogue are presented as coextensive. Leadership means a position at the cutting edge of history and at the cutting edge of style. The final logical link, the comparison of *bankara*, the unconventional look of poor students, to punk, an English working-class phenomenon in its origins, posits them as historically equivalent explosions of "youthful energy," eliding the vast cultural and historical specificities separating the two. This move exemplifies the tendency of the fashion industry to reduce historical and political difference to consumable elements of style. But perhaps the most disturbing aspect of the ad is the aestheticizing of politics. Walter Benjamin links this tendency to processes of objectification and self-alienation that enable "mankind" to "experience its own destruction as an aesthetic pleasure of the first order" (242). In Benjamin's case, this meant a celebration of the beauties of war thematized in fascist ideologies. Though the contemporary historical situation in Japan does not immediately recall the burgeoning militarism of the 1930s, certainly there is cause for disturbance in the encoding of class and poverty as mere ingredients of style. Finally, the ads erase and even implicitly celebrate an entire history of Japanese expansionism and imperialism, in which Gotō was centrally implicated as party to the annexation of Manchuria. In fact, this complicity is recuperated as avant-gardism.

Selectively stressing the ways Meiji leaders such as Gotō responded to the Western challenge, the ad copy erases imperialist histories and creates subject-positions for readers that allow the transfer of desired qualities to the consumer through the purchase of the product. In this case, the Japanese suit positions the buyer within a masculinized, nationalist legacy embodied in the personae of Great Men such as Gotō Shimpei. Clad in such a suit, the Homme Deux man can aspire to a similar position of greatness, defined through key masculine attributes: powerful leadership, a vanguard spirit, resourcefulness. Here, power and style are coextensive.

Specular Women

A final campaign puts another distinctive spin on these themes. If Gotō Shimpei and other Meiji leaders embody a masculinity based on political power and resourceful response to the West, if Muramatsu constructed a masculine essence based on an indomitable, ineffably Japanese spirit that resexualizes the male body, this campaign introduces heterosexuality as the necessary next step for the full construction of Japanese masculinity. It features similar prominent historical figures in full-page headshots, but the commentary this time comes from contemporary women, followed by the copywriter's text. Aimed at female consumers who purchase attire for their husbands and sons, these campaigns appear in the very proper women's magazine *Katei Gahō*.[12] If in the other phases of the campaign, femininity serves as the ground for the figure of active masculinity, here "woman" emerges as the dialectical opposite for the existence of "man": his audience, his mirror, his guarantor of heterosexuality. Fully reinscribing the gender binary, the ads invoke the female gaze as indispensable to the full performance of masculinity.

A particularly striking example features Nobel Prize-winning novelist Kawabata Yasunari as seen through the eyes of actress Kishi Keiko, who narrates their relationship as the classic pairing of the naive young ingenue and the worldly, seductive, dangerous older man. Kishi Keiko, a well-known actress, celebrity, and longtime Parisian resident, embodies cosmopolitan grace; Catherine Deneuve and Grace Kelly come to mind as cross-national parallels. One of Kishi's best known roles was Komako, the provincial geisha in the film version of Kawabata's novel *Snow Country*. She alludes to this experience and to her first interaction with Kawabata, who at one point dissolves into an image of Shimamura, Komako's lover in *Snow Country:*

> The first time these penetrating, quiet eyes, burning with passion, gazed at me, I was in high school. I stood transfixed. . . . *Sensei* [Kawabata], who that day had come to see me play the role of Komako, stood there cutting a romantic figure in a suit, framed by the snow-capped mountain in the evening light behind him. For an instant, I felt dizzy, as though *sensei* and Shimamura had become one. The night of my wedding reception in Paris, when *sensei* had done us the honor of acting as go-between, he gracefully picked up with his slender fingers a spear of asparagus that had appeared on the dinner table and elegantly ate it, the way French connoisseurs might. I've never met another tuxedo-clad Japanese man who could eat asparagus with such style. Even now, the fiery eyes of Kawabata Yasunari *sensei*, who could wear both kimono and Western suits with breezy nonchalance and a uniquely refined sensitivity and aesthetic sensibility, live on within me (Kishi Keiko, actress).
>
> Through Kawabata Yasunari's works, brimming with beauty and acute insight, we are taught about the existence of the aesthetic consciousness at the foundations of the Japanese heart and mind. Beginning with his Nobel Prize lecture, and continuing with "Japanese Culture and Beauty," "The Existence and Discovery of Beauty," these works continued to take this message abroad. Beauty is the world's common language. Is it not the work of the next generation to continue to translate this message into concrete forms and theoretical structures and impart it to the world?

In this passage, we find the copywriter engage a self-Orientalizing that deploys tropes of Japan as the land of the aesthetic, suggesting that aesthetics can ground claims to Japanese uniqueness, excellence, and moral superiority. Indeed, Japan can assimilate the best of the West while teaching the West about real beauty. Skillfully, Comme des Garçons places the *Nihon no sebiro* directly in line with the works of Nobel-Prize-winning Kawabata, as heir to his legacy of creative genius and international acclaim. Taking on Kawabata's mission of imparting the Japanese aesthetic sensibility to the world, *Nihon no sebiro* takes the necessary next step required of "our" generation by translating this Japanese aesthetic into material forms such as clothing. The suit thus becomes the concrete embodiment of an essentially Japanese cultural superiority.

Kishi's testimonial completes the performance of racialized, nationalist masculinity; it is a brilliant gesture. Known for her cosmopolitan elegance,

171

Kishi acts as idealized Other: judge, mirror, and appreciative audience. Under her refined and knowledgeable gaze, Kawabata becomes a "real" man, who is sexually appealing but slightly dangerous, an older man of the world much like his character Shimamura from *Snow Country*. Such a man is at ease even in the most rarefied European circles, possessed not only of the savoir-faire to navigate the customs and manners of the French élite, but also with the confidence to break with those customs. The gendered subject created here is cosmopolitan, acutely intelligent, passionate, and elegant. He is unafraid of being his own man, sufficiently self-possessed to wear either Western or Japanese clothing with panache. An alluring image indeed.

Thus, the ad takes the construction of a satisfying Japanese masculinity to the next necessary level, heterosexualizing the subject. Muramatsu used the indomitable, implicitly martial spirit as an essence of masculinity; Meiji political figures attest to the linkage of style with masculinity as political leadership. But the full (hetero)sexualization of the Japanese man can be fully realized only through the reinscription of the gender binary. Kawabata is troped as the attractive, dangerous, famous older man, Kishi as young, nervous, naive. Yet Kishi is also the intended audience for the construction of maleness, the mirror through which heterosexual masculinity can be performed and seen. Although women are by definition in the position of relative subordination, they also are given the power to adjudicate and mirror who counts as a "real man."

Thus, gender, race, sexuality, class, nation, and the transnational intersect in this picture of *Nihon no sebiro* and the man who wears it. He is both subject of masculinity and object of (female) desire. These advertisements construct a gendered Japanese identity. They create a subject of desire and the potential to fulfill that desire with the product they offer. The text recreates a sense of inferiority to the West—an inferiority implicitly gendered as feminine—and offers a means for transcending the very discomfort it has discursively produced and amplified, one with its own complex history in the realm of geopolitics. Against a history of penetration, occupation, and cultural domination by the West and a historical situation positioning Japan as economically preeminent, they create a masculine dominance that refigures penetration as creative assimilation, constructing a raced, heterosexualized body that will be able to resist further penetration by the West. This body can articulate the anger of having been racialized and denigrated; it is a body that can perform Japan's global economic power. It is also a body implicated in imperial histories and continuing neocolonial projects. These colonizing imperatives are elided on the one hand through a focus on Meiji as a period of nation-building that sought parity with the West, suppressing the traces of militarism and expansionist aggression that accompanied the building of the nation-state. On the other, the suit as *sebiro* invokes Britain's class elitisms and the British imperial project, tacitly placing Japan in the role of Britain's heir. All these complexities of subject formation can be condensed in a startlingly simple act: buying "The Japanese Suit."

Contradictions animate the politics of reception in no less striking form when one removes the campaign from its domestic context. Lata Mani (1990) has written eloquently about the multiply mediated agendas at play when one writes for multiple and perhaps discrepant audiences. Analogously, the campaign takes on unexpected shades of meaning when we place the Japanese suit within a sedimented history of U.S.-Japan relations and the history of Japanese Americans and of raced Asian American bodies. Despite the urgently necessary problematizing of Japanese rivalry with U.S. dominance and the uncritical celebration of nationalisms and imperialisms in the ad campaign, The Japanese Suit can produce unexpected readings when positioned in an Asian American politics and history. For example, given a Japanese American history of incarceration, Japan-bashing discourses, and the recirculation of insidious racial tropes as a result of the trade wars, the construction of gender in the Homme Deux campaign can be seductive. The businessman is probably the most familiar contemporary stereotype of Japanese masculinity. The bespectacled, camera-carrying, buck-toothed, asexual, emotionless automaton, the corporate soldier who threatens to invade the American economy, is here recuperated as a vehicle for ethnic and racial pride in an historical situation when anti-Asian racism continues unabated.[13] In such a climate, even an *ad campaign* that reclaims the businessman in a positive way can be compelling at one level. Asian and Asian American men single out emasculation and desexualization as their distinctive oppressions, and certainly that emasculation is countered deftly here in the construction of a Japanese masculinity that is (hetero)sexualized and powerful in the world. On this plane, the advertisements skillfully and seductively mobilize counter-Orientalist discourses in the service of commodification and the provocation of consumer desire.

Equally seductive is its use of the materiality of clothing to refigure normative identities. In industrialized societies clothing in standard sizes acts as a vehicle for the production of standard human beings, materially constructing who is normatively human. One of the innovations of the Japanese avant-garde

173

was to make clothing in only one size, which is then adapted to different body shapes, as are kimono. For example, in the U.S. accoutrements of authority in the academic and corporate worlds—lecterns, desks, chairs, plane seats in first-class—are obviously not constructed with many Asian American women in mind. The size and scale of objects constitute seemingly trivial but profoundly telling practices of marginalization. From this perspective, the notion of garments made especially for one's size and body type is deeply satisfying. As a strategically essentialist deployment of identity, as an intervention in Orientalist discourses, the Japanese Suit campaign mobilizes issues that could be profoundly significant, both for its intended Japanese audience and within a racialized U.S. context. The seduction seems all the more insidious and poignant when we note that a raced body worthy of pride appears in an *advertisement* deployed in the service of capitalist accumulation. Given advertising's *raison d'être*, this surely indicates the skillfulness of the ads in pulling on issues that deeply compel potential consumers.

The campaign's seductive and problematic resonances lead me to ask what is at stake not only for the producers/creators and consumers, but also what is *our* stake, and what are our interests as analysts? Here, the use of an unlikely object—an ad campaign—as a locus for the production of problematically alluring identities also leads me to interrogate further those arenas often presumed to be beyond commodification; for example, art or the academy. Indeed, our consideration of The Japanese Suit lays the groundwork for our examination of another site where the discourses of nationalism and the transnational are deeply imbricated with figurations of masculinity: the world of social theory. On closer scrutiny, perhaps the ad campaign and our supposedly disinterested academic theorizing may share more than might be apparent at first glance.

GENDER AND RACE IN THE TRANSNATIONAL CIRCUIT

Recent years have witnessed an explosion in the scholarship on transnationalism. Perhaps its most striking manifestation is the appearance of several journals, including *Public Culture*, *Diaspora*, and *positions: east asia cultures critique*. These institutional sites in the academy mark an epochal change through de-essentializing moves that disrupt bounded notions of the nation-state and of a coherent "culture," tracing border transgressions and theorizing heterogeneities that subvert conventional categories. For example, the inaugural issue of *Public Culture* does battle with the European and American monopoly on social theory and with schemas that associate modernity with the West and with homogenization:

> We seek to deparochialize debates about modernity and cultural hegemony, and to widen the tradition of intelligent observing of places and their practices . . . In general, we oppose the view that the emergent transnational cultural forms and flows of today's world are radically homogenizing, and that the burgeoning cosmopolitanisms of the world are but thin replicas of an experience we in the West are connoisseurs of 'always already' *Public Culture* 1 (Fall 1988): 1.

Such interventions have been valuable and contestatory. However, in examining the work of two exemplary figures who are among the most prominent theoreticians of transnationalism, I will address problems inherent in cultural politics and attempt to highlight the *contradictions* and tensions that animate critical interventions. Arjun Appadurai and Paul Gilroy seek to displace Eurocentric hegemony in defining what counts as theory and what counts as legitimate academic inquiry in a series of important strategic moves: they disperse the subjects of theory far outside the bounds of Europe, write this work into a canon of intellectual thought, disrupt essentialist identities. Their interventions have been part of a major conceptual advance in the academy. But oppositional stances are never free of complexity and contradiction, and in academic discourse as in the world of high fashion, contestations of some social forces may involve a reinscription of others. Here, the mutually constitutive, racialized discourses of the national and the transnational are riven by crosscutting forces of gender and class, and I will argue that the work of these theorists presumes a diasporic, always already masculine subject.

Arjun Appadurai has been a pivotal figure in the development of transnational studies as co-founder of *Public Culture* and author of a body of work that traces "global flows," from *The Social Life of Things* to his present work on what he calls "postnationalism." *Public Culture* has occasioned some of the most exciting contemporary writing in cultural studies and anthropology, infusing spirit and liveliness into the anthropological community and beyond. Yet at times this focus on the public, the transnational and the cosmopolitan can and has come at the price of the local, the domestic, and the out-of-the-way, whose implicit devalorizing is arguably present in the very title *Public Culture* and its insistence on the urban and the cosmopolitan. Kamala Visweswaran (1994) has

175

commented incisively on Appadurai's essay on global ethnoscapes (1991), articulating skepticism about his valorization of deterritorialization as a spur to the imagination. She treats critically his marshalling of examples and evidence (a novel by Julio Cortázar and a film by Mira Nair) from highly disparate historical and political contexts, thus erasing specificity and the politics of location from which each artist speaks. In part invoking Caren Kaplan's arguments on deterritorialization, Visweswaran continues:

> Appadurai's project partakes of a transnationalism devoid of any politics of location or constituency, for it is difficult to discern in his schema whether subjects choose deterritorialization, or deterritorialization has chosen particular subjects. . . . Uncritically theorized notions of deterritorialization project too comprehensively a 'global homelessness' and displacement, trivializing the political particularities of the phenomenon and erasing the 'resolutely local' homesites necessary both for First World anthropologists to interrogate their own privilege and for less privileged subjects to claim home as a place of nurturance and protection.
>
> Is it coincidence, then, that while many feminist theorists identify home as the site of theory, male critics write to eradicate it? (Visweswaran 1994: 110, 111).

The gendering of the diasporic imperative is both more subtle and more explicit in a recent Appadurai essay, "Patriotism and Its Futures," in which he argues for postnationalism as both a descriptive term and a utopian horizon of possibility. Here nationalism and transnationalism are gendered in interesting and contradictory ways; masculinity is treated as both coextensive with nationalism and the origin of nationalism's transcendence. Nation is associated with men and with fixed identities: "For those of us who grew up male in the elite sectors of the postcolonial world, nationalism was our common sense and the principal justification for our ambitions, our strategies, and our sense of moral well-being" (Appadurai 411–12). He suggests that challenges to the bounded integrity of the nation-state have come from various quarters, including those one could call feminist and perhaps even gay/lesbian: "Does patriotism have a future? And to what races and genders shall that future belong?" The question suggests that feminists and people of color have made moves to subvert the masculinity of the nation-state.

Simultaneously, the transnational is marked masculine; indeed, Appadurai reveals its paternal origins: "My doubts about patriotism (patria-tism?) are tied up with my father's biography, in which patriotism and nationalism were already diverging terms. My father's distrust of the Nehru dynasty predisposed us to imagine a strange, deterritorialized India, invented in Taiwan and Singapore, Bangkok and Kuala Lumpur, quite independent of New Delhi. . . . So there is a special appeal for me in the possibility that the marriage between nations and states was always a marriage of convenience and that patriotism needs to find new objects of desire" (413). Here, the language of kinship, patrilineal affiliation, and courtship is striking, but consistent throughout is a privileging of the postnational as originating in the paternal. The postnational, then, is complex and contradictory: both paternal in origin and open to gendered multiplicity.

The postnational is also profoundly raced. Whereas the U.S. nation-state is a space of whiteness, the postnational is marked by whiteness that cannot contain its colored and other heterogeneities. A laudable and impassioned political imperative underlies this formulation: to combat the racist essentialisms that mark the lives of those defined as racially marked citizens. In a moving passage, Appadurai speaks of his oscillation "between the detachment of a postcolonial, diasporic, academic identity (taking advantage of the mood of exile and the space of displacement) and the ugly realities of being racialized, minoritized, and tribalized in my everyday encounters" (422). Certainly, those of us who are "of color" in the United States find this passage richly resonant. If racism is linked to forms of nationalist essentialism, then for Appadurai postnationalist space becomes a utopian one, where hybrid, heterogeneous identities can be recognized as legitimate, and where debate, multiplicity, difference, can be celebrated: "In these postnational spaces, the incapacity of the nation-state to tolerate diversity (as it seeks the homogeneity of its citizens, the simultaneity of its presence, the consensuality of its narrative, and the stability of its citizens) may, perhaps, be overcome" (428).

However, in this subversive challenge to fixity and confining unity, Appadurai makes a problematic second leap, seeing the racially marked body as *mired* or *imprisoned* in specificity. Perhaps most tellingly, throughout the article postnationalism and deterritorialized identities are associated with freedom and possibility; the too-celebratory valorization that Visweswaran so acutely noted results in an implicit enshrining of a diasporic Master Subject. First, he describes hegemonic deployments of the trope of the tribe, decrying nationalist/racist essentialisms that marginalize racial others: "As many of us find ourselves racialized, biologized, minoritized, somehow reduced rather than enabled by our bodies and our histories, our special diacritics become our prisons and the trope of the 'tribe' sets us off from another, unspecified America, far from

177

the clamor of the tribe, decorous, civil, and white, a land in which we are not yet welcome" (422–3). When Appadurai invokes the "detachment of the post-colonial, diasporic, academic identity" and the "ugly realities of being racial-ized, minoritized, and tribalized" or troping "special diacritics" as "prisons," the contrast writes a longing and a desire. Though "tribe" or "prison" refers to the dominant racial/nationalist imaginary, he appears in some ways to accept its terms and yearns for transcendence of the specific, of the shackles of the raced body. But who emerges when we have thrown off the shackles and escaped the prisons of specificity? I would argue that it is precisely the detached, exilic Master Subject. Abdul JanMohamed (1991) calls this the posi-tion of the "syncretic border intellectual" who stands apart from the "home country" or the country of residence. Tsing (1993) further elaborates the dif-ferent stakes and political battles engaged from postcolonial and minority dis-course positions, in which the goal of the former is to escape racial marking, the second to embrace it to combat erasure under the sign of the (always already white) universal subject. Appadurai's diasporic subject ideally pos-sesses no racial marking and is apparently endowed with sufficient resources to *choose* to some degree the space of "exile and displacement." Although I passionately concur with Appadurai's challenge to the forces of racism in the United States, his choice of weapons proves problematic. Despite gestures toward feminism, the text implicitly reinscribes the whole subject of liberal discourse in the guise of a traveller who can enjoy the dizzying free play of dif-ference on global terrain, thereby minimizing the historically, culturally spe-cific power relations that constitute and inscribe that difference. In contrast to Appadurai's (always already male) longing for the transcendence of specificity and locality, perhaps it is precisely careful attention to the power relations con-structing particular sites—including the postnational—that will prove enabling. It is of these processes, not (only) of deterritorialization, but of *reter-ritorialization* (Kaplan 1990; Visweswaran 1994) that so many feminist schol-ars write. The production of locality, community, and home, can provide a provisional safe place for those "on the margins," whose "homelessness" is not chosen.[14] Though critically important and contestatory on one level, Appadu-rai's strategies reinscribe a problematic gender and class politics at another.

The potential contradictions animating progressive, oppositional work on the transnational emerge in Paul Gilroy's landmark formulations. His book *The Black Atlantic* (1993) makes key contributions: (1) It examines African dias-poras on both sides of the Atlantic, combatting African American hegemonies in the discourse on Black identities as well as essentialist Afrocentrisms emanating from all quarters; (2) It positions Black intellectuals as equals within the canon of Western philosophy; (3) His analysis highlights hybridity and heterogeneity, subverting assertions of racial, national, or other forms of purity; (4) The book convincingly proposes that performative genres count as vibrant, vigorous forms of theorizing and vehicles of cultural identity formation. A tour de force, the book has been an influential text in the recent focus on diaspora.

Like Appadurai, Gilroy engages a gender critique. For example, he notes the masculinist biases of the many male theorists he discusses, pointing out their theoretical premises, which often entail the implicit or explicit subordination of Black women. For some, nationhood is coextensive with the patriarchal family; others idealize Black womanhood as the symbol of the integrity of Black community. Further, Gilroy takes on the sexism of some forms of rap, arguing that "gender is the modality in which race is lived. An amplified and exaggerated masculinity has become the boastful centrepiece of a culture of compensation that self-consciously salves the misery of the disempowered and subordinated" (85). He goes on to argue that relations between Black women and Black men form the ground of racial identity, and writes critically on conventional gender relations: "Without wanting to undermine struggles over the meaning of Black masculinity and its sometimes destructive and anti-communitarian consequences, it seems important to reckon with the limitations of a perspective which seeks to restore masculinity rather than work carefully towards something like its transcendence" (194).

However, argumentation pivots on one's choice of antagonist, and Gilroy's primary project involves attaining coeval status among the Fathers of European high theory and white, male progressives such as E. P. Thompson, who write nationalist, working-class histories that erase race as a significant axis of identity. Gilroy's battles presuppose an intellectual patriline, and he thus stops short of more thoroughly problematizing theory as a man's game. Despite gestures toward feminism, then, ultimately the potential contributions of this scholarship to the very problems Gilroy treats is of secondary concern. When the discussion turns to hybridity and heterogeneity, this presumption is particularly telling. Rather than theorizing the simultaneity of race, class, gender, sexuality, and the like in the formation of the transnational, Gilroy tends, strategically, to overprivilege the commonality of Black culture shared in diaspora, as Jacqueline Brown acutely observes.

179

The place given feminist scholarship becomes apparent in Gilroy's analysis of the work of Patricia Hill Collins. Taking her as representative of feminist theory in general—highly problematic given the multiplicity of contemporary feminisms—he questions her Afrocentric feminist standpoint theory that would base its claims on an unproblematized "experience" and the reinscription of the whole subject of liberal discourse. Here, the criticism is well taken, as Gilroy rearticulates many poststructuralist feminist criticisms of standpoint theory.[15] Ultimately, however, it appears that the critique of Hill Collins is deployed simply to justify the validity and usefulness of the Hegelian dialectic. The text continues: "For all its conspicuous masculinism and Eurocentrism Hegel's allegory is relational. It can be used to point out the value of incorporating the problem of subject formation into both epistemology and political practice. This would also mean taking a cue from a politicized postmodernism and leaving the categories of enquiry open" (ibid.). Feminist criticism here serves as a straw woman, a vehicle to recuperate Hegel. Another interpretive strategy might have made alliance with poststructuralist and materialist feminisms which also challenge standpoint theory, while simultaneously engaging sophisticated critiques of the recirculation of Hegel and other fathers of Theory.[16]

A related issue arises in Gilroy's intriguing appropriation of the Bakhtinian chronotope. He offers both the ship and the railroad as dense articulations of particular space/time conjunctures. Since the chronotope of the ship invokes the Middle Passage, it stands primarily for the period of slavery and the forcible removal of Black men, women, and children from Africa. The ship features equally in the lives of key Black figures neglected in (white) British histories, among them histories written by leftist progressives. Gilroy focuses on the sailor and the Pullman porter as emblematic of the historically overdetermined travels characteristic of the Black Atlantic: the sailor "crossing borders in modern machines that were themselves microsystems of linguistic and political hybridity" (12), and the Pullman porter "who benefits from the enhanced mobility provided by modern technologies but does so in a subordinate role, managing the travel experiences of others and servicing their needs at the expense of those of his own family" (133). Both are tropes of masculinity that were ideologically and empirically central to Black Atlantic diasporic experiences. However, their inscription in the narrative immediately points toward the text's exclusions: the experiences of Black female subjects in creating, articulating, and perhaps subverting this always already masculine discourse. Jacqueline Brown notes that is is crucial to take into account the complex, differential figurations and appropriations of diaspora, where class and gender also nuance identities mediated through race. Her study of Black Liverpudlians and their articulations of diaspora through identification with Black Americans carefully differentiates the ideological centrality of the seafaring man and the very different and more punitive discourses that affect Black Liverpudlian women, whose lived versions of diaspora might, for example, involve relationships with Black American sailors. She argues:

> It is precisely issues of class, sexuality, and gender—as these form the terrain for local negotiations of power—that split the category Black, providing people with quite different motivations for seeking affirmation from Blacks elsewhere. The most serious elision, then, in Gilroy's work concerns the possibility that actors may assign mutually contradictory meanings to the Black cultural productions they appropriate (7).

Attention to this degree of complexity and specificity represents the next level of political and theoretical intervention.

What then can we say about the circuits of the transnational? One striking commonality appears to be the interdependence or inextricability of nationalism and transnationalism. Binaries of nationalism and trans- or post-nationalism, hybridity and essentialism, recur throughout the disparate sites of geopolitical formations, high-fashion advertising, and academic discourses. For far from being superseded, the national has obviously summoned striking allegiances in the contemporary period, where the national/racial essentialisms of the Japanese Suit ads are but one instance in an age of phenomena like the resurgence of Eastern European nationalisms. As Katherine Verdery noted, "Is it that the increase in transnational/trans-statal processes, through which capital is being further concentrated on a global scale, generates at the same time movements of resistance cloaked in the mantle of particularism and specificity? That is, do we have yet another dialectic of concentration/centralization and resistance, with transnationalism and nationalism constituting one another mutually?" (17). For Appadurai in particular, this contemporaneous or mutually constitutive feature of identity formation seems elusive; rather, the term of postnationalism is (over)privileged, thus constructing a linear narrative of redemptive possibility. For Gilroy, the hybrid and the heterogeneous are associated with the diasporic. Yet, these may also be inextricably bound to practices of essence fabrication. Analysts such as Naoki Sakai write of the ways universalism and particularism, essentialist nationalism and internationalism, are mutually constitutive discourses. Further, there is the political, contextually specific necessity to assert essentialist identities, as theorized in Chela Sandoval's notion of oppositional consciousness and Spivak's mobilization of strategic essentialism. At this point, a return to the Japanese Suit campaign may offer insight, for Japanese fashion is precisely a transnational phenomenon shaped fundamentally by nationalist discourses, whether in the tropings of the Japanese designers as such by an international fashion press, or the ways the Japanese Suit ads depend upon transnationalism, cosmopolitanism, and global geopolitical histories that are used precisely to undergird a masculinist, racial, class-specific, nationalist essentialism.

In all sites, the imbrication of these national/transnational discourses with those of gender and race are inescapable. In all, the combatting of racisms (and in the case of the academic analysts, nationalisms) have resulted in the reinscription of gender dominance; in the cases of Appadurai and of the ads, class elitisms are pervasive. In part, this is indicative of the complexity of cultural politics and the contradictions potentially animating the deployment of any oppositional strategy. Yet the matter is more complex. Despite gestures toward feminist criticism, both Appadurai and Gilroy figure intellectual debate as a patriline and miss opportunities to make links with the vigorous theorizing of multiplicity, heterogeneity, and category crossings in the work of women of color like Chela Sandoval, Kamala Visweswaran, Gloria Anzaldúa, Marta Savigliano, Jacqueline Brown, Lisa Lowe, and others. Such alliances might have drawn further attention to the complexity and multiplicity of levels at play in discussions of hybridity and heterogeneity.[17]

The contradictory cultural politics animating both the ad campaign and the work of the two male critics speaks eloquently to the salience of the *positionality* of our critiques and to the particular battles we therefore choose to engage. Like the Japanese Suit campaign, with its argument for the distinctiveness of raced bodies, their work is understandably appealing in their challenges to racist and nationalist essentialisms, whether in the domains of (always already male) European high theory or in white feminism. Still, interventions at one level can be compromised by reinscriptions of power at another; the workings of masculinities in the world of theory instantiate those kinds of reinscriptions. Class also emerges as such a force in Appadurai's work, which presupposes a diasporic, cosmopolitan subject largely able to *choose* the ways he can ride the currents of transnationalism. One wonders, then, who and what are elided in these formulations. What of those people who have little choice of when and where to move, those who cannot move at all, or those who must politically assert a specific, local identity for specific political ends? Such questions and new feminist scholarship on diaspora highlights the necessity of attending carefully to differential appropriations of phenomena such as transnationalism.

Accordingly, foregrounding positionality enjoins us to scrutinize what is at stake given *particular locations*, for only the Master Subject can presume to speak from everywhere and nowhere. Edward Said proposes the metaphor of the academic as traveler, who transgresses national and other boundaries, as a replacement for the image of academic as potentate, issuing decrees of truth from the Ivory Tower. The image of the traveller is surely compelling. Yet even this notion may be wanting, for Said claims that "the image of traveler depends not on power, but on motion, on a willingness to go into different worlds, use different idioms, and understand a variety of disguises, masks, and rhetorics" (1994: 17). In light of scholarship calling attention to the political, sometimes imperial, relations implied in tourism and travel and the likely detachment of the traveler from local struggles, I would seek another image: someone whose travels are not desultory, but who has a stake in being *somewhere*, making commitments to build or to transform those somewheres. Undertaken from a site of privilege, such an image invites charges of Orientalist noblesse oblige; undertaken from sites of lesser privilege, this is the position Abdul JanMohamed calls the "syncretic border intellectual," what Kamala Visweswaran calls "homework," what I have called engagement in a common struggle.

My project in juxtaposing the work of these male analysts of the transnational with the Japanese Suit campaign is not to trivialize the former, but to occasion reflections that may count as homework. Conventional discourse posits the relationship of the academy to the fashion world as one of depth to surface, the monastic conceit of pure, profound intellectual pursuit invidiously contrasted with the mindless celebration of shallow trends and superficial decoration. Subverting the surface/depth binary is a compelling challenge in light of the moralizing fashion provokes, with its obvious enmeshment in processes of commodification and objectification. I hope to have suggested in this article and in other work that matters are much more multiply nuanced, and that limited contestatory moves—always riven with contradiction—can occur "even" in this world of "surfaces."

Subverting the surface/depth binary thus becomes a way of interrogating our own sites of privilege, for we in the academy can hardly claim to inhabit a pristine space apart from the forces of commodification, commercialization, or the pursuit of marketable difference. We all participate in a capitalist publishing industry; some chase crossover dreams (sell-out, accessibility, or both?) with trade books and lucrative contracts. The persistence of the myth of originary genius and the enshrining of the author (despite his "death"), feeds the need, in commodity capitalism, for the marketable difference that makes individual careers, even as "new" ideas develop and extend a larger conceptual vocabulary and reflect transformations in the world. Inevitably then, concepts like "the transnational" or "diaspora" become forms of assimilable, consumable difference. The "star" phenomenon is certainly another aspect of our regime of consumer capitalism, where the discourse of originary genius intertwines with those of celebrity and the hunger of the market for the "new" and the "hot."

By making such arguments, I am not attempting to imply that I somehow speak from a pristine space outside these forces. This is precisely *not* an argument for a right-wing anti-intellectualism or an unproblematized empiricism that sees cultural studies or theoretically vigorous work as merely trendy. The lives of all academics and all denizens of consumer capitalist societies are inextricable from the forces of commodification. The question is not how one can transcend it—as though one could—but how within it one can make interventions that matter. At some level, like the authors of the Japanese Suit campaign, we who write are out to sell our writing, our theorizing, our political challenges. This does not necessarily negate our efforts to be contestatory. Rather, perhaps this is the most realistic appraisal of one kind of inevitably complicitous intervention in such a commodified world as ours.[18] Our enmeshment in capitalism and the contradictions enacted when we seek to make moves that are purely contestatory emerge as themes in both the ad campaign and in our academic interventions. Academia and fashion are not exactly *the same*, nor are the challenges to Orientalism and racism made by the ad campaign as effective as the theoretical/political challenges made by the critics I discuss. Nonetheless, precisely because we presuppose a radical disjuncture between these worlds, I have suggested that there might be fruitful cause for reflection in holding them together for a moment. The Japanese Suit shows us how consumption might work when it pulls on issues compelling to the people who are its prospective consumers, offering wish-images that, at the very least, articulate our deep desires and fears even as it does so in obvious service of capitalist accumulation. These complexities also appear in the domain of the

academy and point us toward the contradictions that animate our own enterprise. Both the academic conceit of disinterested scholarship and the progressive conceit of liberatory intervention are belied in the scholarly work on the
transnational and diaspora, where critical developments at one level can reinscribe other power relations at another. Yet neither set of contradictions should
immobilize our attempts at critical intervention. They lead us instead toward a
critical scrutiny of our own sites of enunciation, an explicit recognition that the
battles one chooses to fight and the positions from which we mount our arguments matter, and matter crucially. In the end, both ad copy and academic theory return us to the questions we posed at the outset: Where are we positioned?
What is at stake?

ENDNOTES

1. Numerous works have dealt with advertising, the articulation of subjects, and the provocation of consumer desire from a variety of theoretical standpoints. For some well-known
formulations see Stuart Ewen, *All-Consuming Images*; Wolfgang Haug, *A Critique of
Commodity Aesthetics*; Judith Williamson, *Decoding Advertisements*; Michael Schudson,
Advertising: The Uneasy Persuasion.

2. For other analytic work on fashion and men's clothing, see, e.g., Valerie Steele and Claudia
Kidwell, *Men and Women: Dressing the Part*; Elizabeth Wilson, *Adorned in Dreams*;
Richard Martin and Harold Koda, *Jocks and Nerds: Men's Style in the Twentieth Century*.

3. A political slogan from the Meiji restoration and a response to Western penetration.

4. 1868–1912, when Commodore Perry "opened" Japan to the West.

5. See, e.g., Harumi Befu, ed. *Cultural Nationalism in East Asia*.

6. Thanks to Emiko Ohnuki-Tierney and Sumiko Iwao for pointing this out.

7. The campaign won a design award for advertising from a Japanese fashion industry trade
paper. Akiko Kozasu, an editor with *Marie Claire Japan* and a longtime Comme des
Garçons supporter quotes industry experts who pointed to the tension and the exemplary
use of Japanese typography in the ads.

8. Quoted in Miyoshi, p. 57.

9. See, e.g., Ivy 1988 and Stanlaw 1992 on the semiotics of the use of loan words and different scripts in Japanese. The latter account centers on this issue but fails to link it adequately to a constitutive political history of occupation and penetration by the United
States.

10. At a joint Comme des Garçons/Yohji Yamamoto men's show, I overheard this example of
the use of *shibui*. During the Yohji half of the proceedings, a Black man with sunglasses
and dreadlocks, dressed in black leather, appeared on the runway. As he posed in front
of us, I heard some young Japanese women behind me gasp loudly, "*Shibui!*"

185

11. One, with a leading postwar politician, Conservative Prime Minister Yoshida Shigeru, again trumpets the theme of world powers setting world style. Since Meiji, the ad asserts, there have been just a handful of men who could take that quintessentially British object, the suit, and make it distinctively theirs. The text constructs a narrator who claims a desire to possess a *Nihon no sebiro* appropriate for the public position or face of Japan at this moment, when Japan has become an international player.

12. One, for example, features Shiga Naoya, author of *A Dark Night's Passing* and the founder of the White Birch literary group. Commenting on his work is the author Mori, who is married to an Englishman. She writes with lively humor of her husband's reaction to Shiga's photograph. There is something recognizable in Shiga's contemplative expression, she says, that made her English husband sit bolt upright. This ineffable Japaneseness is linked to a gentlemanly, tastefully elegant style that transcends cultures—a style so distinctively Japanese and so compelling that an Englishman is forced to do a double-take.

13. See, for example, the final chapter of this volume, which deals in part with Michael Crichton's *Rising Sun*.

14. See Visweswaran 1994, Kondo (this volume), hooks 1990, Martin and Mohanty 1986.

15. See, e.g., Donna Haraway; Judith Butler 1987.

16. Cf., e.g., Judith Butler, *Subjects of Desire*.

17. See George Lipsitz's review of *The Black Atlantic*.

18. Elliott Shore writes eloquently of the dilemmas of socialist journalists at the turn of the century. How does one put one's message across? Does one adopt strategies used by more mainstream, even popular culture venues, in order to attract readers? Does one accept advertising, or implicitly condone labor practices associated with capitalist firms?

STRATEGIES OF INTERVENTION

PART THREE

6.

the narrative
production of home
in asian american theater

Community, then, is the product of work, of struggle; it is inherently unstable, contextual; it has to be constantly reevaluated in relation to critical political priorities; and it is the product of interpretation, interpretation based on an attention to history (Martin and Mohanty 210).

HOME. FOR MANY people on the margins, is, to paraphrase Gayatri Chakravorty Spivak, that which we cannot not want. It stands for a safe place, where there is no need to explain oneself to outsiders; it stands for community; more problematically, it can elicit a nostalgia for a past golden age that never was, a nostalgia that elides exclusion, power relations, and difference. Motifs of home animate works by peoples in diaspora, often peoples of color, who may have no permanent home,[1] people on the margins such as gays and lesbians, for whom home was rarely if ever safe, and women and children, where the "haven" of home can be a site of violence and oppression. Martin and Mohanty focus on the narrative production of home and identity by white Southern lesbian writer Minnie Bruce Pratt. Their problematic recognizes the desire for safety and the construction of an identity while it interrogates that construction, noting its suppression of differences within, highlighting its always provisional nature, and examining its enmeshment in networks of power. Pratt, Martin, and

Mohanty highlight the necessity and inevitability of a desire for a home in an inhospitable world, the accompanying dangers of that desire, and the continuing need to create homes for ourselves.

I take up the problematic of home and community as racial and ethnic identities, produced and created through narrative, discourse, and performance. The site is Asian American theater in Los Angeles, more specifically, a play called *Doughball*, a December 1990–January 1991 production at East/West Players in Los Angeles, the oldest existing Asian American theater company in the country. Perry Miyake, a Sansei, or third-generation Japanese American from Venice, California, wrote the play, and the production starred Steve Park, the Korean grocer from Spike Lee's film *Do the Right Thing*, and formerly a regular on the television comedy *In Living Color*. I examine the narrative and performative production of home as a work of collective memory and as a safe place in the text, in the production itself, and in the specific site of East West Players and of Asian American theater in Los Angeles. The essay ends with the implications of productions like *Doughball* for a cultural politics, addressing particularly the question of the political weight of realist representation.

"HOME" IN ASIAN AMERICAN LITERATURE

The narrative and performative production of home, community and identity is a particularly urgent issue in the case of Asian Americans. As I noted in the introduction, the term "Asian American" itself bears the marks of the civil-rights and student struggles of the 1960s. It was created to displace the term Oriental, a word eschewed for its stereotypical associations with exoticism, despotism, and inscrutability, and for its reinscription of the East/West binary defining the East in terms of the West. Minimally, Asia names a continent, not some phantasmatic landscape. "Asian American," then, is an historically specific, constructed, political identity, a specific response to a particular historical situation in North America, where people of Asian descent are lumped together regardless of national origin, and where violence, racism, prejudice against any Asian American becomes an act of violence against all Asian Americans. "Asian American," then, is above all a coalitional and, as I have argued, a performative identity.

Given this particular sedimented history, Asian Americans have a specific relation to the notion of home. For mainland Asian Americans, surely one of the most insistent features of our particular oppression is our ineradicable foreignness. The fiftieth anniversary of the forced imprisonment of Japanese Americans was commemorated in 1992. Certainly the incarceration of Japanese Americans in concentration camps was attributable at least in part to this elision of Japanese Americans with Japanese nationals, a savagely ironic situation, given that exclusion laws prevented Issei, the immigrant generation, from becoming citizens until the passage of the MacCarran-Walter Act in 1952. No matter how many generations Asian Americans are resident here, no matter how articulate we seem, we inevitably attract the comment, "Oh, you speak English so well," or its equivalent, "Where are you from?" which somehow never seems to be adequately answered by Oregon or Illinois or New Jersey. The question, "Where are you *really* from?" is sure to follow.

We continue to see this elision of Asian and Asian American in a historically specific climate nuanced by events including World War II and the Korean and Vietnam Wars, Japan-bashing, anti-Communist ideologies, and post-1965 immigration from Asia. In the *Los Angeles Times*, this 1991 article appeared, headlined "Japanese-Americans Stung by Vandalism at Center."

> Members of a judo class were shocked when they arrived recently at a Japanese-American community center in Norwalk and discovered 'Go Back to Asia' and other epithets smeared on the walls in white paint.
>
> It was the third time in a week that the center had been vandalized . . . . it was the racial graffiti that stirred painful memories for some of the older members of the Southeast Japanese Community Center who recall being taken from their homes during World War II (Avila).

Nor is it only Japanese Americans who suffer from the confusion of Asian with Asian American. The emblematic case, a "mournful reference point"[2] (Commission on Wartime Relocation and Internment of Civilians 301) among Asian Americans, is that of Vincent Chin, the Chinese American engineer beaten to death with baseball bats by two unemployed "all-American" white auto workers who blamed Japan for their plight.

Given the continuing confusion of Asians with Asian Americans, perhaps it is not surprising that one of the most insistent themes in Asian American literature and theater is a preoccupation with the claiming of America as home. This motif animates the work of countless Asian American artists: Maxine Hong Kingston, Shawn Wong, Jessica Hagedorn, among others.[3] Perhaps it is most eloquently encapsulated in a poem from Mitsuye Yamada's *Camp Notes*

191

(1976). Yamada is a Nisei, a second-generation Japanese American, and as the title suggests, the volume deals mostly with experiences from the concentration camps where Japanese Americans were imprisoned during World War II. She ends the volume with a poem called "Mirror Mirror," a dialogue with her son Doug.

> People keep asking me where I come from
> says my son.
> Trouble is I'm american on the inside
> and oriental on the outside
> No Doug
> Turn that outside in
> THIS is what American looks like

As a resonant postlude to this book thematizing the dislocation of the camps, the poem functions as a testimony to the ongoing legacy of the camps: the continuing racism defining America as white, and the internalization of that definition by young people of color. Equally, it stands as an affirmation of an Asian American identity. Yamada thus refigures America, recognizing that one need not be Euro to be American.

Even more fundamentally, Asian American playwrights problematize notions of a singular home and of a singular identity. Dislocation, contradiction, unforeseen cultural possiblities, multiple geographies of identity exceeding the boundaries of nation-states, emerge as motifs. Jessica Hagedorn, Filipina American musician, performer, and writer, states in her introduction to her play *Tenement Lover*:

> In all my writing there are always these characters who have a sense of displacement, a sense of being in self-exile, belonging nowhere—or anywhere. I think these themes are the human story. When it comes down to it it's all about finding shelter, finding your identity. I don't care whether you're an immigrant or native-born, you're discovering who and what and where you are all the time. When I think of home now I mean three places. The San Francisco Bay area really colored my work. New York is where I live. But Manila will always have a hold on me. What is the threshold of my dreams? I really don't think of myself as a citizen of one country but as a citizen of the world (79).

For Hagedorn, multiple, site-specific identities enable her to transcend the boundaries of nation-states, yet also create contradiction and dislocation. The notion of belonging to the world subverts and refigures any singular notion of identity and rootedness in only one place, where stable geography reproduces the stability of the bounded monad, the singular self. Rey Chow says it this way: "The question, 'When are you going home?' can be responded to in the following manner: home is here, in my migranthood" (Chow 48).

David Henry Hwang captures the traces of history in Asian American identities in his one-act play *As the Crow Flies*. Mrs. Chan, a Chinese American grandmother, narrates her complex geography of identity:

> The day I arrive in America, I do not feel sorry. I do not miss the Philippine.
> I do not look forward live in America. Just like, I do not miss China, when I
> leave it many years ago—go live in Philippine. Just like, I do not miss Manila,
> when Japanese take our home during wartime, and we are all have to move to
> Baguio, and live in haunted house. It is all same to me. Go, one home to the
> next, one city to another, nation to nation, across ocean big and small. We are
> born traveling. We travel—all our lives. I am not looking for a home. I know
> there is none . . . (104).

This relentlessly antinostalgic passage arises from a realism born of having "no options," in Hwang's words. Geopolitical upheaval, dislocation and migration have been a way of life for Mrs. Chan, even if she is now comfortably ensconced in her upper-middle-class suburb.

Hwang treats the cleavages of class, race, and different sedimented histories as they operate in the lives of Mrs. Chan and her African American housekeeper, Hannah. Neither has a home, but whereas for Mrs. Chan home is an impossibility because of constant dislocation, migration, and endless travel, Hannah's situation stands at the opposite extreme. This passage is narrated by Hannah's alter ego/ghost, Sandra Smith:

> She spends most of her life wanderin' from one beautiful house to the next,
> knowing intimately every detail, but never layin' down her head in any of 'em.
> She's what they call a good woman. Men know it, rich folks know it. Every place
> is beautiful, 'cept the place where she lives. Home is a dark room, she knows
> it well, knows its limits. She knows she can't travel nowhere without returnin'
> to that room once the sun goes down. Home is fixed, it does not move, even as
> the rest of the world circles 'round and 'round, picking up speed (105–6).

Home here spells confinement, loss, and the relentless fixity of the intersections of gender, racial, and class oppression that secure and maintain Hannah's position as a domestic. The endless and relentless migration of Mrs. Chan's life is counterpointed to the relentless fixity and closure of Hannah's, articulating the differences of race, class, and history that separate the women. Though in unequal class relation, neither woman has options, and each asserts her triumph over the need for a home. Their shared bleak realism, their cauterization of nostalgic desire, are belied by the yearning Mrs. Chan and Hannah both feel for home, one that, according to Hwang, can only be "metaphysical." Lured—indeed, impelled—by the promise of home, they pursue the crow, the bringer of disaster:

> They run on faith now, passing through territories uncharted, following the sound of their suffering. And it is in this way that they pass through their lives. Hardly noticing that they've entered. Without stopping to note its passing. Just following a crow, with single dedication, forgetting how they started, or why they're chasing, or even what may happen if they catch it. Running without pause or pleasure, past the point of their beginning (107).

Having no other options in life, having neither home nor the luxury to indulge in the desire for home, they cannot erase their longing. For them, home is attainable only in death.

DOUGHBALL AND THE NARRATIVE PRODUCTION OF HOME

Perry Miyake's *Doughball* was produced at East West Players as a Christmas play during December of 1990 and January of 1991. The review in *The Los Angeles Times* characterized the production as "uneven." Though some of the acting was favorably reviewed, the closing sentence reveals the reviewer's ambivalence: "The title refers to a game of chance played at the annual Venice carnivals fondly rekindled here, but with only random, not tight focus" (1990). Although this is not precisely a pan of the play, and though the reviewer does much to credit the acting of several of the key members of the cast, the impression is of yet another earnest, well-intentioned but not fully realized production.

Postponing the inevitable, I attended the closing performance more out of a sense of duty than desire. The lead actor, Steve Park, had been among a group of Asian American actors who had spoken at our teach-in protesting the performance of Gilbert and Sullivan's *The Mikado* at the Claremont Colleges.[4] I should further preface my reactions by saying that the playwright and I are exactly the same age and that I went to the performance with a friend of Basque descent from my hometown in Oregon, who graduated from high school a year after I did. ("The Bascos and the Buddhaheads used to run together," as he so eloquently put it.) Expecting clumsy earnestness, my friend and I found a production of incredible intensity, authenticity, and luminosity. As the play began, my skepticism ebbed as I felt transported into the space and time of my high school. My friend and I kept looking at each other in amazement: "My God, that's Mrs. Y———!" "And they're like B——— and R———!" We could rename all the characters, because we knew them all. And I laughed at that production the way I have rarely laughed before or since: I laughed the laughter of recognition. As the play continued, I was even more startled by the two young women in the play, uncanny refractions of my own high school self: one, the bookish valedictorian with a crush on the protagonist David; the other, the protagonist's dream girl, who herself dreamed of leaving her confining world for Stanford and for France. Emerging from the theater, I felt slightly drunk, as though the intensity of the experience had been too much for my body to assimilate. Then it struck me forcibly: Asian Americans never laugh the laughter of recognition because we are systematically erased from view. We never see ourselves portrayed the way *we* see ourselves. Small wonder I experienced this play with almost physical force, in my whole being. Small wonder I spent the subsequent week in a fog, musing about the place of Stanford and of France as utopian landscapes for Sansei girls. And small wonder that mainstream critics were unable to understand the play fully. Instead of exoticism, they were exposed to the less spectacular, but infinitely more resonant, small truths of everyday life: the truths of home. As I felt with *M. Butterfly*, I was consumed by urgency to write about this play, to document its resonance, for never in my life have I seen anything so "true" to "my experience."

Now, what might such a reaction mean? Rather than simply taking that experience as transparent or foundational, poststructuralist suspicion of notions like truth, authenticity, and experience, require a critical interrogation of those terms. What writing or performative practices *created* the effects of authenticity or verisimilitude? How can we account for the discursive production of a culturally essentialist Japanese American identity? In other words, just what was so homey about this play?

First, and most important, there was no exoticism, still a rarity when Asian Americans are depicted in mainstream venues. In *Doughball*, there were no fake Oriental accents, no Asian women as wilting flowers, no quasi-Japanese music, no Oriental splendor. Steve Park explained it to me this way: . . . "I think Asian American theater tries to pander to the white audience too much.

195

And that's what I liked about *Doughball*; there was no sense of that in *Doughball*." I think this may be a critical factor in the lukewarm mainstream reception of the play. For a Japanese American, the absence of Japonaiserie means we can see ourselves represented "authentically," not as whites with an exotic veneer, but as normal, everyday Japanese Americans.

A key feature producing authenticity effects is the sensuousness of language: its textures, its familiarity, its evocative power. Especially resonant for Sansei, who as a rule do not grow up speaking Japanese, is what one might call "family Japanese": phrases for food, words about the body and bodily function, epithets signalling intense feeling, phrases that bring a start of recognition and stir memory. Take this example, from David's irrepressible mother:

> YUKI
> I was over there, but Frank had to go *benjo*, so I'm here now! Oh, Wayne, did you get some *udon*? They're probably running out so you better get some if you want some! (57)

Yuki uses the word *benjo*, a very rough slang word for bathroom, one that would raise eyebrows in contemporary Japan for its crudity. It is, however, a word that most Sansei would know. In Japan, it would be particularly horrifying to hear an urban woman saying this; for me, it elicits childhood memories. The energetic admonition to eat, with *udon*, noodles, as the lure, eloquently captures the interactional styles of many tough, dynamic Nisei women. To the credit of Miyake and of Alice Kushida, who gave a vibrant, unerringly "authentic" performance, Yuki embodied this energetic toughness.

Another exchange enacts a particularly Sansei identity:

> ERIC
> Ooh, negative vibes, man. Bad *bachi* . . .,
> DAVID
> Okay, we'll hang out here and if she shows, cool (24).

This is quintessential West Coast Sansei language: the California slang combined with a reference to Japanese American family talk; *bachi* as divine retribution—*bachi ga ataru*, *bachi* will strike, you'll be punished, for some misdeed. It can also used be as a disciplinary admonition, especially for young children, as in: "Don't touch that—it's dirty, it's *bachi*."

Derogatory epithets are another linguistic practice spurring memory; these Japanese phrases occur only among intimate relations with friends, family, and the Japanese American community—after all, these are the only people who can understand the insult. Two fathers speak:

MITS
Who's crying? I don't cry. I complain a lot, but I don't cry.
FRANK
Yes, you, *monkutare* (24).

The *tare* here is a particularly rough, rustic suffix. *Monku* means "complaint," so *monkutare* is a complainer, a kvetch. The suffix is combined with other words to create salty epithets associated with family and friends in the Japanese American community, for only intimates can fight in this way or understand the insult: *unkotare*, shithead, a term appearing in the play, and *bakatare*, stupid idiot. These expressions are extremely crude and regionally provincial; middle-class Tokyo residents would laugh at their quaintness. Accordingly, these expressions define for Japanese Americans a particularly familial world that is neither Euro-American nor Japanese, but Japanese American.

Small epiphanies and moments of recognition like these demonstrate the role of linguistic practices in defining a community.[5] These languages in Japanese American plays enable the creation of a Japanese American identity transcending a particular family's idiosyncrasies. As an Asian American, often one does not know what is peculiar to one's family and what is common to a larger community. Or, if you believe that you are engaging in practices that are typical of your ethnic group, you still may not be sure "what is Chinese tradition and what is the movies" (Kingston 6). What these linguistic practices accomplish is to create the sense of recognition and authenticity, asserting and affirming one's belonging to a family and to a distinct culture.

The play discursively produces home and community just as forcefully through its embeddedness in a specific geography: Venice, California. When the play went into production, Perry Miyake took the actors on a tour of the part of Venice where he grew up; he took me on the same tour when I interviewed him. This is not the Venice of rollerblading and Muscle Beach and Dennis Hopper, but the Japanese American and Chicano Venice on Centinela Avenue, the Venice of Mago's, the fast-food joint where you can still get avocado cha-shu burgers and teriyaki burritos, of the funky, 50s drugstore where the boys used to stand for hours reading comics, of Kenny's Cafe, where you can enjoy Hawaiian Japanese favorites like Spam-fried rice and Portuguese sausage and eggs. The play itself occurs during a summer carnival at the Japanese American

Community Center in Venice, still a lively hub of community activity. This Venice has a lived-in feeling of family and communities that have existed for at least a generation; artsy glitz has little purchase here. *Doughball* attempts to write this Venice into collective memory.

A fourth element in the discursive production of home arises from the resonance of sensory memory, and through its deployment, a Proustian evocation of a world. In particular, foods, sounds, and smells serve as symbolic vehicles of ethnic identity. One eloquent example is a monologue delivered by Wayne, the protagonist's cousin, a Vietnam vet who is mostly mute until David decides he wants to join the army and go fight in Vietnam. To discourage David, Wayne speaks, uttering this soliloquy on home:

> I love the smell of rice cooking in the evening. It don't smell like death no more.
>
> I sit in our kitchen, on the same old chair I sat on since I was a kid. Mom's at the sink chopping vegetables, wearing that same old apron she always wears. Dad comes in the back door and stomps off his boots in the back porch.
>
> There's hamburger okazu on the stove. Hamburger okazu. Poor man's sukiyaki. Same ol' shit I was so sick of eating six days a week before and now I can't wait. Hamburger, onions, green onion, string beans, eggplant, sugar-shoyu, tofu, and that wiggly shit that looks like worms. All cooking in that big ol' black cast-iron frying pan.
>
> I smell the rice cooking. I hear the lid rattling on the rice cooker. Sun's going down outside the kitchen window. And I can't believe I'm back.
>
> Mom puts a big bowl of okazu in front of me, raw egg on the side, chawan full of hot rice in my left hand, hashi in my right. Dad says, 'Itadakimasu,' and nothing ever tasted better.
>
> So I eat. I savor. I enjoy. And I don't look up 'cause there's tears in my eyes. I'm home. Goddammit, I'm home (94–5).

Just as a world emerged from Proust's teacup and his tisane-drenched madeleine, so an entire landscape of memory arises from the cast-iron pan full of hamburger okazu, memories that go beyond the Venice J.A. community, certainly to "mine" in Oregon and I suspect to others as well.[6] Sounds—the rattling of the rice cooker, the stomping of the boots—the smells of rice, the cast-iron pan and the description of the food in it, the phrases of fragmentary Japanese most Sansei know—*hashi*, "chopsticks," *chawan* "rice bowl," *okazu*, a meat and vegetables main dish, as well as the hot rice and raw egg, indispensable accoutrements to *sukiyaki*—create family and home from memory, inscribing a larger set of practices that define Japanese American culture.

Through the erasure of exoticism, through linguistic practices, and through exploring the evocative power of sensory memory, Perry Miyake and *Doughball* created a Japanese American community and culture. As he put it:

DAVID
    I miss this. Being somewhere where you don't have to explain yourself, and what you are.
ANDREA
    Home (101).

HOME, IDENTITY, AND POLITICAL CHANGE

Given this, what more does one say about the discursive production of home in a naturalistic play such as this? What kind of political weight can it sustain?

Recent work of poststructuralist feminist critics attempts to assess the political consequences of deploying certain kinds of narrative strategies. Some have argued for the subversive potential of particular strategies that tend to privilege particular tactics in advance. For example, Catherine Belsey argues that expressive realism is associated with the constitution of author and reader as autonomous, whole subjects; with certain Aristotelian notions of art as mimesis; and with a particular moment in the development of capitalism. Realist representation minimizes contradiction. The conventional narrative structure introduces disruptions in the social order, and then through plot and character development—a development that elicits audience identification—the play or text arrives at a narrative closure that re-establishes order. For Belsey this forecloses political possibilities and leaves codes of representation intact. Jill Dolan, a feminist critic of theater, also tropes realism as politically conservative and inadequate to the kind of materialist feminist theatrical practice she envisions as subversive. Her argument is given particular weight by her analysis of several plays that deal with lesbian issues, in which the realist narrative inevitably leads to a closure in which the lesbian—in particular the butch lesbian—ends up dead, vilified, recuperated to the heterosexual norm, or some combination of the above (1988, 1990). Both she and Belsey would call for a text that problematizes the process of representation, foregrounding contradiction and disrupting easy identification. One way of doing so would be through Brechtian alienation effects, calling attention to the theatricality of theatrical production: for example, having the actors address the audience "out of their roles" or undercutting

199

psychological realism by staging a series of seemingly unrelated vignettes that cannot be recuperated into a smoothly flowing narrative line. Certainly such critiques of realist representation are incisive and well taken. Realism can lull the spectator into an overly easy identification that reinscribes the whole subject who freely chooses to give her/his labor and to exercise "free choice" in consuming the products of capitalism. As Belsey eloquently argues:

> The ideology of liberal humanism assumes a world of non-contradictory (and therefore fundamentally unalterable) individuals whose unfettered consciousness is the origin of meaning, knowledge, and action. It is in the interest of this ideology above all to suppress the role of language in the construction of the subject, and its own role in the interpellation of the subject, and to present the individual as a free, unified, autonomous subjectivity. Classic realism, still the dominant popular mode in literature, film and television drama, roughly coincides chronologically with the epoch of industrial capitalism. It performs . . . the work of ideology, not only in its representation of a world of consistent subjects who are the origin of meaning, knowledge and action, but also in offering the reader, as the position from which the text is most readily intelligible, the position of subject as the origin both of understanding and of action in accordance with that understanding (67).

Given what can be described only as cogent and incisive critiques, one must then ask whether *Doughball* is indeed simply a fond rekindling of memories. Is it merely nostalgic? Does it inscribe a golden age, a mythical community that fails to see its own exclusions and never really existed? Does it rely on a realism that privileges narrative closure and an insidious reinscription of the whole subject? And must that realism be transcended and disrupted in order to be politically subversive?

First, there is inevitably a sense in which *Doughball* and other realist narratives can be read as having this conservative political weight. *Doughball* relies on psychological realism and on the production of the familiar; without a doubt it elicits the "identification" of the spectator. Any narrative is exclusionary in some ways, and this is most definitely a Sansei *man's* text, privileging a male point of view of that historical period, and in its warm nostalgia it idealizes to some extent this very problematic moment in history and in the life of the protagonist. Critics indeed focused on the play's nostalgia, finding it aesthetically and politically retrograde. Miyake countered with the following: "The reviewers are all intellect, no heart. I write from the heart. They see that and they say, 'Oh that's just sentimental . . . nostalgic. Ping [Wu, an Asian American actor who has been active in the *Miss Saigon* protests] was saying, 'So what if it's nostalgic; it's *our* nostalgia.' They expect us to be satisfied with *their* nostalgia" (personal communication).

I think Miyake and Ping Wu are on to something here, and that the issue is considerably more complex. We must ask who is creating this nostalgic home, for whom, and for what purpose. Morley and Robins point out the politically insidious construction of a European homeland, a home that would enshrine Eurocentrism and shore up defensive boundaries against threats from non-Europeans in what they call "a fortress identity" (3). How different this seems, for example, from Black lesbian feminist Barbara Smith's invocation of home, the house on 132nd Street off Kinsman in Cleveland, where she learned about feminism from the women in her household. Hers is a home that stands for claiming one's Blackness, a claim that one does not leave "the race" when one is a feminist or a lesbian (xxii). The questions of who and for whom are crucial in these examples. The Heimat is part of a fortress identity addressing (white, northern) Europeans, an attempt by the center to retain its power. Differently positioned, Barbara Smith's home is a safe place for other African Americans and lesbians. And Perry Miyake implicitly addresses Asian American, and specifically Japanese American viewers without explaining and without exoticizing for a mainstream audience. To reiterate Steve Park's comment, there was no "pandering to a white audience" in this instance. Perhaps at this particular historical moment one kind of political intervention would subvert precisely in its verisimilitude, in its "authentic" representation of a "reality" of marginal peoples in ways not captured in dominant cultural representations. Perhaps, in these instances, it is precisely the realism of the narrative that is politically effective.[7]

Further, perhaps the term "realism" itself must be problematized and opened to the play of historically and culturally specific power relations.[8] The speaker's position, the intended audience, the stakes, and the larger discursive fields of history and power through which meanings are constituted are not mere contexts that nuance an essentialized meaning; rather, these are essential in determining the political weight of any narrative strategy. Indeed, I would argue that the authenticity effects and conventional narrative line of *Doughball* support a politically urgent project: a Sansei's attempt to write Sansei identity into existence. My own experience of drunkenness from the laughter of recognition was followed by anger that Asian Americans in general, Japanese Americans, Sansei (as we get more and more ethnic- and generation-specific), are systematically erased from representation in mainstream media. Perhaps worse, when we are depicted it is only in the most stereotyped way, thus subjecting us to psychological violence rather than offering affirmation—or even recognition of a fully human existence. Miyake himself said this, in a statement both apocalyptic and poignant:

> [F]or once, we got to present ourselves as we are, onstage. I believe we haven't yet defined ourselves onstage and I really do fear that a whole generation of Asian Americans, us Sanseis, will be ignored not only by the mainstream media, but by ourselves, meaning Asian American theater groups, simply because we are too far removed from the immigrant experience, and we will become extinct without a trace of our art, our self-expression, to be remembered by. (personal communication)

Again, though this statement could be taken as disingenuous given the relatively large number of Sansei men whose work has been produced in Asian American theaters, his statement for me captured the urgent necessity fueling the desire to "write ourselves into existence." Miyake writes for himself and for other Japanese Americans first; his implied spectator is not from the dominant culture. The question of realism, then, must be a question of realisms in the plural, realisms deployed by positioned subjects with different stakes, who constitute themselves within shifting fields of power and history.

The realist impulse in *Doughball* is equally linked to a sense of urgency arising from the specificity of geography and place, and the historical circumstances in which Miyake writes. He desires to write a moment into history, for his play is an act of collective memory, a nostalgic remembrance of the time when there was a community. Miyake was born and grew up in Venice, left it for a number of years, then returned. He commented on the changes: "It just got to be a less friendly place, and it was strange to be living at home and feeling sort of out of place. I wanted to capture that time again in high school, because no one else was writing about that period, our generation" (interview). With preservation and historical memory as goals, Miyake actually *creates* a history and a community by paying his respects to his experience. His Venice is poised between relocation and redevelopment, a moment of seeming calm and safety before other forces disrupt it anew. It is also the midst of the Vietnam War, and the everyday concerns of the boys—girls, mostly—are shadowed by the specter of the draft. David, the protagonist, and Mits, his father, talk about changes in the community:

MITS

Boy, I'm getting too old for this. Maybe next year they'll just have some kinda high-tone, *kanemochi*,[9] black-tie dinner and skip the carnival.

DAVID
Skip the carnival?
MITS
They gotta raise big bucks to build a new community center. Pave this parking
lot over.
DAVID
They gotta have a carnival. Where are all the junior-high kids gonna hang out?
MITS
The way they're talking about getting rid of all the old stuff. Japan's getting rich,
starting to whaddayacallit?—redevelop Little Tokyo, just move all the Issei out.
They don't give a damn about us.
DAVID
Yeah, but this is Venice.
MITS
Maybe we're too small for them to get their paws on. We still gotta rebuild this
place. Judo dojo's falling apart. This place is old. (*looks around*) We stayed here
when we got outta camp and finally came back.
DAVID
Where?
MITS
Here. (*points to porch*) Dojo was the mess hall. (*points USL*) Kitchen was in the
same place. (*points USC*) All the families stayed in the rooms where the offices
are until they found a place to live. (*looks around*) They even had to put up tents
in the parking lot. No room for everybody coming back out here. That's how old
this place is. Falling apart.
DAVID
I could do without the dirt.
MITS
Nah, when this place is all cement, it's gonna be too cold. Too clean. Lose touch.
(83–4).

Relocation and impending dislocation are themes here, and in an interesting
way this passage enacts the contradictions of Japanese American identity. The
site of the community center holds memories of dislocation from imprisonment
and of coming home. At the moment of the play, it provides the funky, down-
home space for the creation of Japanese American community in events like
the summer carnivals or Obon festivals. But it is disintegrating, as the memories fade and the community disperses. And the new threat is symbolized by
Japan. Accordingly, Japanese Americans find themselves caught between, if
you will.[10] The grounds of the Venice Japanese Community Center have in fact
been paved over, as Miyake showed me, and he views part of his mission as

preserving in memory the time when it was exactly that, a provisional safety zone amidst past and impending dislocation.

In order to assess these moves to write history and identity and to analyze the political weight of plays like *Doughball*, one must consider elements of production. The process of putting up the play mirrored this creation of a provisional home for the cast, crew, and playwright. At first plagued by various illnesses, injuries, car accidents, deaths in families (Miyake himself lost a close relative), and by an initially tense relationship between actors and the director, Patricia Yasutake, the cast built solidarity through the production. Lissa Ling Lee, who played Andrea, the class valedictorian, described the atmosphere to me:

> This experience was really unique, everyone here was very supportive of each other, which is really usually not the case in Hollywood. I think because of the fact that we were Asian American actors, we had more of a need to see this project come together, rather than just ourselves shine. So we tried to help each other. It was very different. I can't really compare it to anything else.

In fact, the cast actually had occasional reunions and, in Steve Park's words, "after the show we'd do *Doughball* things, like *Doughball* went to see *Hedda Gabler*, and we were going to try to go see *Canton* (*Jazz Club*) together, but it was overbooked . . . That's rare, that after the show we'll be like, 'Oh let's do this together.' " The themes of the play and the actual production in which initial strife led to solidarity among cast, crew, and writer created a shared, provisional home that writes Asian American identity.

The home of *Doughball* can be further placed in the context of sites such as East West Players, the oldest Asian American theater troupe in the country. Over the years the company has sponsored workshops and classes in various aspects of theatrical production including acting, and now, playwriting, a way of producing producers of Asian American identity. The first David Henry Hwang Playwriters' Institute presented in April of 1992 staged readings of the first plays, portions of or complete one-acts, from the Institute. (Among the fledging playwrights was this author.) Partially a participant-observation technique, enrolling was also encouraged and inspired by the work of writers like Perry Miyake and by the vibrant Asian American theater and performance art scene in Los Angeles.

Doughball's geography of identity and creation of home must also be located within Los Angeles, perhaps the center for the production of Asian

American art and culture at this historical moment. Other vibrant Asian American theater companies exist in San Francisco, New York, Minneapolis, and Seattle, but the relative stability and continuity of an organization like East West Players, the relative receptiveness to Asian American theater in mainstream venues such as the Mark Taper Forum, as well as in smaller, Equity-waiver theaters and alternative performance art spaces like Highways, make Los Angeles an exciting place to be now for a person of color and an Asian American. California at large should continue to be a key locale for cultural production by peoples of color, as whites in the state are rapidly becoming a plurality rather than a majority, and as diasporic communities and communities of color continue to create, narrate, and perform themselves.

Given these multiple layerings of home, community, and identity, I want to argue for the political weight of plays like *Doughball.* Three points must be underlined here. One has to do with the question of audience reception and realist representation. Seeing theater and performance of, by, and about Asian Americans—whether the narrative strategy is realist, non-realist, avant-garde, or some combination of strategies—has among its potential effects the empowering of other Asian Americans. The question of realist representation, then, must take into account not only narrative strategy, but also effects on actual audience members, mindful of an historical context in which there is a general subversiveness in simply being able to see progressive plays by and about people of color. Second, I wanted to gesture toward the implications of such moves for anthropological ethnography. As more of us anthropologists from the borderlands go "home" to study our own communities, we will probably see increasing elisions of boundaries between ethnography and minority discourse, in which writing ethnography becomes another way of writing our own identities and communities. And writing that identity in the context of writing one's scholarly work creates a narrative space in the dominant discourse, a space that could refigure the disciplines as home for us (cf. Kondo, forthcoming). Certainly, "going home"—not only to *study* one's own community, with all the asymmetries of power that term implies, but also to help *create* it—gives one a wholly different relationship to the usual anthropological project of distanced observation and studying down. The distant ethnographer/observer can become a participant fully engaged in a common struggle of great political urgency, in which we can contribute as much as we receive.

Finally, the debate about the political effects of realist representation must move beyond the familiar positions based on binarized and dehistoricized notions of realism and avant-gardism. The lulling of the spectator into the transparency of reality, the reinscription of the whole subject, the elicition of nostalgia that masks oppression and difference are all recognizable effects of realism. Other approaches that call attention to the representational frame itself also draw predictable charges: elitism and lack of accessibility to large audiences. Usually the counterattack is to argue that realism is just as constructed as other forms of representation, and that to consider avant-garde representation beyond mainstream audiences is itself an elitist presupposition (Trinh 1991, 87–8).

Perhaps these questions cannot be answered in the terms in which they are posed. Rather, they must be answered specifically, and in reference to particular productions, texts, audiences, venues. For though I think the work of feminist poststructuralist literary critics like Belsey and Dolan is on the mark in many ways, I think the prescriptive nature of those readings is unwarranted given their purely formal and textual basis and their essentialized reading of realism. That is, the literary critic, through her analysis of formal properties of the text, can trace out the political weight of certain textual strategies for an idealized conventional audience. But doing so elides the question of realisms in the plural, received and interpreted by diverse, multiply positioned audiences, in all their complex and contradictory messiness. I cannot call myself a typical viewer of *Doughball*, but I do want to highlight the fact that seeing *Doughball* led in my case not (only) to an idealization of a Japanese American community that never was, but to rage and anger that Asian Americans generally, and Japanese Americans specifically, are so seldom depicted "realistically" in the media. That is, precisely the realist moves in *Doughball* spurred me to action: provoking a problematizing of representations of Asian Americans by the dominant culture, motivating the writing of this paper and, in part, my decision to take the playwriting class. The realism of *Doughball* heightened the felt necessity to create homes for ourselves, however problematic and provisional, figuring home not as an essentialized space of identity, but as an historically, culturally specific construct inseparable from power relations. Rather than privileging certain representational strategies in advance, I am arguing for a more complex view of the relationship between aesthetics and politics and for more thoroughgoing studies of reception that would go beyond the positing of the idealized author and the idealized audience, positioning sites, venues, productions, and audiences within larger matrices of power, history, and culture.

Though *Doughball* makes no attempt to subvert codes of realist representation, I think one must seek its political and aesthetic value elsewhere: for example, precisely in its deployment of reality effects. It underlines the salience of Chela Sandoval's incisive analysis of "oppositional consciousness" in U.S. Third World feminism. She describes the contextually specific tactics Third World feminists engage, arguing that one cannot necessarily privilege in advance and for all time the utility of any *particular* tactic. "Differential consciousness" is a mode of "weaving 'between and among' oppositional ideologies" (14), and it mobilizes a "tactical subjectivity with the capacity of recentering depending upon the kinds of oppression to be confronted" (ibid.). Chandra Mohanty and Biddy Martin make a similar point:

> Basic to the (at least implicit) disavowal of conventionally realist and autobiographical narrative by deconstructionist critics is the assumption that difference can emerge only through self-referential language, i.e., through certain relatively specific formal operations present in the text or performed upon it. Our reading of Pratt's narrative contends that a so-called conventional narrative such as Pratt's is not only useful but essential in addressing the politically and theoretically urgent questions surrounding identity politics (194).

I want to concur with Sandoval and with Martin and Mohanty and end by saying that Perry Miyake's *Doughball* draws our attention to the *constructedness* of home, identity, and culture, underlining the necessity for people on the margins to create, produce, and assert our identities. Its specific locations (Venice, East West Players, and Los Angeles), its framing by a particular history of dislocation, (the Vietnam War and urban redevelopment) underscore the historically and politically constructed nature of those identities. Indeed, as I stated at the outset, the term "Asian American" itself is inextricable from history and politics, as an identity forged through the student struggles of the '60s—before then, after all, we were merely "Orientals." Asian American theater, including productions like *Doughball*, and sites like East West Players, Highways, Pan Asian Repertory in New York, Asian American Theater Company in San Francisco, continue to explore the aesthetic and political possibilities of such identities. However problematic the notion of home, whatever differences within are effaced, and however provisional that home may be, *Doughball*, East West, Los Angeles, and my ongoing experiences as a documentor and perhaps producer of Asian American theater highlight for me the continued urgency to create our homes and our identities for ourselves. As Elaine Kim has argued, "claiming

America for Asian Americans means inventing a new identity" (147). I would suggest that such an identity would be neither Asian nor American if the latter means "European," nor does it mean hyphenated "Asian American," if that means *riding* on the hyphen "between two worlds." Rather, I think Asian American playwrights, writers, and artists are creating identities that defy binary categorization into "Asian" or "American" or into some mediating third term. They are articulating for Asian Americans something new, something that exceeds previous categories. Despite the human suffering incurred through dislocation, incarceration, and diaspora, the historical experiences of Asian Americans can become a source of strength, the openness of identity a field of possibility. As performance artist Dan Kwong urged us, we must continue to "tell our stories," we must continue to write ourselves into existence.

ENDNOTES

1. See, for example, Sid Lemelle and Robin Kelley, eds. *Imagining Home*, on the role of "Africa" as homeland in the African diaspora.
2. A phrase describing the effect of "relocation" on the Japanese American community.
3. Elaine Kim (1990) provides a cogent analysis of the oppositional quality of the Asian American claim on America as home.
4. See the final chapter for an account of this teach-in.
5. The winter production at East West Players in 1992 was R.A. Shiomi's *Uncle Tadao*, a play thematizing the lingering memories and pain of relocation, brought alive by the redress campaign of the 1980s. Again, the small details of language created authenticity effects, particularly through Sab Shimono's brilliant portrayal of a Nisei man. Small expressions, inflections, and intonations reminded me of home: the use of the term "high-tone" to mean "classy" or "elegant" and the particular way Niseis pronounce that word; Shimono's pronunciation of "goddamn," which many Nisei men will pronounce "gotdamn," and so on. A Hawaiian-born and -raised Sansei colleague commented on the word "yakking" and its familiarity to him; up to that point, he had thought that it was strictly a Hawaiian J.A. term, but Shiomi is a Japanese Canadian playwright from Toronto.
6. I invoke Proust both to deflate the kind of elevated world of the Mundane allowed "great French literature" and to elevate the work of Asian American theater, to argue that the same attention can be paid the evocative power of sensory memory in both settings.
7. Of course naturalistic representation may not be the only mode of "capturing reality."
8. Cf. Emily Apter's work on "colonial realism."
9. Rich person.
10. As an analyst, this strikes me as problematic. Japanese capital has sometimes been behind redevelopment, as, for example, in Japantown in San Francisco, when the build-

ing of the Japanese mall displaced many Japanese American residents—but never without the key intervention of white developers. In one sense this passage inevitably feeds the current Japan-bashing discourse which is dangerous and life-threatening for Japanese Americans. On the other hand it does the work of distinguishing Japanese Americans from Japanese and demonstrates the ways that Japanese Americans' lives are shaped by larger forces of war, racism, and global capitalism.

7.

interview   with
david   henry   hwang

DAVID HENRY HWANG, the author of the Tony-award winning *M. Butterfly*
discussed in Chapter One, is perhaps the best-known Asian American playwright. His works include *F.O.B.* (1979), written while he was an undergraduate
at Stanford University, *The Dance and the Railroad* (1981), *Family Devotions*
(1981), the science fiction music-drama *1000 Airplanes on the Roof* (1988), *Face
Value* (1993), and his most recent full-length play *Golden Child* (1996).

Hwang was among the most visible spokespersons for Asian American
artists during the *Miss Saigon* casting controversy, which I discuss in the con-
cluding chapter. His play *Face Value* thematizes these protests in a farce about
mistaken racial identity. This phone interview took place in 1993 after *Face
Value* had closed on Broadway.

DK: Just let me preview the general areas. My book is about the performativity
of race and gender, so let me ask you about *Face Value* and *Bondage*, and then
about the transfer of your plays to film, and then your work in different media—
opera, with Prince—followed by some general questions.

DH: O.K.

DK: I wonder if you could tell me the story of *Face Value*: its genesis and maybe how you are thinking about changing it now.

DH: O.K. The play started out because I was disoriented and confused by everything that happened with *Miss Saigon* and with that casting dispute, and the way in which it seemed so difficult to be able to get any sort of meeting of the minds between the two sides. I found that a little discouraging and dispiriting, and I therefore felt like I wanted to write something about it. But I wasn't quite clear what. So I started out with this premise of two Asian Americans who decide to go in whiteface to disrupt the opening night of this Broadway musical where a white actress plays an Asian. And as I started writing it, it seemed to me that a play like *What the Butler Saw* by Joe Orton[1] could be an interesting model, because Orton takes some elements of farce and uses them to blur the lines of gender, and I thought it would be interesting to do the same to blur the lines of races and explore what it really means to play another race. What does it mean to take on the skin of another race?

It's a play that took a long time to write, to get a first draft of. I think it took five or six months to get a first draft, which is very long for me. At the time that I got a first draft, it was still very long and unwieldy, and I thought it would still need a lot of work. But there were various people who were interested in producing the play. Stuart Ostrow,[2] who produced *Butterfly*, committed to it early. And he got Scott Rudin, who had previously been known basically as a Hollywood producer—and a very successful Hollywood producer—and was interested in getting into stage. Scott came on board as a co-producer, and the Jujamcyn[3] theaters also came on board. So those were our three producers. And we got Jerry Zaks[4] as a director because Jerry has a great record both with comedy and also with more serious plays that explore certain issues like John Guare's *Six Degrees of Separation*, which Jerry also directed on Broadway.

Now, once we went into rehearsal, I had always proposed to Stuart that maybe one way to do this play—because I felt like it needed so much work—was to do a number of different out-of-town tryouts. Rather than doing the traditional "go to one city and then go to New York," it would be great if we could go to two or three different cities. I suppose, in retrospect, what I was looking for was sort of a development process like the type that August Wilson[5] uses, where you really take a long time to polish it up—except he uses the not-for-profit theater system, and this would have been a commercial equivalent of that and would have been prohibitively expensive. So, as a result, I suppose I had a certain amount of hubris when that didn't work out and felt that I would be able to fix the play in a couple of months, and we would be able to bring it to Broadway, and it would be fine. And, you know, that didn't happen. We got bad reviews in Boston, and then by the time we had gotten to New York, it still wasn't working, and we didn't have really the money to continue to keep it open and to continue to make changes. So we made the decision that it would be better not to open it and therefore allow the play to have some future life than to open it and blow its chances. I guess that it's theoretically possible that it could have opened and gotten good reviews, but basically we didn't feel that it was where it should be, and I think that was the primary thing that motivated us.

I have a grant to rewrite and redo the play at Trinity Rep in Providence. I'm thinking that one of the mistakes that I made on the approach to the play is that I conceived it—maybe because of Orton—I conceived it too much as a physical farce. If I was using a French farce as a model I was thinking of it as a Feydeau farce with a lot of action and movement and doors. Whereas I now think that really what this is, is more of a comedy of manners and therefore would—if we're using French playwrights as analogies—be more like a Molière farce or a Marivaux farce, which is about the way the people behave with one another, in which the plot is not quite as convoluted and not quite as "you need a joke a minute." Those are really the lines along which I'm reimagining the play.

DK: Are you in the process of rewriting now? Are you working with Oskar?[6]

DH: I'm working with Oskar, and we're hoping to have a script that we can do a reading of by this fall. Right now, actually, I'm working on another play, a new play, but I'm planning to get to *Face Value* next. In the meantime, I've been outlining plot sketches and stuff like that, for when I get started.

DK: I was also going to ask you about gender and race as performatives. I'm just wondering about audience reaction and about joking about race at this particular historical moment. I wonder if you had more insights about that. Did you also not take Shakespearean comedy as a model as well?

DH: I think there's definitely the use of asides and the *Midsummer Night's Dream* quality of it. In the previous draft there was a triple wedding at the end of the play. So all of those are very Shakespearean in influence.

DK: I'm just wondering whether race is somehow different, that somehow gender-bending is . . .

DH: Well, I think that was one of the interesting things we found in Boston. By the time we got to New York, we were scratching our heads and feeling that there is, as Scott Rudin put it, "something wrong in the alchemy of the evening." It wasn't something that we could exactly all put our fingers on, otherwise we would have been able to solve it. But there is something extremely uncomfortable about joking about race, trying to make people laugh at these situations. As many people have said, there's something transgressive about laughter, and I think there's so much sensitivity and anger and resentment and fear and all those things that swirl around these subjects right now, that for people to feel relaxed enough to be able to laugh about this sort of subject is very difficult. I think that's one of the challenges that I'll continue to face no matter how I structure the play and no matter who my farcical model is. At least a Molière structure allows us to have a greater discussion of the issues, which I think will make people somewhat more comfortable about it. Or at least give them an opportunity to breathe, as opposed to jumping into something controversial and uncomfortable head first, and trying to make the jokes just come. I think we have to allow for the fact that people are not going to feel at ease with this material in the beginning.

DK: Did you have a chance to probe different kinds of audience reactions, say Asian American audiences versus more mainstream ones?

DH: Not that many people saw it in Boston since we got bad reviews, which also didn't help either because you're in a huge theater with a hundred people in the house, which is not very good. But the Asian American Resource Center in Boston did a benefit evening. Gish Jen[7] introduced me at a talk we gave afterwards, and—I don't know, it's always hard for the playwright to judge, because except at academic conferences, if people don't like your work they usually don't tell you. But in that context, anyway, it seemed like everybody was really quite taken with the piece. Gish introduced me by saying that she felt that in watching this, the use of Shakespearean or farcical techniques applied to her own situation. (She) felt like it was a piece of clothing that she'd always seen and never been able to wear that had now been tailored to her, which I thought was a lovely thing to say. So I don't think that it's a given that all works transcend cultural differences. I think some do and some don't. It's possible that this is just always going to be a play that I hope at least is going to be more interesting to Asians than to a mainstream audience. But, you know, we'll see.

DK: A number of your plays have a theme of unmasking—certainly *M. Butterfly, Face Value*, and *Bondage*.[8] Is there some insight that you could give on that issue?

DH: I've lately come to think that unmasking is maybe part of a larger theme that seems to me to travel through the works, which is the fluidity of identity: the way in which different characters in the plays always transform into other characters or trade identities. I think one way in which this manifests itself, particularly in the more recent plays, has to do with the conscious taking on of a mask, and then the decision either to act in such a way that is consistent with the mask or to defy the mask. That seems to me to be a more general way of looking at the body of work.

DK: Could you tell me what you're working on now?

DH: I'm working on something which is sort of surprising to me because I had ideas for writing one play and when I started writing, I found that I was writing something else. It's essentially a play about something that happened in my family about three generations ago.[9] So it's kind of a memory play which is told from the point of view of a contemporary Asian American. In that sense it's a little surprising to me because it's a little more conventional than some of the stuff that I've been used to doing lately, at least in form. But it has to do with the decision of my great-grandfather to convert to Christianity. What I'm finding as I work on it is that it's an interesting way to explore the notions of traditional vs. nontraditional. It's an ironic juxtaposition in the sense that, at least for a mainstream audience, the decision of a Chinese person to take on a Western religion—is that a conventional decision? Obviously it's antitraditional in terms of Chinese culture. In terms of a Western audience, it would be taking on a traditional culture and family values and all that kind of thing. So looking at it from the standpoint of an Asian American who narrates the story, I think it takes on a more interesting irony than I might have initially expected. But overall, it's still a somewhat more conventional play than I'm used to writing.

DK: In a couple of your interviews you mentioned wanting to extend your writing in more Chekhovian ways.

DH: I think this falls in that category. I'm just interested in challenging myself in different ways and becoming a better writer in different areas. The Brechtian/Stoppard/Shavian ideological models that I've been influenced a lot by—I've learned a lot from those models, and I think that I've been able to incorporate interesting forms and juxtapositions and ideological arguments, but I still don't feel that I necessarily have a very good grasp on the minutiae of humanity: what it is to really create characters that are real in their details. That's an area (where) I feel I could use some work, so this play gives me an opportunity to try to stretch that part of myself.

DK: And also, I suppose, working the subtext in ways. Could you describe some of the process of transferring *M. Butterfly* to film?

DH: Basically, I guess I had a fairly conventional Hollywood experience—in the sense that I was a screenwriter, and the work sort of resembled what I wrote and sort of didn't.

DK: (*laughter*) Are you at liberty to say how?

DH: Sure. Basically, I did a first draft and David Cronenberg became interested in directing it. We had a meeting and he suggested that I might go back more closely to the play, because the first draft that I did of the script worked really hard to find filmic equivalents to the theatrical devices and metaphors that were used in the play and went pretty far in terms of things like bombs falling on Vietnam. David felt that that distracted from the story. In hindsight I'd agree with him. I think that the first draft was an attempt to reconceive the story in cinematic terms, which was a necessary part of my process but was not, I think, as successful as it could have been. So I did a second draft that we both felt was much closer to target. It was closer to the play and yet at the same time, I made it a point to expand on certain notions in the play and to find filmic equivalents to the theatrical metaphors that were used. Some were more surreal or dream-like. At the time, David was editing *Naked Lunch*, so I figured, oh, he'll really love all of this stuff. To give an example, there is a scene in the play which a lot of people like: the one where Song changes from a woman to a man between the second and third acts. And the question is, how do you duplicate that on screen? It's not particularly effective just to have somebody change because we've seen so many special effects. I felt that in film one of the things that's important is point-of-view. For instance, when you see a comedy on film the audience doesn't laugh necessarily on the joke line. The audience often laughs on the reaction shot. They see someone else reacting. So somebody else on screen becomes our eyes, in effect. So I'd written this scene where, after Song and Gallimard are arrested, Gallimard is still protesting that he doesn't believe that she's a man, and the French security people take him to one of these rooms with the one-way mirror. They have Song go in the other side so Gallimard can see Song, and they don't tell Song, obviously, that he is being observed. They just tell him to change. And so then it crosscuts between a very casual Song undressing, washing off his make up and all that, and Gallimard's insane reaction and denial in the adjacent room. I thought that was a very interesting equivalent of that moment.

So David, I guess, decided to make a much more naturalistic picture. I didn't get to be around for filming, and I didn't get to see the picture until the final test preview in Santa Monica. So by then it was pretty much already locked. I have some respect for the picture. I think that the choices that David made were things that he believed and that they were his own artistic vision. I just think that his vision was not entirely dissimilar but somewhat different from my own, and therefore I can't really accept the film as my own child. I think in that respect it's very much a typical screenwriter experience. I saw the film twice. I saw it once in this preview, and I saw it at the opening at the Toronto Film Festival. I just saw it a week ago—it was on cable—so this is my third time watching it now, after a couple of years. And watching it again after this time, I think I've realized that one of the reasons the movie, for me, doesn't quite work, is that nobody in the movie—to put it kind of glibly—is having any fun.

DK: It's very somber.

DH: Yeah. You don't see Gallimard getting off on what he's able to accomplish and this fantasy of being the triumphant Pinkerton and the conquering Western man and all that. *And* you don't see Song's sort of glee at his manipulation and the way his disguise works and the way that he's being adored. Everybody's just so depressed all the time!

DK: Indeed, aren't they? Even the cinematography.

DH: Yeah, yeah, and everything's very dark. I've always thought of Gallimard in terms of the film as somewhat of an analogue to Lawrence of Arabia. Because when Lawrence takes the Arab army and they start blowing up the trains and Lawrence is skipping along, there's that famous shot where he's skipping along the top of the train that's been blown up, and we see him in shadow—that's when he starts to believe that he can only be killed by a silver bullet. There's that kind of madness that comes with believing that you're suddenly becoming greater than just a man. And that's what I think should have happened to Gallimard in the film and didn't.

DK: So basically with Cronenberg you didn't have that much input.

DH: No. Since David's used to writing and directing his own pictures, I think that he basically felt that once it was his, it was his.

DK: For me one of the things that was striking in comparison to the play is that the Orientalist critique was much muted and the love story part highlighted.

DH: Right. Well, I think that David would probably say this himself, I don't think that this is something that he would feel bad about in any way. I think for David it was always a piece about the delusion of romantic love. Period. And I think that the political aspects were vaguely interesting to him to the extent that they affected his main theme, but they weren't really what he was about. So, consequently, I think there's some hint of the politics, but you see that the filmmaker has no particular passion for that.

217

DK: That certainly came through. (I have) some similar questions about *Golden Gate*, which I liked much more than the reviewers.

DH: Yeah, I think *Golden Gate* should have been a better picture. On the other hand, I think that it was better than it was reviewed.

DK: I can't quite understand the reviews, to be honest, because I thought that there was a lot of graceful writing, and the white man dies in the end, and the acting was good: Matt Dillon was great; Joan Chen was great.

DH: Now, that picture turned out very differently from the script also, but that was something in which I was consulted, and for some reason—I'm not quite clear why exactly—we did film it similarly to the script. Or John Madden did. We did a test preview of it, and people really didn't like it. Asians, whites, nobody liked it. So the film started getting recut and changed around. Part of me feels that was a script which had, in its original form, a lot of metaphors in it and a lot of symbols and shifting moods. I think that maybe there's only a very special handful of directors that could have done it. Maybe that's one possibility. Another possibility is something that I'm trying to understand in the nature of film. Which is that one has to respect the verisimilitude of the medium.

DK: It's exactly that, isn't it?

DH: Coming from the theater I'm really in love with metaphor. Whenever you put a symbol in the movie, it falls a little bit flat. Even in *The Joy Luck Club* which I think basically works as a movie—whether or not you agree with this point-of-view or that point-of-view. Except there's the one moment where Rosalind Chao, who I think gives a great performance, has that speech where Andrew McCarthy has come back. Roz is in the rain and she's going, "I ate opium to die," and she's intoning essentially the words of her grandmother or great-grandmother. I don't know if that completely works. Even that little bit of transcendent symbolism, it sort of works in the picture, but it's a little iffy. I guess I'm recognizing that there's a fly-on-the-wall quality that film demands. You're actually *in* China or you're actually *in* San Francisco, and people expect that it's supposed to be real. That's one of the aesthetic differences that I'm learning about between stage and film.

DK: Absolutely. Once in awhile—I don't know what you think for example of *Mishima*, that Paul Schrader picture or—it's so rare.

DH: See, *Mishima* comes off to me as a little bit academic.

DK: No wonder I like it. (laughter)

DH: Yeah, I did like it and all, but it felt a little like an essay: here, and here, and here, and you add these up, and this makes sense in terms of why he killed himself.

DK: In essence, does this mean that you plan to direct someday, or would like to?

DH: I think I'm still planning to direct someday. As I think you know, *Golden Gate* was originally written as something for myself to direct, and that didn't work out because I wasn't at the point in my career where that could happen. But now I'm a little further along; I've had some movies made, even though they weren't hits, and [that] in the ladder of things makes me more eligible to direct movies. So I think that is something I'm going to do someday, but I do appreciate the education I've had over the last few years in movies. It hasn't exactly been easy in the sense that I would rather those movies had been hits. But if I go to direct a picture now, I do feel that I do know more about movies than I did two or three years ago. It's not a form that has come as naturally to me as stage. However it is, I'm hard- or soft-wired for things like metaphor and shifting tone. All of those things are very difficult to pull off in a picture.

DK: Well, speaking of differences in media, then, I'm wondering if you could talk about your collaborations in music, the Prince one first.

DH: The Prince thing is very simple to talk about. We had talked and met right after *Face Value* closed—that would have been right after spring of '93—and he was interested in possibly our doing a Broadway musical together. I've always been a huge Prince fan, so I was just happy to try it out and see if anything was going to come of it. I wrote a script that he really liked and he wanted to do, except that when he first told me the idea, I had the impression that it was something that he wanted to be in. Then, by the time it was done, he wanted to produce it, but he didn't want to be in it. And I felt like it was a piece that was very much designed for him to star in, and I felt like if it wasn't going to be him, then it really didn't make sense. So, the only thing that's really come out of that is a little monologue of it, that's going to be published in this Asian American erotica anthology that Geraldine Kudaka is editing,[10] and then the song "Solo" which was on *Come*.[11] That really just came about because Prince had sent me the tape of a song called "Solo" which, at the time, was sort of a ballad actually. No, it's a ballad now, it *was* a heavy-metal song. He said that he wanted some words to speak with it, like he was going to put in sort of a

219

poetry reading section in middle or something. I said, "I don't really write lyrics, and I can't write anything that rhymes." And he said, "Don't worry, you just write some stuff and I'll make a song out of it." So I faxed him just some blank verse. He used some of it and changed some stuff around, and sent back a tape a few days later, and it was a ballad. And then about a year later, I got a call from his production company, and it was going to be on this album. So, that's fun.

DK: Oh, I see. I thought maybe you had a hand in the music, because immediately when I heard it I thought, "Oh, this must be the one."

DH: Right. No, unfortunately I didn't have a hand in the music, I mean, unless it was only in the subconscious sense, though I think that Dan Kuramoto[12] and I are going to hang out a little in a few weeks and try and compose some music together. I think it might be for the next album.

DK: The collaboration with Philip Glass. How does it work when you're working with a . . .

DH: With Philip it's very easy. *The Voyage* was a proper libretto that I basically wrote before there was any music. We did a few drafts of that, and then he just set it to music. *A Thousand Airplanes* was a monologue against a Glass score. Philip is very easy to work with. He basically feels that each person in the collaboration knows more about his or her area than he does, and he doesn't interfere too much.

DK: And in terms of the casting of *A Thousand Airplanes*, if I remember correctly—did you alternate on the road with a white man and Jodi Long?[13]

DH: There were a couple of white men that did it, there was a white woman that did it and Jodi Long also did it. It was with just sort of anybody. I guess it was truly blind in that respect.

DK: I thought that was an unusual casting move. I wanted to move on and ask you what you see in terms of Asian American theater now. Who do you think is doing interesting work? What would you like to see generally, in American theater?

DH: I guess I'm looking at this point to people that can do work that transcends category. That's one of the reasons that Anna Deveare Smith is very interesting and attractive to us because I think she transgresses these different boxes that we've been put into as writers or performers. I really think that's where the next step is.

220

One of the things that *Face Value* attempted to get at, and I suppose *Bondage* also, is the whole question: What is the inherent meaning of race? Or, are the only meanings that race is associated with those which have been imposed upon it? I think most of us would say that race in itself—besides the fact that you have slightly different physical characteristics from people in other races— that doesn't have any greater intrinsic value in terms of temperament, intelligence, mentality. Most of us would not agree with Charles Murray. And if that's the case, then I think that a lot of the boundaries that we have used and talked about and fought for in the 60s through the 80s continue to evolve and change, and some of them are still relevant, and some of them aren't. I think that when you get into a world where there are more biracial children, where minorities do become a plurality, and, therefore, the intra-ethnic battles become as fierce if not more so than those between people of color and the white establishment, then we really begin talking about a new parameter and a new set of rules, and we have to redefine where it is that we stand. I think that that's an uncomfortable position, not only for the mainstream, but also for us. I think that for people of color it's uncomfortable because we have to redefine what it is that *we* are, and what are the symbols of *our* identity. So I suppose people who are doing that sort of work seem to me to be the most interesting. I think the stuff that Han Ong does is fascinating. I don't completely understand all of it, but I think he and Jessica Hagedorn have been doing this sort of stuff for a long time. This doesn't fall into the theater category, but the fact that Desmond Nakano[14] is directing his first picture, and it's about the white/black thing, I think is significant also. I think the more that we can mix it up, the better we all are. Which is somewhat contradictory to the fact that I'm at this moment writing a play about my great-grandfather. But, you know, every now and then you have to do that, too.

DK: I agree with you. Along similar lines, in one interview you talked about how, in the Reagan years, there seemed to be no exciting ideas in the air. Do you think that this is a more interesting historical era?

DH: I think this is a very interesting historical era—not, again, the most comfortable, simply because everybody's so pissed off.

DK: Aren't they!

DH: There's so much anger, and everybody feels that they're getting the short end of the stick. Everybody feels that they're being ripped off. And we can argue; I have my own opinions—and most of them I'm sure probably agree with yours—about who actually *is* getting ripped off. But I think that fact is that we at least have to acknowledge that the people who feel these things *really feel them*, you know, and start from there. I think that it's easy for us as people of color to say, "This is ridiculous, you have no right to feel this," to white men for instance. And I don't know if that's the most constructive place to start. I think that the constructive place to start is to acknowledge that whether or not anyone has a right to feel anything, these feelings are real and they have to be dealt with, and then take it from there.

DK: Any ideas how? I have to deal with them everyday in my classroom!

DH: Well, you know, I was reading something about the Fourth Reich skinheads. They were being interviewed in British *Esquire* or something like that. And they were talking about the fact that a lot of them—I think they went to Long Beach High School—and they couldn't go up to the second floor because the second floor was the Black floor or something. Some of them went up to the second floor and they got beat up. Now, from an historical perspective we could say: well, that's very much an exception and doesn't really conform to the power structure that these people are living in. But on a moment-to-moment basis, we have to, I think, say that their experience of racism is not dissimilar to our experience of racism when we were in high school. So that if, then, we grow up, and we become writers or artists or politicians or whatever, and some of our political perspective is born out of certain humiliations that we had in high school, growing up, etc., then I think that it's understandable that theirs are also. So what do we do with that? I guess it was me that said—Anna Deveare Smith quotes me as saying—that to have an honest conversation about race between people is more intimate than sex. And I guess acknowledging at least a certain *individual* legitimacy to being angry for *all* sorts of people. It may allow us to form at least some beginnings of trust that are necessary to have that discussion. The reason we can't have that discussion is that we don't trust each other. We feel that we aren't going to be validated if we state our opinions and people are just going to put us down. Those of us who are, say, Asian Americans, I don't think we can come up with a solution in the abstract, and we can't come up with a solution in isolation. But I do think that this sort of thing of trust needs to be looked at more carefully.

DK: As I said, it can be trying on a daily basis. There really is a lot of rage out there, and I think you're right that people are feeling that existentially what they confront individually may feel similar.

DH: And if it feels similar but it doesn't have the same sort of political or historical reality, is it still legitimate? You know? It is on some level, it isn't on another level.

DK: To me it's more about loss of privilege and the rage that it's about, but it is interesting. And so are we talking then in terms of white male artists like (David) Mamet or Michael Crichton? (laughter) How are you seeing this manifested?

DH: The body of work of Michael Douglas lately? (laughter) I think definitely. Look, there's been such a rush of people trying to claim they're politically incorrect these days that it's sort of absurd that people on the one hand are going, "Oh, all the politically correct people are taking over." And on the other hand, all the people who are making money, the subjects that are selling and the books that are selling, the radio talk show hosts that are selling, are all people who are proudly declaring themselves to be politically incorrect. It's this weird contradiction, this weird fact that denies what it is. It reinforces this idea that this political correct notion is something that was created by the right in order to reinforce the ideas of the right—and it's working.

DK: It seems to be, very effectively. I just wanted to ask you quickly if you're working on a new project.

DH: I'm working on something new. I have a Hollywood movie coming out around Christmas. It's based on this bestselling novel called *The Alienist* that's been on the charts last year, and it's about a serial killer in New York in 1895. Teddy Roosevelt's police commissioner at the time. Scott Rudin, who produced *Face Value* is also producing *The Alienist*, so he asked me to write it. It's going to be a Paramount picture and maybe it'll do well. I think that it's good. I suppose, in order for me to gain more power and ability to do what I want in Hollywood to have a hit, but I feel somewhat conflicted about it, too.

DK: And then I just have one question that's not about theater at all, actually, but a question for you that's about fashion consumers, since my book is also about that. You wear Comme de Garçons. Do you buy other Japanese designers' clothes?

DH: Do I buy other Japanese designers? I buy a fair amount of Miyake. Let me see.

DK: And do you buy other designers as well, and do you see anything specifically in the work of Kawakubo or Miyake that is attractive to you?

DH: Hmmm. Well, I do buy other designers as well. Lately I've been buying a fair amount of Gigli.[15] But the thing that has always appealed to me about Kawakubo is whenever she does something which is basically conventional in

223

form but has one thing that's off-kilter about it. Those are the things that appeal to me most. My favorite pieces of hers are . . . the black blazer with the flowered buttons, and a couple years ago she did a series where there were black blazers that had extended lapels with little strips of color down the lapel. Just the little touch like that, to throw it off-center is basically what appeals to me about her work. With Miyake I suppose it has to do with the silhouette, and there's also a monk-like quality to some of the things that he does that appeals to me in some strange way that probably goes back to something puritan in my upbringing. And the fabrics.

DK: His fabrics are beautiful. Well, thank you.

DH: O.K. Well, good luck.

ENDNOTES

1. British playwright and farceur.
2. Producer of *M. Butterfly*.
3. Producers of, e.g., George Wolfe's *Jelly's Last Jam* on Broadway.
4. Broadway director, known for his work in musical comedies.
5. African American playwright. Author of *Fences, Joe Turner's Come and Gone*, and *Two Trains Running*, among others.
6. Eustis, Artistic Director at Trinity Repertory Theater and former Associate Artistic Director at the Mark Taper Forum in Los Angeles, where we both served as dramaturges on Anna Deavere Smith's *Twilight: Los Angeles 1992*.
7. A Chinese American novelist.
8. *Bondage*, a one-act play, takes place in an S-and-M parlor. An Asian American man and a white woman (she is the dominatrix), both clad in leather from head to toe, don the roles of different races, in a constantly changing dynamic. The dénouement is their unmasking.
9. The play Hwang mentions is *Golden Child*. Commissioned by South Coast Repertory in Costa Mesa, California, it premiered in November 1996 at the Public Theater in New York. *Golden Child* subsequently opened in a revised version at South Coast Rep in January 1997.
10. Geraldine Kudaka and Russell Leong, eds. *On a Bed of Rice: An Asian American Erotic Feast*. New York: Anchor, 1995.
11. A CD by the artist formerly known as Prince.
12. Leader of the jazz fusion group Hiroshima.
13. An Asian American actress; she played the character of the mother in the ABC situation comedy *All-American Girl* (1994), in which comedienne Margaret Cho starred.

14. Director of *White Man's Burden*, starring John Travolta and Harry Belafonte, in which black and white roles are reversed.
15. Romeo Gigli, a Milanese designer known for his precious fabrics and collections that have drawn inspiration from, for example, Byzantine costume. Like Kawakubo, Miyake, and Yamamoto, he is a designer's designer.

8 .

art, activism, asia, asian americans

IN THE INTRODUCTION I wrote of the politics of pleasure and argued that we must take such a politics seriously in order to appreciate its power even as we interrogate its effects. These modes of appreciation and critique are essential when we analyze racial representation in popular culture. The pleasure we experience in images, spectacle, and narrative can be simultaneously seductive, insidious, empowering, life-giving. A strategically deployed critical consciousness would require a sensitivity to this complexity. Such a pursuit would comprise at least two general forms of subversion.[1] When we speak of an oppressive politics of representation in film, theater, and television, the dominant minimizes oppositional critique through the pleasures of narrative ("It's such a beautiful story"), of the visual (spectacle, cinematography), and through a sharp distinction between fiction and fact ("It's just a story"; "It's just a satire"). One tactic depends on deconstructing the dominant and exposing these ruses of power. Another tactic could be called a strategic deployment of authenticity that would create alternative visions to oppressive representations: spaces where those of us on the margins could "write our faces." Here, the pleasures for Asian American audiences would be those of self-recognition and empowerment. Though radical separation from the dominant is impossible, these faces might

227

be ones we could at last recognize as ours. Both tactics and their myriad context-specific variations must be part of a repertoire of activist strategies.

Whatever the risks, we must continue to explore those strategies in the face of continuing racism, for to remain silent ensures a smooth, seamless reproduction of power relations. For Asian Americans, this includes deconstructing hegemonic representations of Asia that—like it or not—make a profound impact on Asian American lives. Such elisions abound. Cambodian children are shot in Stockton; Asian American women pushed in front of subway trains by Vietnam vets with post-traumatic stress disorder; Asian Americans meet up with everyday racisms, from outright racial epithets to the well-intentioned racisms of "You speak English so well"; white Asianophiles, whatever their sexual persuasion, fetishize Asian Americans in terms of sexuality and submissiveness. The ineffable "foreignness" of Asian Americans continues to bristle with life-determining significance, and as long as that is so, we must continue to interrupt the reproduction of structures of racial domination reflected in the reproduction of whiteness as universal norm and the specific, phantasmatic constructions of its various colored Others.

Such interruptions require outspoken critique and organized efforts to effect social transformation, exemplified in three interventions in which Asian American artists, activists, and academics have been prominently involved. The *Miss Saigon* controversy and its aftermath engage multiple modes of political/artistic intervention, including organized protest, educational efforts, satire, and counterhegemonic cultural production. Perhaps this elaboration indexes the undying persistence of the *Madame Butterfly* trope recirculated in *Miss Saigon*. The second involves the latest incarnation of Japanese male stereotypes—the businessman as corporate soldier—in Michael Crichton's novel and film *Rising Sun*. Mobilizing martial metaphors alive with historical resonances from the Pacific War, *Rising Sun* creates a sinister Japanese threat that skillfully, seductively draws upon a venerable Orientalist tradition. Finally, we turn to local institutional interventions that have made a difference, through the case of an organized teach-in/protest that occurred around a performance of Gilbert and Sullivan's *The Mikado* at the Claremont Colleges, where a concerted organizational effort linking Asian American faculty with other faculty of color and with other campus progressives—including Women's Studies and gay/lesbian groups—was one pivotal step in bringing about the establishment of a fledgling Asian American Resource Center and a still nascent Asian American Studies program.

228

The continuing need for actions such as those I describe might seem discouraging, a Sisyphean task of battling the "changing same." Yet, in the spirit of the Chicana artists with whom I began the book, I would also argue that these interventions illustrate useful, sometimes even life-giving, strategies. None is perfect or beyond complicity or recuperation, yet all are interventions that have made a difference.

DEAD BUTTERFLIES

Perhaps no recent debate over Asian American representation has galvanized Asian American artistic communities or captured the attention of mainstream media as has the casting controversy over *Miss Saigon*. It remains for Asian American theater artists a historical and political watershed that forced the mobilization of actors and community, spawning numerous artistic and political interventions that represent an array of tactical possibilities.

The controversy began when producer Cameron Mackintosh designated Jonathan Pryce, a white actor who had played the Engineer in the London production, to repeat the role in *Miss Saigon*'s Broadway premiere. In response to pressures from Asian American activists and actors, Mackintosh reportedly "looked under every rock" for an Asian or Asian American for the part, but he claimed to have failed in his quest. With the deadline looming, Actors' Equity refused to grant the card Pryce needed to work in the United States. Their decision recognized the objections raised by Asian American actors that Asian or Eurasian parts should be cast with Asian Americans, since historically, both Asians *and* Eurasians had been played by whites. Indeed, the category Eurasian was often deployed precisely in order to hire white actors: David Carradine in *Kung Fu* is but one example. Asian American artists like Dom Magwili and Ping Wu argued that Mackintosh had in fact used this tactic, since the libretto makes no reference to the Engineer as a person of mixed race (Cf. "Fallout Over *Miss Saigon*"). Mackintosh subsequently revoked his decision to bring *Miss Saigon* to Broadway. This spelled the loss of millions of dollars of revenue and a substantial number of jobs for the theater world. Succumbing to Mackintosh and to protests from some of its members, Equity reversed their initial decision. *Miss Saigon* opened on Broadway in February 1991 with Jonathan Pryce as the Engineer.

The parameters of the debate expose the assumptions and limitations of liberal humanist ideologies. *The Los Angeles Times* devoted a special page to the controversy immediately following the Equity decision to refuse Pryce his card. On the Right, Charlton Heston called the decision "racist" and declared his shame to be a member of Equity. Fueling his indignant reaction were his claims that actors as a group are more discriminated against than are people of color. Two producer-directors, one Asian American and one white, read the issue as one of artistic freedom, since directors and producers should be able to cast whomever they choose, race notwithstanding. Here, the argument was that "the best person" should get the part. Velina Hasu Houston raised the issue of multiracials. In her view, neither side was in fact right, for Eurasians are neither white nor "pure-blooded" Asian Americans. Finally, actor/writer/director Dom Magwili noted the political and historical forces involved. He argued that casting a white actor as an Asian *or* Eurasian is *traditional casting* that gives whites license to portray people of color, while people of color cannot even play themselves. This traditional casting, he argued, is racist casting.

With the exception of Magwili, most writers subscribed to the common liberal humanist assumption that the individuals involved are shorn of history and beyond or outside power relations. Heston ignores the racial stratifications and divisions within the category "actor"; certainly, Heston himself enjoys wealth and celebrity. He erases the historically constructed power relations that allow whites to play Asians and Asian Americans, while the reverse has never been the case. His cry of "racism" (or its cousin, "reverse racism") assumes that any critical discussion of race by people of color is racist. Such a view mistakes hurt feelings or individual inconvenience for systematic historical domination. Similarly, the producers' invocations of artistic freedom mobilize a liberal individualism that authorizes us to do what we please, without regard for the consequences. Their fear of censorship arises from a faulty analysis of power relations. Asian American activists and Equity are hardly in a position to dictate or silence; rather, they were attempting to compel Mackintosh to take seriously the issue of historical inequality and to search more assiduously for a talented Asian American actor—of whom there are many—to fill the role. Here, as often happens, who counts as the best is racially marked, where supposedly objective standards are in fact imbued with power relations. Defining the parameters of debate solely in terms of artistic freedom fails to give equal weight to artistic *responsibility* to various communities. Velina Hasu Houston's poignant argument about the specificity of Eurasians and the ways people of mixed race are often marginalized by members of all their constituent racial groups, is at one level indisputable. However, like most of the other writers, she fails to account for the historical overdetermination of the decision to allow a white actor to play Asian *and* Eurasian. In this case, the "white" and "Asian" halves are not equally weighted in political terms. A clear analysis of the issues must take into account the historically constructed, *systemic* power relations that informed Mackintosh's casting decision. In short, it matters who is doing the casting, for whom, for what purposes, and where those subjects and institutions are located in larger matrices of power.

In the mainstream media, focus on the casting controversy served to obscure other protests and other issues. Ultimately, the casting controversy is—or should be—a relatively minor aspect of the *Miss Saigon* story, for the striking feature here is the problematic politics of representation. *Miss Saigon* is a "colored museum" of Asian stereotypes, including the tenacious trope of Asian women's sacrifice and death. Asian American groups vociferously denounced the oppressiveness of these images, picketing *Miss Saigon* on its opening night on Broadway; gay Asian Pacific American groups made similar interventions when the Lambda Legal Defense Fund used *Miss Saigon* as a fundraiser for the Fund. Yet by that time, the story of *Miss Saigon* was old news, and the protests scarcely garnered media attention. When *Miss Saigon* opened in Los Angeles in late January 1995, I submitted the following piece to The *Los Angeles Times*, which was published after almost a month had elapsed and at less than half its original length.[2] Given that the longer piece deals substantively with the politics of representation and issues of institutional complicity, I reproduce it here:

> *Miss Saigon* opened on January 25 as the inaugural production of the newly renovated Ahmanson Theater. The blockbuster musical was the subject of live TV coverage, a cover story in the *Times Calendar* section, and extensive advertising hype. We have all heard about the controversy surrounding the Broadway production: should Jonathan Pryce, a white actor, play the Eurasian engineer or should the role go to an Asian American actor? However, reportage in both New York and Los Angeles has erased a far more urgent issue, the focus of protests among Asian Americans on both coasts: *For what kinds of Asian roles are we competing?* In New York, Asian American groups asking such questions picketed at opening night; in Los Angeles, many Asian Americans actively object to the stereotypes staged in *Miss Saigon*. Yet, aside from two letters published in the *Times Calendar* section, coverage of this side of the story has been conspicuously absent.

What are our objections to *Miss Saigon?* In the play Kim, a Vietnamese bar girl and prostitute, falls in love with Chris, an American G.I. in Vietnam. He returns to the U.S. as Saigon falls, and in his absence she bears him a son. In the meantime, Chris marries a white woman, but when he discovers Kim to be alive in Thailand, he returns with his American bride to search for his son. Ultimately, Kim kills herself to ensure her son's "escape" to a "better life" with his father. An update of the opera *Madama Butterfly, Miss Saigon* admittedly seems a mild improvement over the Puccini warhorse: the U.S. soldier, Chris, feels sorrow upon abandoning his Asian paramour; a song, "Bui-Doi," decries the plight of Amerasian children. Deploying deeply problematic narratives of East-West relations, *Miss Saigon* restages and conveniently expiates American guilt over Vietnam.

This expiation occurs through the recirculation of all-too-familiar Asian stereotypes: *extremes of sexuality*, represented in the *prostitute and the pimp*, the shy *lotus blossom*, and *asexual, faceless peasants and cadres*; *Oriental despotism* in the statue of Ho Chi Minh and in Kim's Vietnamese suitor, and its inverse, *Oriental subservience*, in the phalanxes of soldier hordes; *the sleazy, sneaky Oriental*, in the person of the Engineer, and familiar paternalistic narratives, such as *White man saves Asian woman from Asian man*, and *Asian woman dies for white man*. However updated, *Miss Saigon* is simply a case of "the changing same."

So what of the many Asian American jobs that *Miss Saigon* represents? Having had the misfortune of seeing *Miss Saigon* on Broadway for the book I'm writing, it is difficult for me to imagine a more disempowering, heartbreaking spectacle than the sight of gifted Asian American actors displaying their creative talents as pimps, prostitutes, lotus blossoms, and faceless Orientals. Equally disturbing is the fact that Cameron Mackintosh has apparently established schools to train Asian American theater professionals to populate further productions of *Miss Saigon.* Presumably we are to be grateful, even happy, for these opportunities. True, *Miss Saigon* gives Asian American actors jobs: jobs fleshing out the white man's fantasy, jobs that allow us to participate enthusiastically in our own oppression. Too often, artists of color are still the hired help, recruited to fill out the vision of a white playwright or director. In the name of empowerment through employment, *Miss Saigon* instead secures Asian American subordination.

There are, of course, notable exceptions in the work of artists of color. I was part of the creative team on Anna Deavere Smith's play *Twilight: Los Angeles 1992* at the Mark Taper Forum, part of the Center Theater Group that is also sponsoring *Miss Saigon*. In *Twilight*, Smith took on the bristling tensions around race and the historical oppressions that led to the L.A. uprisings. Given the Taper's putative commitment to racial diversity, it is particularly disappointing that *Miss Saigon* arrives in L.A. under the aegis of the Center Theater Group as the Ahmanson's inaugural production. I hope that progressive people of all races will think twice before spending $65 on this multimillion-dollar celebration of racial stereotypes. Let us register our protests. Boycott *Miss Saigon*. No matter how seductive the spectacle, racism is still racism.

Concerted forms of political activity around *Miss Saigon* arose across the country.[3] In the Twin Cities, for instance, the Pan Asian Voices for Equality (PAVE) organized a protest of *Miss Saigon* that embraced a coalition of African Americans, Native Americans, Asian Americans, feminists, and gays and lesbians. Widely covered in the local media, the demonstrations, pamphlets, articles, and teach-ins aimed to encourage debate and to draw attention to the depiction of Asians. As part of their intervention, Asian American Renaissance staged a counter-performance called *Missed Saigon* that dealt with stereotypes perpetuated in the play and the larger issues of power and culture it raises.[4]

What were the effects? Though the theater did not cancel performances or alter their performance schedules, they did make some concessions. Fifteen thousand complimentary tickets originally designated for schoolchildren were withdrawn in light of PAVE's objections that the musical presented stereotypical images to young children without a dissenting point of view. The theater also agreed to provide an insert with each playbill, written by an Asian American woman who specializes in media portrayals of Asian Americans (*Asian American Press*, December 3, 1993, 2). Moreover, the protest committee sent me Xeroxes of numerous letters from people I assume to be white, attesting to the value of the interventions. A few people sent in donations, some in the amount of the ticket price ($50.00). One cancelled her subscription to the Ordway Theater performance series. Asian Pacific community organizations also solicited information and presentations from people on the committee, which were positively received. These small but significant signifiers of the protest's impact deserve to be marked. Yet, given the unequal distribution of resources, it is unrealistic at best to expect a small group—or even a major Broadway production like *M. Butterfly*—to derail permanently the circulation of persistent hegemonic fantasies like the Butterfly trope, for one cannot at one stroke eliminate the geopolitical relations, the masses of capital, and the overdetermined histories that create and perpetuate these insidious ideologemes.

So stated, the Gramscian "wars of position" seem bleak. But perhaps we should mark an equally important effect of the protests and the organizing: an enactment of political identity and "community."[5] In such instances, this enactment is part of the intervention, giving Asian Americans the occasion to grapple with critical issues and to make alliances amongst the various Asian

Pacific groups and with other subaltern groups. Perhaps this outcome is as important as subverting the dominant. David Mura puts it this way:

> Whatever the effect of the anti-*Miss Saigon* activities on people outside the community, it's clear that the protests are part of a larger sea change occurring in the consciousness of Asian Americans and other people of color throughout this country. That sea change is something neither the Ordway nor *Miss Saigon* nor its mainly white middle-class patrons can stop. Increasingly, Asian Americans and other people of color are demanding that we be able to present our own images, to tell others how we see ourselves (*City Pages*, February 9, 1994).

Telling others how we see ourselves can sometimes involve the use of theatrical hyperbole as political strategy. Performance artist and playwright Ken Choy and performance artist Juliana Pegues, both members of the artistic organization Asian American Renaissance, staged a "die-in" at Minneapolis' Ordway Theater at a performance of the opera *Madama Butterfly*. Standing up in the midst of the proceedings, they screamed, "No more Butterfly!" and fell down repeatedly to simulate their deaths. Choy was tackled, Pegues manhandled, as both were forcibly removed and charged with disorderly conduct.[6] Notable here is the theatricality of their challenge, reminiscent of ACT UP and its deployment of hyperbole. Equally important are the stakes as performers these artists have in *Madama Butterfly*. Their artistic life is constricted by the limitations described by Butterfly and other Oriental stereotypes, for unless Asian American artists write our own roles, there will be few alternatives to a life of playing lotus blossoms, dragon ladies, pimps, rapacious businessmen, or, as actor/director François Chau wryly stated, "druglords, bodyguards to the druglord, druglords on the run." Dramatically focusing attention on the paucity and the oppressiveness of roles for people of color in mainstream productions, Pegues and Choy, in concert with other members of Asian American Renaissance, mounted a critical and theatrical statement of protest.[7] In short, Asian American artist/activists have, through conventional and unconventional means of political mobilization, interrupted the smooth recirculation of hegemonic racial representations.

REWRITING OUR FACES: *FACE VALUE* AND *BUZZ OFF, BUTTERFLY*

234

To subvert the dominant can involve recognizable forms of political activity. But cultural production is always already political, and performance can enact its subversions textually and on stage. Satire and parody are valuable tools for politically committed artists, providing ways to subvert oppressive representations through performing their absurdity. Deconstructive readings depend upon invoking and then deconstructing or subverting the dominant; David Henry Hwang's *M. Butterfly* does precisely this. Hwang transposes his deconstructive critique into the register of farce with his first full-length play to follow *M. Butterfly*: *Face Value*, his satire of the *Miss Saigon* controversy. Hwang knows the controversy from the inside, as one of the original instigators of the *Miss Saigon* protest; along with actor B.D. Wong, he served as one of the spokespersons for the movement.

The version of *Face Value* that played on Broadway is a farce of mistaken racial identities in a physically comic style. It brings to mind comedies such as *Much Ado About Nothing*, as well as farces that pivot around mistaken gender identity, such as *Twelfth Night* and Marivaux's *The Triumph of Love*. In *Face Value*, a white actor in yellowface is set to star on Broadway in a musical called *The Real Manchu*. Two Asian American activists dressed in whiteface are planning to disrupt the opening night performance from the audience. Two white supremacists, mistakenly believing *The Real Manchu* to be about "real Orientals" and believing the lead actor to be Asian, lurk in the wings, ready to hold up the proceedings. There begins the comedy of mistaken racial identities. By the last scene, all the characters except for the white supremacists are coupled with someone of another race: the male Asian American activist/actor with a young white actress who had been the white actor's mistress; the white actor with the Asian American woman activist/actress; the white producer with the African American stage manager. A white supremacist conveniently named Pastor (he is one) has a change of heart and marries them all, in a wedding scene à la *Much Ado About Nothing*. Whatever one may make of the politics of this narrative closure (for example, why must the people of color all be heterosexually coupled with white people?), *Face Value* offers an intriguing proposition: that race is a mask that is in some sense performative.

A complex politics of reception was at work during the production of the play. *Face Value* was slated to open on Broadway in March 1993. Producers took it on the road to Boston, where it opened in February to dismal reviews and small houses (due no doubt to the combination of the reviews and winter storms). The play went into previews on Broadway in March, and—in view of audience reaction, poor box-office performance, and the artistic and production team's assessments—*Face Value* closed before it officially opened. Whatever one makes of the success of the production as a theatrical/artistic endeavor (since I did not see the production, my remarks are based on a reading of the text alone) the politics of this chilly reception suggest that Hwang had touched a nerve about race.

The Boston press coverage confirms this suspicion. Kevin Kelly of the *Boston Globe* wrote, "*Face Value* illuminates very little. It proves as *shrill as its real-life stimulus* [my emphasis]. Worse, for all the intensity of its message, it's labored and unfunny." Whether or not the play was "labored and unfunny," the phrase that resonates with political significance is "shrill." For those whose stake is continued oppressive racial representation, both the *Miss Saigon* protests and Hwang's play were forms of political critique. One wonders whether the critic's less than complimentary appraisal of the *Miss Saigon* disputes affected his reading of *Face Value*. Furthermore, audience nervousness around race may indicate that a farce about race, especially by a person of color, may be too unsettling at this historical juncture. Hwang opined that audiences, both in Boston and on Broadway, were unsure whether or not it was all right to laugh. This nervousness and uncertainty are not uncommon in the mainstream reception of work by people of color: Jessica Hagedorn and Han Ong's collaborative work *Airport Music* at the Berkeley Repertory Theater is one recent example that comes to mind.[8] In such instances, racial critique from people of color can provoke guilt. Perhaps it is especially disturbing when that critique comes from Asian Americans. Hwang tells of a white woman in the audience who proclaimed her shock that *Asian Americans* were raising issues of racism (1994). She clearly viewed Asian Americans as model minorities, assuming that racism for us is no longer an issue. Her anger/guilt/doubt/surprise may have been shared by many members of the audience.

Hwang stated that he intends to rework the play as a comedy of manners in the style of Molière, rather than its present incarnation as a physical farce. The delicacy and nuance of comedies of manners may yield more fruitful ways of coming to terms with the prickly issues of race. However, the broad parody of the lyrics to *The Real Manchu* also allows us to see the absurdity of hackneyed anti-Asian tropes:

JESSICA AND CHORUS
Don't get sentimental
he's a crafty Oriental
he's inscrutable
CHORUS
(You know his conscience is gone)

JESSICA
He's inscrutable
CHORUS
'Cuz he comes from Canton
JESSICA
He's inscrutable
CHORUS
(And he hates women's rights)
He's Fu-u-u—
ALL
Cruel yet transcendental
He's a crafty Oriental
CHORUS
He's inscrutable
JESSICA
(You know, he's greedy and brown)
CHORUS
He's inscrutable
JESSICA
And he's bound for your town
CHORUS
He's inscrutable
JESSICA
(You can't read him at all)
CHORUS
He's inscrutable
JESSICA
'Cuz his eyes are so small
ALL
He's Fu
Fu Manchu
JESSICA
Gesundheit!
CHORUS
Fu Manchu!
JESSICA
God bless you!
. . . .
BERNARD
   Ni hao mah
   I come from land so far
   I'm Fu
   That's spelled F-U to you . . .

> Those foolish whites don't know . . .
> I will soon rule their land . . .
> I'll buy Miss USA
> And ship her to Japan   (*Act I, Scene 4*)

Here, Hwang lampoons a panoply of pernicious stereotypes of Asians, particularly Asian and Asian American men: Oriental despotism and its correlative, Oriental patriarchy; inscrutability; lust for white women; and stereotypical characteristics, such as slanted eyes and unpronounceable or nonsensical names. The Yellow Peril, Japanese invasion, and Fu Manchu's will to world domination are invoked and rearticulated in the register of parody. Taken to an extreme, the stereotypes seem at once ludicrous and hilarious. Here, farce works as a tool of deconstructive critique.

Finally, *Face Value* elaborates the leitmotiv of Hwang's work: the fluidity of identity. While *F.O.B.* treats the shift from the mythic to the mundane and *M. Butterfly* thematizes shifting gender and sexual identities, in *Face Value* and Hwang's one-act, *Bondage*, it is race that shifts and changes. These later plays suggest that race, too, is performative, but there are limits to its fluidity. For example, in the last three plays, a dramatic unmasking occurs, revealing a truer self whose vulnerabilities are thereby exposed. This suggests that shifting identity is not simply a free play; rather, certain identities are socially and culturally constructed and their borders patrolled. They cannot simply be jettisoned. Though Hwang's ideas are still in formation as *Face Value* is rewritten, his interventions around race are provocative and invite further reflection on performances of race and on race as a performative.

Chinese-Hawaiian gay performance artist Ken Choy takes up the battle with dominant cultural representations on multiple levels. He deploys satire as a political tool in his performance art, and he was among the organizers of the *Miss Saigon* interventions in the Twin Cities. Trained at the University of California at Irvine and performing in Los Angeles out of Highways Performance Space, Choy lived in Minneapolis after winning a Jerome Playwriting Fellowship and stayed some two years before returning to Los Angeles. His performance piece *Buzz Off, Butterfly*, is a series of vignettes loosely connected by a narrative about the plight of performance artist Ken Chow, who shuttles between unsupportive parents and uncomprehending grant agencies. Many episodes articulate the poignancy of self-Orientalizing Asian Americans who engage in versions of Bhabha's "mimicry," including a young Asian American who wants to be Chuck Norris's son, or "Ken Markewitz," an Asian American who thinks is

Jewish, or, in "Ode to a Butterfly," an Asian American gay man who literally becomes a butterfly, wings and all. Choy begins cocooned in diaphanous white, complaining about his Midwestern, beer-guzzling, chest-haired, dominatrix white male lover, to whom Ken must play Butterfly. "Why," Choy asks, "have I become a classified ad?" adding, "Subservience. . . Ain't it grand." As the piece progresses, the character becomes more and more defensive of that subservience, acquiring first one wing, then another.

Buzz Off, Butterfly thematizes the colonizing of the minds, bodies, and lives of Asian Americans. Choy quite clearly stated to me his intentions in the piece; he means to depict someone who is deluded and who through that delusion becomes in fact insane. The last word is eloquent here. *Buzz Off, Butterfly* ends with a spectacular display of Choy's wacky performative energy in a hilarious and disturbing explosion of epithets entitled "The Angriest Asian in the World." The "angriest Asian" represents for me the inevitable outcome when subaltern people succumb to the seductions of mimicking the dominant. Indeed, Choy has explicitly invoked his anger as a source of creative inspiration: "I'm very issue-oriented so issues make me angry. So, I find something I'm very angry about and that stirs something inside me and I try to think of an unusual and unique way of presenting that" (Sigmund 1992).

Choy's work leads us outside the text, to consider issues beyond the levels of representation, including venue and the genre of performance art as a contestatory practice. My intent is not to erect a binarism between performance art and "conventional" theater; rather, I want to point out the different levels at which these genres can operate and at which they can be appraised. Choy premiered these pieces at Highways, a gay/lesbian and multiracial performance space founded by Tim Miller (one of the "NEA Four"), among others. His work highlights the importance of venue; for example, Highways has fostered senses of community for gays and lesbians and people of color, nurturing a host of young artists, including Choy. Equally pivotal, Highways-sponsored performances give space, time, and voice to different racial and sexual communities; for instance, *Buzz Off, Butterfly* was part of an annual series of Asian American performance and visual art, "Treasure in the House," curated by Dan Kwong and Dylan Tranh.

In formal terms, work like *Buzz Off, Butterfly* operates against naturalistic conventions. For example, the genre often depends upon an episodic structure that disrupts notions of the well-made play and linear narrative. Moreover, there is for the performer an accessibility to performance art that refuses the requirements of spectacular theatricality—or overproduction, depending on one's perspective. The material requirements are minimal: a body; a voice; perhaps a few clothes—or none; a few lights; perhaps some music, perhaps not; and stories based on personal experiences. The result can be an intimacy of theme, form, and practice that allows access to many who might otherwise be prevented from telling their stories. Similarly, for an audience a smaller venue like Highways is a far more intimate experience of spectatorship than witnessing the proscenium stage at a Broadway theater. There can be a kind of empowering accessibility about a piece like *Buzz Off, Butterfly* in such a setting.

The interventions I have described use different genres—mainstream theater and drama, on the one hand, performance art, on the other—and are directed at somewhat different audiences. Broadway's overwhelmingly white, mainstream, and upper-middle-class clientele constitutes one key site of intervention. The presence in mainstream venues of work by people on the margins is crucial in terms of interrupting the pleasures of spectacle, of the familiar (and often racist or sexist) revival, of uncontested racial stereotypes, of easily digestible entertainment that serves only to confirm the audience's prejudices. Performance art like the Ken Choy piece and the series of which it was a part occurs in smaller, more intimate venues offering accessibility to artists and to educated, middle-class audiences, including gays, lesbians, and people of color. Whatever the venue, these productions must be set within an increasingly vibrant Asian American performance scene, the national sea change David Mura invokes. Creating Asian American culture becomes a way to write our faces and, in the process, to rewrite the contemporary meanings of race.

TRADE WARS AND CORPORATE SOLDIERS

If the *Madama Butterfly* trope in its many guises continues to circulate as a mechanism for the continued oppression of Asian American women and gay men, then the contemporary straight male counterpart is the Japanese businessman. He is a corporate soldier, an automaton whose polite demeanor conceals a samurai spirit devoted to the company and to the nation. Feeding fears of a "Japanese invasion" and "takeover," he is among the most salient Orientalist stereotypes in the contemporary American imaginary. Nowhere was this trope more visibly circulated than in the novel and the film *Rising Sun*. Both have provoked considerable controversy among Asian American communities and caused consternation among progressive American scholars of Asia.

Rising Sun imparts an ominous sense of the impending threat to American autonomy posed by Japanese business. From the outset, it establishes familiar terms of discourse rooted in essentialist national identities: the U.S. and Japan as two separate and distinct nations/races, whose ways of life are opposed and mutually hostile. The specter of "trade wars" so familiar from the American news media looms in the book from the opening aphorisms. The first is attributed to an American, Phillip Sanders, who is allowed a proper name: "We are entering a world where the old rules no longer apply." Underneath we read, "Business is war," a "Japanese motto." Note that no specificity or individuality is allowed the Japanese characters. Is this a particular company? An individual? Or is it, as the attribution suggests, a motto familiar to all Japanese, a clarion call to which an entire nation responds? These epigrams introduce the tone and the themes of the book: the word of individual American warning precedes the bald statement of collective Japanese martial intentions.

Set in Los Angeles, *Rising Sun* introduces us to narrator/protagonist Smith, a special-services liaison officer and a police lieutenant who is called upon to investigate a murder in the new headquarters of the Nakamoto Corporation on the gala opening-night festivities. Veteran John Connor, an "expert on Japanese culture," acts as Smith's adviser on "Japanese customs," in the manner of a hunter instructing a neophyte on how to deal with wild animals: "Control your gestures. Keep your hands at your sides. The Japanese find big arm movements threatening. Speak slowly. Keep your voice calm and even" (15). Such passages have the effect of creating Connor's authoritative voice—the we-know-them-better-than-they-know-themselves Orientalism is striking here—and solidifies the impression of Japan as an alien Other, imbued with an unfamiliar essence that can be comprehended only through professional translation and mediation.

Rising Sun trumpets a wake-up call to Americans, alerting them to the pervasiveness of the Japanese threat and advocating a response in kind, lest America "turn Japanese." Indeed, the book represents the U.S. as engaged in a battle for its very existence as an autonomous nation. To fend off this enemy, the first step is precisely to recognize Japanese efficiency. For example, a Black man who works monitoring the security cameras in the Nakamoto Towers describes his family's experiences working in Japanese auto factories and in the old GM plant. American practices were slipshod and inefficient; overpaid, arrogant,

241

and ignorant management imperiously gave nonsensical orders to production workers, while "the Japanese" collaborated with line workers to solve problems. "I tell you: *these people pay attention*" (45).[9]

The Japanese threat to American autonomy is all the more formidable because—in addition to their efficiency—they are ineffably strange, engaging in practices "we" would label unethical or inconsistent. Here Connor patrols the borders of essentialized cultural and racial difference. His pseudo-social scientific pronouncements about Japanese behavior attest to the deeply alien nature of the economic enemy. (This passage might have been based in part on my own *Crafting Selves*, which discusses, among other things, shifting and contextually constructed identity in Japan.) Crichton embellishes this notion to create a transposed version of the sneaky, crafty Oriental through the term "inconsistency," though this is not a term used in my book. The Japanese of *Rising Sun* seem all the more dangerous because their inconsistency—hence inscrutability—is located in cultural norms.

> "It's annoying," Connor said. "But you see, Ishigura takes a different view. Now that he is beside the mayor, he sees himself in another context, with another set of obligations and requirements for his behavior. Since he is sensitive to context, he's able to act differently, with no reference to his earlier behavior. To us, he seems like a different person. But Ishigura feels he's just being appropriate . . .
>
> Because for a Japanese, consistent behavior is not possible. A Japanese becomes a different person around people of different rank. He becomes a different person when he moves through different rooms of his own house."
>
> "Yeah," I said. "That's fine, but the fact is he's a lying son of a bitch."
>
> Connor looked at me. "Would you talk that way to your mother?"
>
> "Of course not."
>
> "So you change according to context, too," Connor said. "The fact is that we all do. It's just that Americans believe that there is some core of individuality that doesn't change from one moment to the next. And the Japanese believe context rules everything" (54).

Perhaps Crichton, himself the possessor of an anthropology degree, wanted to render this "social scientific" analysis in an evenhanded way. But the passage describes "the Japanese" as a monolithic whole, incapable of consistency, prone to lie in American terms. This "the Japanese" may do not out of pernicious individual intent, but because their "culture" deems such behavior to be normative. Blame here then rests at the level of culture. The subtle implication is that such cultural norms could be even more insidious precisely because they shape the behavior of individual Japanese, imbuing Japan as a whole with a proclivity for what we would, at best, call inconsistency, and which would strike most of "us" as "lying." And because it is posited as an immutable cultural essence, such behavior is by implication virtually incorrigible.

"The Japanese" become even more deeply, ineffably Other as we make further discoveries about "their" sexual practices. The dead blonde is the mistress of playboy Eddie Sakamura, who kept her in an apartment complex with other call girls. The specter of Japanese conquest through the seduction of white women looms here. One of them invokes the well-worn stereotype of bizarre sexuality as the flip side of the "polite" Japanese veneer:

> "And to them," she said, "their wishes, their desires, it's just as natural as leaving the tip . . . I mean, I don't mind a little golden shower or whatever, handcuffs, you know. Maybe a little spanking if I like the guy. But I won't let anybody cut me. I don't care how much money. *None of those things with knives or swords (my emphasis)*. A lot of them, they are so polite, so correct, but then they get turned on, they have this. . . this *way*. . ." She broke off, shaking her head. "They're strange people" (64).

Rising Sun thus recirculates the hackneyed trope of the polite, conventional, repressed Japanese businessman, who conceals a penchant for the sadistic, a notion I have criticized elsewhere (1984). The reference to swords, laughable were it not invoked so seriously, signals a transhistorical Oriental despotism emergent in "their" conquest of "our" women and metaphorically, "our" country. Surely, Crichton suggests, this same cruelty fuels Japanese dedication to the economic wars.

This crafty Other has succeeded in infiltrating the top echelons of "our" government and business. Geopolitical intrigue heightens through a plot element introducing trade negotiations between the Nakamoto Corporation and a U. S. firm. The Senate Finance Committee is holding hearings on the issue, and its chair, we discover, made love with the dead call girl on the boardroom table before her murder. Clearly, Crichton is drawing a picture of a Senate and government riddled by politicians beholden to the Japanese, who are figured as the foreign presence that has penetrated the national body on multiple levels.

Such a penetration is particularly degrading and to be feared when it involves races like "the Japanese," who are troped as alien and as fundamentally less worthy than "we." Connor's authoritative pronouncements explicitly thematize race; here he puts the Japanese in their place while attributing racism to *their* cultural proclivities, not to his own characterizations.

"The Japanese think everybody who is not Japanese is a barbarian. . . . They're polite about it, because they know you can't help the misfortune of not being born Japanese. But they still think it. . . . The Japanese are extremely success-ful, but they are not daring. They are plotters and plodders" (196).

Uttered in Connor's voice, these derogatory statements have an authoritative ring. The Japanese may have the upper hand now, but clearly all is not lost. "They" are, after all, merely "plodders"—hardworking but uncreative, suc-cessful only because of their dedication to work and their devious business practices. Representing "them" as clannish and endowed with a racist superi-ority complex, Connor not so subtly allows us to counter by asserting "our" own superiority.[10]

Racial discourses are amplified with the introduction of Smith's romantic interest: the beautiful, half-Black, half-Japanese computer whiz, Theresa Asakuma, who simultaneously embodies the exotic-erotic and the computer-nerd stereotypes. She analyzes the doctored tapes that erroneously depict the murderer as playboy Eddie Sakamura; her zeal is driven by revenge for the dis-crimination she experienced while growing up in Japan, both as someone of mixed race and as someone with a physical disability. Again, Japanese racism makes American racism pale in comparison:

You Americans do not know in what grace your land exists. What freedom you enjoy in your hearts. You cannot imagine the harshness of life in Japan, if you are excluded from the group. But I know it very well. And I do not mind if the Japanese suffer a little now, from my efforts with my *one good hand* (261).

Though one could hardly make an argument for Japan as a multiracial utopia, and though oppressive forms of racial, caste, and other forms of discrimina-tion undeniably exist, the matter is considerably more complex. For example, John Russell writes eloquently on the racial formations shaping various Japanese responses and tropings of African Americans, which he argues were mediated through the West (1991). This level of complexity never enters Connor's analysis.

Connor neatly preempts any attempt to problematize American racism when he invokes the Chrysanthemum Kissers, academics who kowtow to Japanese con-tacts lest their sources of information disappear. "Anybody who criticizes Japan is a racist" (204). In *any* fieldwork situation—no matter where it might be—relationships are crucial, but the assertions Connor makes are simply unfounded. Criticizing Japan is not the problem—no nation is beyond criticism—but those criticisms must always be appraised on multiple levels: the tropes they engage, the analyst's positioning in a geopolitical matrix, and subject's stake in that critique. Rather than coming to terms with his own positioning, Crichton's character merely provides a convenient justification for American racisms. For Connor, racism lies at the level of individual prejudice, rather than with larger systemic inequality.[11] He fails to recognize that his experiences of "racism" reflect partial—and only partial—loss of white male privilege. As Said would argue, he confronts Japan as first and foremost a white male citizen of a country accustomed to dominating world geopolitics in this century, and that legacy endures, despite a changing geopolitical/economic order.

At stake throughout *Rising Sun* is a white *masculine* subjectivity that must preserve its boundaries at all costs. Threats to the dominance and to the integrity of the boundaries of such an identity proliferate, and in the face of such threats, this subjectivity must eschew an infantilizing, feminizing dependence on others. For example, according to Connor, America has gone wrong by underestimating the formidable Japanese threat to "our" autonomy through "our" debilitating dependence on Japanese capital. This theme is transposed into the "drunken uncle" metaphor when he tells Smith of meetings various Japanese industrialists held in Los Angeles, ostensibly to determine the fate of the U. S. Smith is indignant, but Connor replies:

> Do you want to take over Japan? Do you want to run their country? Of course not. No sensible country wants to take over another country. Do business, yes. Have a relationship, yes. But not take over. Nobody wants the responsibility. Nobody wants to be bothered. Just like with the drunken uncle—you only have those meetings when you're forced to. It's a last resort (193).

On the one hand, this passage supports Connor's own self-presentation as eschewing Japan-bashing for an approach that is critical of the U.S. Yet this seeming even-handedness cannot mask a preoccupation with restoring American masculinity to its "rightful" dominance. The drunken uncle is an adult who should be authoritative, responsible, and in control—but his lack of control elicits caretaking efforts from, presumably, a nephew (the subjects presumed in the book are always already masculine). The uncle is lacking in masculine authority and ideally must be restored to his proper, responsible, *senior* position. The desire to reinstate white American men as global leaders animates the allegory.

The novel closes in a symphonic orchestration of stereotypes, with "business-as-war" the leitmotiv. And the viciousness of the war exacts many casualties.

Internally, competition among *keiretsu* is associated with the torture and the death of Eddie Sakamura, whose father's company belongs to a rival of the Nakamoto *keiretsu*. The merciless Ishigura is revealed as the killer of the blonde woman, for she is merely a pawn in the plot to blackmail Senator Morton into changing his views on the MicroCon sale. Like a good corporate samurai, Ishigura then jumps off the terrace to his death in order to spare himself and his company the shame of his crime. With heavy-handed symbolism, he is engulfed in cement, immolated in the foundations of the building owned by the company to which he had devoted his life. Predictably, Orientalist stereotypes and the demands of narrative closure dictate that he will commit suicide.

This very predictability becomes the source of our pleasure as readers, and here the politics of pleasure must be interrogated. Crichton is a master of his genre. It is no surprise that *Rising Sun* was a bestseller. He adeptly deploys the techniques of the whodunit to keep the reader turning the pages: breathless pacing, cliffhanger chapter endings, clever plot twists. Even readers like myself who were predisposed to be critical can be drawn in—for we want to know *who committed the murder*. Here, genre conventions create suspense, providing the seductive tease and the satisfying resolution. Mainstream audiences can pleasurably encounter Orientalist stereotypes that are sufficiently attentive to historical context to be familiar yet different. The Orientalist stereotypes have the ring of authenticity, rearticulating all-too-familiar martial metaphors extant since before the Pacific War.[12] Crichton masterfully orchestrates these pleasures in a riveting narrative—hence its heightened insidiousness.

How more precisely does that insidiousness operate? First, the book firmly reinscribes national, racial, and cultural essentialisms; such processes have never been more problematic than in this era of transnational capitalism. Certainly, the suggestion that the U.S.—or any other major economic power—has been an innocent in geopolitical terms seems disingenuous at best. The presumption of a nation-state based form of capitalism fails to account for the presence of multinational capital and for the economic interpenetrations of the economies of multiple nation-states. In an era of global flows of information, technology, and capital, where does the Japanese economy end, where does the American one begin? What does the invocation of these national essences reveal and obscure? And what is at stake in this essence fabrication?

Second, because *Rising Sun* is written from a site of embattled U. S. white masculinity, Crichton's characters' aggressive reassertion of national, cultural, and racial essence occurs at a moment when that identity is on the verge of being deposed from its accustomed site of privilege. Inevitably, the threat to masculine dominance is sexualized and gendered. In *Rising Sun*, the transgressive threat of penetration comes from an alien and formerly "inferior" feminized Other. In the novel and film *Disclosure*, Crichton writes a similar scenario, but this time the threat is the femme fatale: the sexually voracious, power-hungry woman executive who uses every conceivable strategy, including accusations of sexual harassment, to "fuck" both literally and figuratively the male protagonist. In the film, Michael Douglas adds to his body of work performing threatened white masculinity, this time fending off the advances of, and finally outwitting, his former lover/boss/corporate adversary Demi Moore. In *Rising Sun* and in *Disclosure*, Crichton articulates the anxieties of white men who must patrol the boundaries of their essential identities to remain on top, for above all, they must *avoid being fucked*—by women, by the Japanese. In this way, Crichton brilliantly captures the sense of white male outrage and loss represented in the recent attacks on affirmative action and the anti-immigrant sentiment of California's Proposition 187. Riding the Zeitgeist, he has created seductive blockbuster entertainment that clearly touches a national nerve at a moment of historical transition.

The publication of *Rising Sun* raised consternation and protest among Asian Americans and scholars of Asia, who raised the kinds of arguments I have outlined here. Crichton staunchly denied allegations of Japan-bashing, arguing that he was, if anything, "America-bashing." Though the book is indeed critical of present American business practices, one could hardly label Crichton a basher. Further, his presumed bashing is deployed in order to resecure the dominance of white masculinity as it confronts the threat of infantilization, penetration, and feminization. The criticisms of the U.S. aim to restore us to "our rightful position" of global leadership, while criticisms of Japan construct an alien, hostile enemy through the circulation of numbingly familiar racial images of despotism, bizarre sexuality, cruelty, inconsistency, inscrutability, and a self-immolating devotion to work.

Critical reaction among American scholars of Japan and among Asian Americans was immediate. Crichton, a Harvard alumnus, was a member of the Visiting Committee for the Department of Social Anthropology at Harvard and is a member of the Harvard Board of Overseers. Robert J. Smith of Cornell, an eminent anthropologist of Japan, resigned his position from the Visiting Committee when he read *Rising Sun* and distributed the letter of resignation to scholars of Japan, including myself. In it, Smith decried the racist representations of Japan

in the book, saying that he had dedicated his life to combatting these very stereotypes. Among the local interventions in Los Angeles, historian of Japan Miriam
Silverberg gathered scholars of Japan to critique the book. Asian American
groups across the country gathered to protest the racist depictions of Japan represented in the novel.

Responding to criticisms from Asian Americans, several changes were
incorporated when the book was made into a film. The most obvious is the race
of the perpetrator: the murderer in the film is a white Nakamoto employee.
However, the racial alteration from Japanese to white is only marginally better.
Indeed, it appears at least equally insidious, for the Japanese thereby prove
successful in infiltrating, even "brainwashing," Americans who will collaborate
with them. The language of war is inescapable.

Further, the casting of actor Wesley Snipes, an African American actor, as
Smith sets up a complex discourse around race given the media attention
accorded to Black/Asian, and specifically, Black/Korean, tensions. (In the
novel, Smith is racially unmarked.) It shows the inadvertent naiveté or the cal-
culating cynicism of the filmmakers around race, for selecting Snipes has a
divide-and-conquer function: the filmmakers can claim they are not racist
because they have introduced an African American character; this in turn
gives them license to reproduce various pernicious Asian stereotypes. Yet
Snipes is not allowed to escape his position of subordination as a man of color;
he is allowed to challenge Connery's veneer of authority, but he cannot go too
far. For example, at one point, Snipes jokes defiantly that Connery is acting like
a "massa," which is indeed accurate. Yet the filmmakers fail to recognize that
simply calling attention to the authority of the white man over people and cultures of color does not depose that authority. Snipes is still junior to Connery;
Connery provides the brains, while Snipes is there mostly for the ride.

Given the plot changes and the change in the race of the perpetrator, several well-known Asian American scholars with whom I spoke considered the
film version of *Rising Sun* to be far more innocuous than the novel. With this
expectation in mind, I went to the movie and found myself reeling in horror. It
took me some time to recover from what I found to be a highly disturbing experience. Cinema's powerful materiality, the use of image and sound, created the
palpable presence of an ominous Japanese threat that begins from the first
frames. A red rising sun flashes onto screen to the refrain of insistent, relentless drumming, much like the relentless Japanese threat the film will present
to us. The dark cinematography, the sleek, monolithic black tower, the images

of Los Angeles in the rain, create a high-tech vision reminiscent of *Blade Runner* and *Black Rain*. The director creates a cold, cruel, hyperefficient Japanese world that evoked for me Vincent Chin and Japanese American internment.

The film vividly recirculates other stereotypes not present in the book. Oriental decadence and the colonizing of the white female body by the alien other is depicted on screen through Eddie's use of a nude blonde woman's body as a table laden with sushi, which he picks from her stomach as he reclines with his harem on a large bed. Stan Egi portrays Ishigura, but the costumers and makeup artists have dressed him in an ill-fitting, cheap-looking suit, with slicked-down hair. An unflattering picture to say the least, this costuming choice contributes to the sleazy Oriental stereotype and would hardly be appropriate in a high-powered Japanese corporate setting. Furthermore, Egi is clearly directed to play the character as unappetizingly obsequious; though his actions are far too exaggerated for an actual Japanese, he apparently fits the director's notion of a Japanese corporate soldier.

When the film opened, a public outcry arose. Media Action Network for Asian Americans (MANAA), among other organizations, and Asian American journals and newspapers decried the politics of representation in the film. MANAA had attempted to discuss the issues with Twentieth Century Fox, but "after eight months of failed negotiations, including three months of meetings canceled by Fox" (Chung 4), they decided to go public with their concerns. MANAA President Guy Aoki stressed that the organization "took the high ground," never calling for a boycott of the film. Instead, they concentrated their efforts on an educational campaign (personal interview). Picketers greeted the opening of the film in San Francisco and New York, representing coalitions of numerous Asian American political organizations (Chouy 6). According to some Asian American analysts, Twentieth Century Fox deployed divide-and-conquer tactics in their dealings with Asian Americans. On the one hand, the studio attempted to win over some Asian American journalists with all-expense-paid trips to a preview of the film and used the participation of some Asian American actors as "proof" that the film was not racist. Simultaneously, people with Asian American names were excluded from attending Los Angeles-based previews of film; when they called back with other surnames, they were admitted to the screenings (Muto 9). The protests led to a delay in the film's release in Japan, where it lost revenue. Though Twentieth Century Fox never made an effort to work with Asian American groups on the issue of representation, the activism and educational efforts of Asian Americans meant that the pernicious

249

racialisms did not go uncontested, and that Asian American organizations joined together in coalition, in an important enactment of solidarity.[13]

Finally, it seems appropriate to clarify my stakes in this critique of *Rising Sun*. At the end of his book, Crichton appends a bibliography, citing works that he found helpful and consulted while he wrote the novel. My book *Crafting Selves* is on this list. Paradoxically, my aims were antithetical to his: to deploy a strategic humanism that would involve in part the fundamental problematizing of the term "the Japanese." After deliberating on the matter, however, one could attribute such a reading to the strategic essentialisms common in interpretivist and other strains of cultural anthropology that invoke "culture" at the level of language, custom, practice. These strategic essentialisms can be deployed for various ends. In my case, the aim was critique of dominant American concepts—in particular, the monadic, bounded "self" or "whole subject"—in order to further anti-racist and feminist struggle in the United States. For Crichton, descriptions of language and cultural practice can be appropriated for different ends: to further buttress American superiority. On the one hand, this misappropriation could be seen as a risk inherent in any form of explanation that invokes "culture." Armed with a degree in anthropology Crichton can convincingly exaggerate the boundedness of "culture" for his novelistic ends.

Yet perhaps the issue of appropriation is more general. As I learned during my stint as a dramaturge for Anna Deavere Smith's *Twilight: Los Angeles 1992*, based on the bristling histories and tensions that fueled the L. A. uprisings/riots/civil unrest, the work of critics or artists is inevitably interpreted in unanticipated ways. Despite our best dramaturgical efforts to anticipate audience readings of the politics of racial representation, someone always came up with a completely surprising reaction. *Twilight* foregrounded for me the salience of the intentional fallacy, for authorial/dramaturgical intention could never guarantee meaning. In the case of Crichton's reading of my book, the intentional fallacy seems all the more fallacious, for authorial intention not only failed to guarantee meaning, but the text generated meanings antithetical to authorial intent. Once released in language, the subject-positions, histories, and (structurally overdetermined) interpretive schemas of readers and audiences shape reception. We can but do our best to anticipate certain overdetermined misreadings and preempt them, taking seriously authorial responsibility and attempting to do battle with the misappropriations of our work. In the case of a highly popular film and novel such as *Rising Sun*, the stakes are even more urgent. We must continue to challenge the highly resilient structures of racism and male dominance that fuel the recirculation of subjugating discourses such as Orientalism.

THE MIKADO AND INSTITUTIONAL INTERVENTION

The material effects of critiques of representation might seem to be distant from our everyday lives, especially for those of us in the academy. Most obviously, the politics of representation reverberate in the entertainment and culture industries, and on intangible levels we would call psychological. I contend, however, that taking the politics of representation seriously can have *institutional* impact—even in the academy. I argued in my first essay for the profound and potentially transformative effects of feminist and minority discourse. I end this discussion of art and politics with an account of a local intervention around a performance of Gilbert and Sullivan's *The Mikado* at the Claremont Colleges. My narrative figures the *Mikado* protest as a pivotal event within a history of activism and protest that led to greater institutional recognition of Asian Americans at the Colleges. It serves to instantiate successful attempts at political coalition. My perspective is that of a central organizer of the protest; hence, it is both partial and inevitably celebratory. It is a story that will no doubt always remain beyond the bounds of official institutional history.

In September 1990 I had just arrived at Pomona as a newly tenured faculty member and was busily trying to acquaint myself with the new campus. While going through my mail one day, I noticed a listing of coming events at our large auditorium, which we call "Big Bridges." The season was to commence with a performance of Gilbert and Sullivan's *The Mikado*. I groaned inwardly as I looked at the listing. Not again. The last production of *The Mikado* I remembered was in Boston, where the Emperor's Court had metamorphosed into a Japanese company populated by Japanese businessmen, conjoining the Oriental despot trope with that of the corporate soldier. Not again—facing the situation that women, people of color, gays, and lesbians face all too often when oppressive stereotypes recirculate in forms that the dominant considers harmless fun. And as in all such occasions, one must decide what to do. Make a fuss? So much effort, and I just got here. Let it go? Then I would hate myself for being the "silent Asian" who allows an egregious event to slip by without a whisper of protest.

Supportive colleagues and allies eased my dilemma. Historian Samuel Yamashita intended that his students write a critique of the event. But after

251

speaking with Yamashita and other colleagues of color, including Deena González, Sid Lemelle, Ray Buriel, Ruth Gilmore, Lynne Miyake, and Sue Houchins, the possibility of larger collective action emerged. The faculty and staff of color organized ourselves into a consortium-wide "Coalition of the International Majority/National Minority," which rallied around *The Mikado* issue and provided a forum to deal with issues of significance for the faculty, staff, and students of color. The coalition deemed the politics of representation in *The Mikado* to be highly offensive, and its selection as an appropriate form of entertainment at our major auditorium signified the systematic marginalization of Asian American issues at the Claremont Colleges. Despite yearly proposals from Asian American students for an Asian American Studies program and an Asian American Resource Center, and despite the precedent of Chicano Studies and Black Studies programs dating from the 1960s, comprising both academic and student services branches, Pomona College and the other Claremont Colleges continued to ignore the needs of Asian American students. During the graduation ceremony just before my arrival, faculty, students, and the one Asian American trustee sympathetic to Asian American issues had worn yellow armbands in protest and provoked the wrath of the administration, but this had elicited no concrete response. Many of us thought this marginalization of Asian American issues to be linked with the "model minority" stereotype: that Asian Americans are quiet and docile, and hence will not cause trouble; that we don't need "special programs" because we've "made it"; that racism has no bearing on our lives. Given the years of administrative non-response, it seemed high time to forego politeness and make some noise.

For *The Mikado*'s opening night, the Coalition of the International Majority decided to hold a demonstration outside the auditorium. Once the performance began, we would conduct a teach-in and counterperformance at the student ballroom. We mobilized student groups of color, Women's Studies, the gay and lesbian organizations, and sympathetic groups of faculty and staff. Outside the campus, we contacted members of the Asian American artist/activist organization APACE (Asian Pacific Alliance for Creative Equality) that had formed around the *Miss Saigon* controversy. We alerted the media, distributed flyers, and prepared presentations.

I wrote an analysis of the politics of representation of the play, which we then circulated to the faculty and staff of color and to other potentially sympathetic colleagues, giving versions at the teach-in preceding opening night and at the teach-in/counterperformance. The piece singled out the problematic

Orientalist tropes that permeate the text: nonsensical and offensive renderings of Chinese (not Japanese) names, Oriental exoticism and despotism, Oriental proclivities for suicide, and Oriental women as either submissive lotus blossoms or witch-like dragon ladies. Anticipating objections, I took issue with predictable responses to our critique: that *The Mikado* is a cultural classic; that it is simply a satire; that Gilbert and Sullivan were "really" writing about England. I argued that in the light of work by feminist scholars of music and opera such as Catherine Clément, we must ask: for whom is *The Mikado* a cultural classic? Further, in this instance "satire" merely excuses the continued circulation of racist and sexist tropes. In this regard, the choice of Japan as the setting for this satire was overdetermined given the contemporary discourses of Orientalism and Britain's imperialist project. Finally, the choice to stage *The Mikado* at the Colleges effectively preempted the performances of Asian American plays written and performed by Asian Americans, echoing an institutional history that had failed to confront Asian American issues.

Several other faculty provided their cogent perspectives at a teach-in preceding the protest. Samuel Yamashita described Britain's imperialist project at the moment Gilbert and Sullivan penned *The Mikado*. Jennifer Rycenga, a feminist scholar of religion and music, analyzed the Orientalist motifs of the music itself. Theater professor Leonard Pronko presented another point of view, raising the anticipated objections.

The evening of the performance became an emblematic, inspirational moment when coalition politics appeared to fulfill its promise. Hundreds of faculty and students assembled at the Office of Black Student Affairs. From there we walked, phalanxes of people of many colors, to the auditorium, shouting and chanting all the while. One phrase was especially memorable: "El Mikado *es un pecado*," "*The Mikado* is a sin." The demonstration continued in front of the auditorium while we picketed, passed out leaflets, and chanted our protests. When the performance began, we adjourned to the student ballroom.

The teach-in continued for three hours. The faculty repeated and embellished their remarks from the previous teach-in. Samuel Yamashita retold a poignant story starkly revealing the links between Orientalist representations of Asia and Asian American lives. When he taught at a small liberal arts college in upstate New York, each December 7 (Pearl Harbor Day) his car would be trashed—probably by members of the fraternity that held an annual "kamikaze" party every year on that date. Eventually, Yamashita took to hiding his car in the yard of a Jewish colleague.

A group of actors from APACE had driven from Los Angeles to the Colleges to lend their support. Their presence linked our local intervention to larger issues of Asian American representation, and a buzz of excitement accompanied their arrival. Representations of Asians and Asian Americans are clearly of critical salience to actors, who must decide whether or not they can in good conscience play certain kinds of roles. In particular, artists Kim Miyori, Natsuko Ohama, Steve Park, Tzi Ma, and Rosalind Chao spoke of the *Miss Saigon* casting controversy and the importance of continued activism on the part of Asian Americans around issues of representation. Their presence highlighted for us *The Mikado*'s exclusionary gesture that constituted effective silencing of three-dimensional Asian American portrayals in works authored by Asian Americans.

Alliance across different groups, then, became a critically important consequence of the protest. APACE extended our struggle beyond the Colleges, but equally important were local solidarities among people of color and campus progressives. The support of the Office of Black Student Affairs and the Black Studies faculty, the Chicano Studies faculty, and students and staff of color was indispensable to our efforts. Indeed, at the close of the teach-in, the president of the Pan African Student Association rousingly invoked our common struggles around race, culminating in a scathing satire of the Claremont University Center administration. I ended the teach-in with a call-response with the audience, the power of coalition vibrant and alive as we joined together to denounce racist representation and to work for institutional change.

I can venture only an educated guess as to the real impact of *The Mikado* protest. The Deans subsequently began discussions with the Asian American faculty about establishing an Asian American Resource Center. We advertised and interviewed candidates for Director during the spring, and by the following year a fledgling center was inaugurated. Though others might tell a different story, I see the *The Mikado* protest as a critical event that, in combination with years of proposals, petitionings, and graduation protests, helped pave the way for a still fledgling Asian American Resource Center, discussions with Asian American and Asianist faculty around Asian American Studies, and funding for an Asian American Performance Art series. More hires at Pomona and at other colleges are continuing in the Asian American fields, and we hope to establish a Five-College Asian American Studies Department.

From the point of view of official history, though, *The Mikado* protest never happened. At the official opening of the Asian American Resource Center, the establishment of the Center was instead attributed to "student efforts" and to the foresight of the College. These might indeed be key factors. But I would argue that the groundswell of support—especially from other faculty, staff, and students of color, and from other progressive groups on campus such as Women's Studies, gay and lesbian groups, and the differently abled created a daunting coalition that could no longer be ignored.

My tale of *The Mikado*, then, is a guardedly optimistic narrative of a local intervention that speaks to the power of political alliance. Though the institutional gains seem modest—in our especially busy moments some of the Asian American faculty laugh wryly that now it means yet another committee assignment—even these modest gains might never have occurred had faculty and students not researched, lobbied, protested, and raised our voices. *The Mikado* protest foregrounds the power of political coalition and the profound stakes that Asian Americans inevitably have in representations of Asia. Local institutional interventions are one site of political change, where hegemonic representations can be contested.

For all disenfranchised people, these struggles continue daily, urgently, in multiple registers.[14] Local interventions can shift discourses, interrupting a smooth reproduction of dominant imaginaries. When we think about a cultural politics that makes a difference, we must examine their workings on multiple levels. I have suggested that Asian American artists, activists and academics have pursued different strategies of subversion, challenging the seductive pleasures of dominant narratives and using those challenges to shape institutions, hiring practices, and the production of images in the culture industries. When analyzing particular interventions, critics should take into account a multiplicity of factors. For theater and performance, these include: (1) different genres, such as mainstream theater, performance art, and conventional political action; (2) formal interventions in text, thematics, and structure; (3) the ways production and performance can generate and alter textual meaning; (4) venue; (5) audience and reception (critical, academic, mainstream, community); (6) accessibility in form, content, and price, for both the audience and the performer; (7) processes of production (rehearsal and collaboration); (8) grants and funding;[15] (9) institutional structures, as in the case of *The Mikado* and the Asian American Resource Center; (10) the formation of community and political identity.

A cultural politics that makes a difference must be animated by a willingness to locate these and other levels at which any cultural work may simultaneously reinscribe and contest. I would further argue that we must speak of opposition with precision: oppositional for whom, in what ways, under what circumstances. Equally important, these tactics of intervention must engage a notion of critical positionality, for the binaristic notion of cultural politics—resistance OR accommodation—is invariably associated with the assumption that the critic inhabits an inviolable moral space.[16] This Manichean view is better supplanted by a notion of a cultural politics that makes a difference, realizing all the while that interventions are always partial and positioned, and pristine separation or liberation from the dominant is illusory at best.

However, this should not mean that significant intervention is impossible. Far from it. For example, in theater and performance—despite the carefully controlled and limited visibility for artists from disenfranchised groups—it is nonetheless remarkable that even mainstream regional theater has become a site where, increasingly, "others" are "talking back," and that so many of the fine plays of the past few years have been written by people "on the margins," asserting the need for hope and vibrantly affirming life in the midst of daily oppression. I think of Tony Kushner's luminous *Angels in America*, José Rivera's *Marisol* and his witty, lyrical love letter to L. A., *The Street of the Sun*, or on a more interested note, Anna Deavere Smith's *Twilight: Los Angeles 1992*, where our process of multiracial collaboration recapitulated the tensions, contradictions, and utopian possibilities of life in a multiracial society. Given such interventions, I passionately resist a view that consigns all efforts at contestation to the junkheap of recuperation. Though inevitably compromised, spectacularized, and tokenized, some interventions matter.

Such interventions at all levels continue to vibrate with urgency in an historical moment marked by the resurgence of radical conservatism in its many guises. To see culture as a transcendent domain apart from the messy politics of everyday life has become a politically dangerous assumption: it leads to elitism and Eurocentric universalism, while simultaneously justifying Republican budget cuts of a domain deemed to be extraneous to the practicalities of everyday life. On the contrary, the realms of cultural production are constituted through forces such as gender, race, class, economics, politics, even as the sites of performance problematize and enact those larger abstractions. In the face of the attacks on the arts and what may be the imminent demise of affirmative action, cultural production by people on the margins becomes even more potentially contestatory and valuable. Theater, performance, and design have created spaces where Asians and Asian Americans can "write our faces," mount institutional interventions, enact emergent identities, refigure utopian possibilities, and construct political subjectivities that might enable us to effect political change.

Performing alternative visions of cultural possibility on stage, on the runway, or on the streets may not in itself force an about-face of the advancing conservative tide or thoroughly transform the political/discursive structures that shape our lives. But the work of the artists and designers I have discussed in these pages sketches out and performs for us utopian wish-images for gender, race, sexuality, and other dynamic forces. Perhaps they introduce us to new forms of possibility and new forms of intellectual and political intervention. For without the refiguration of the possible, there can be no social transformation; there can be no "about-face."

ENDNOTES

1. Unlike DeCerteau, I make no distinction between "strategy" and "tactics."

2. I initially submitted this version to the Editorials division at *The Los Angeles Times*, which sent it to their Counterpunch section, devoted to opinions and reactions to stories about the arts. The editor there kept my piece and apparently had decided against publishing it after two letters of protest on the opening of *Miss Saigon* appeared in the Sunday *Calendar* section. Eventually, after many delays, the essay was published at less than half its length in a section called Voices, opinions and writings from "the community," under the title "Gripe." Nothing that remotely resembled a call to action made it to print. The label "Gripe" undercut the message by individualizing and trivializing a serious *position* on an issue that was shared by many members of a community. The label casts the critical voices of people of color in terms of sheer negativity, rather than seeing the call to action and the positive political solidarity in such a critique.

3. Locally, Asian American student groups at the Claremont Colleges organized a teach-in around *Miss Saigon*, responding in part to the Colleges' use of the play as a "student activity" sponsored by various student governments. Actors Tzi Ma (who was present at the *Mikado* protest), Ping Wu, and Ken Choy participated. Larger protests in Los Angeles were muted; some leafleting occurred on opening night, but the unfortunate timing of opening night immediately after Christmas vacation and technical difficulties meant that highly visible collective action did not occur.

4. Choy has created another piece entitled *Miss Appropriated*, a collection of performances by various artists, many of whom were involved in protests around *Miss Saigon* and the performance of Puccini's *Madama Butterfly*. The program suggests a similar strategy of wild satire and subversion of stereotypes, including "Death is Our Way," lampooning the supposed Asian proclivities for suicide and brutality.

257

5. About a similar protest in New York, Yoko Yoshikawa describes eloquently the heady atmosphere animating the work of Asian Pacific gays and lesbians who sought to disrupt the Lambda Legal Defense Fund's use of *Miss Saigon* as a fundraiser. She revels in the gay and Pan-Asian character of their coalition—loving descriptions of the different kinds of food, the open physicality—that were part of their meetings, and soberly discusses their multiple marginalization in a gay community dominated by whites and a largely heterosexual Asian American community, as well as a mainstream press which never really understood what queer Asians were doing at this protest.

6. The two were arraigned and fined $25, after charges were lowered to a petty misdemeanor.

7. There was yet another twist to the controversy. The Opera cast Geraldine McMillan, an African American, to sing the role of Cio-Cio-san, in recognition of opera's "tradition of colorblind casting," in the words of the Opera manager. Choy noted, "It seems like a technique of pitting minority against minority." He went on to observe the desirability of colorblind casting "in a perfect world, but the reality is that only Caucasians, and sometimes non-Asians, are allowed to play Asians, and not the other way around."

8. The evening I attended, the handful of Asian Americans in the audience was in gales of laughter while the white audience was utterly silent.

9. For Crichton, the invasion is occurring on multiple fronts. America appears to be losing in the halls of academe as well as in the corporate towers and on the production line. Knowledge of the Other is a tactical necessity during a state of war, and the Japanese have responded with a vengeance. When Smith meets Ishigura, the Nakamoto representative, Ishigura's perfect English is striking. Connor responds, "He must have gone to school here. One of the thousands of Japanese who studied in America in the seventies. When they were sending 150,000 students a year to America, to learn about our country. And we were sending 200 American students a year to Japan" (23). The suggestion here is that acknowledgment of Japanese tactical advantage must be followed by an adoption of their practices in order to restore America's (presumably rightful) economic and political preeminence.

10. Indeed, "we" will learn that our sense of superiority is justified, for "our" racism is deemed to be innocuous compared to that of the Japanese. Later, when discussing the case of a "turncoat" who went from a leading position in the U.S. trade negotiator's office to work with the Japanese, Connor replies to the man's allegations that the Congressional scrutiny of the proposed purchase of Fairchild Corporation by Fujitsu was fueled by racism.

> "This racist stuff. He knows better. Richmond knows exactly what happened with the Fairchild sale. And it had nothing to do with racism."
> "No?"
> "And there's another thing Richmond knows: the Japanese are the most racist people on earth" (219).

Here, the authoritative voice of the "expert" on Japan rings eloquently. Connor's definitive pronouncements provide a condemnation of Japan that can be used to justify all manner of retaliatory practice for, after all, the Japanese are even more racist than we.

11. This racial discourse provides a rationale for American response in kind—or worse. The martial imagery is deployed with full force when Connor and Smith confront the Senator who chairs the Finance Committee deciding on the MicroCon case. The Senator, speaking about his fears of Japanese takeover, ends his speech ominously.

> He dropped his voice, becoming one of the boys. "You know, I have colleagues who say sooner or later we're going to have to drop another bomb. They think it'll come to that." He smiled. "But I don't feel that way. Usually" (230).

This, I would suggest, is one extreme Final Solution that Crichton invokes as a possible strategy in the economic wars.

12. See John Dower's important book, *War Without Mercy: Race and Power in the Pacific War*.

13. Though the battles over racial representation in Hollywood film seem endless, activism laid the groundwork for meetings in 1994 between MANAA and executives at Warner Brothers, which released *Falling Down*, another film with a problematic politics of racial representation much decried by Asian American artists and activists. High-ranking studio executives, including Rob Friedman, president of Worldwide Advertising and Publicity, and director Joel Schumacher met with representatives from MANAA, the Korean-American Grocers' Association, and other Asian American organizations. Though the studio refused to disclaim the racial representations circulated in *Falling Down*, they did agree to produce a public-service announcement about racial tolerance directed by Schumacher, that was shown with film trailers (Guy Aoki, interview).

14. They can be subtle, but they are still battles. Recently I attended a moving performance by Dan Kwong that used the relentlessly cheerful letters of Kwong's mother and uncles while they were in relocation camps as the basis for a piece centered on his grandfather's life and the ravages of internment. During the question and answer session, whites dominated the space of the Japanese American Community and Cultural Center. One woman, obviously wanting to be the "good white woman," tried to differentiate the "evil" stereotypes from what her father had taught her, as though a wide gulf existed between the two, and as though any of us—especially whites—can completely escape the influence of such stereotypes. Another asked questions that betrayed both ignorance of cultural conventions and asserted the I-know-you-better-than-you-know-yourselves strain of Orientalism. Capping off the evening, a white man stood up, called the artist "Dan," as though they were intimates, and pontificated on the necessity for us to tell the stories of "great men"—such as his own grandfather. After the performance, it was clear that the dominant must try to appropriate and domesticate even this, the mournful reference point that touches the lives of mainland Issei, Nisei, Sansei, and Yonsei (first-, second-, third-, and fourth-generation Japanese Americans). Even this experience cannot "belong" to us as such; it cannot be treated with respect. Rather, the dominant appropriates the oppression in which it is centrally implicated in its attempts to allay its own guilt and to prove its own good intentions.

259

15. E.g., *Miss Saigon*, in Minneapolis, cost $41 million and was funded by the established Ordway Theater and by the city.

16. This failure to problematize one's own position rests in part on monolithic, essentialist notions of identity and subjecthood; for example, the first-world, middle-class, heterosexual male critic of color who takes his position to be coextensive with "the race," or white female critics who colonize the category "woman," who is assumed to be always already white.

references cited

Abu-Lughod, Lila. "Writing Against Culture." In *Recapturing Anthropology*, edited by Richard Fox. Santa Fe: School of American Research, 1991.

Aguilar-San Juan, Karin, ed. *The State of Asian America: Activism and Resistance in the 1990s*. Boston: South End Press, 1994.

Anzaldúa, Gloria. *Borderlands/La Frontera*. San Francisco: Spinsters/Aunt Lute, 1987.

Anzaldúa, Gloria, ed. *Making Face, Making Soul/Haciendo Caras: Creative and Critical Perspectives by Feminists of Color*. San Francisco: Aunt Lute Foundation Books, 1990.

Aoki, Guy. President, Media Action Network for Asian Americans. Telephone interview. August 25, 1995.

Appadurai, Arjun. "Global Ethnoscapes: Notes and Queries for a Transnational Anthropology." In *Recapturing Anthropology*, edited by Richard Fox. Santa Fe: School of American Research, 1991.

Apter, Emily. "Ethnographic Travesties: Colonial Fiction, French Feminism, and the Case of Elissa Rhaïs." Davis Center Papers.

Austin, J. L. *How to Do Things with Words*. Cambridge: Harvard University Press, 1955.

Avila, David. "Japanese-Americans Stung by Vandalism at Center." *Los Angeles Times*, November 17, 1991: A3.

"A Bad Fashion Statement." *Newsweek*, February 20, 1995: 8.

Barthes, Roland. *Système de la mode*. Paris: Seuil, 1967.

261

_____. *Writing Degree Zero, and Elements of Semiology*. Translated by Annette Lavers and Colin Smith. Boston: Beacon Press, 1970.

_____. *L'empire des signes*. Geneva: Albert Skira, 1970.

_____. *S/Z*. New York: Hill and Wang, 1974.

_____. *The Pleasure of the Text*. Translated by Richard Miller. New York: Hill and Wang, 1975.

Baudrillard, Jean. *L'échange symbolique et la mort*. Paris: Gallimard, 1976.

_____. *Simulations*. Translated by Paul Foss, Paul Patton, and Philip Beitchman. New York: Semiotexte, 1983.

Beeman, William O. "The Anthropology of Theater and Spectacle." *Annual Review of Anthropology* 22 (1993): 369–93.

Befu, Harumi, ed. *Cultural Nationalism in East Asia: Representation and Identity*. Berkeley: Institute of East Asian Studies, 1993.

Belsey, Catherine. *Critical Practice*. London: Routledge, 1980.

Benjamin, Walter. "The Work of Art in the Age of Mechanical Reproduction." *Illuminations*. New York: Schocken, 1969.

Bhabha, Homi. "Of Mimicry and Man." *October: An Anthology*, Cambridge: MIT Press, 1987.

_____ ed. *Nation and Narration*. London and New York: Routledge, 1990.

Bourdieu, Pierre, with Yvette Delsaut. "Le couturier et sa griffe: contribution à une théorie de la magie." *Actes de la recherche en sciences sociales*. (September 1974): 7–36.

Bourdieu, Pierre. *Distinction: A Social Critique of the Judgement of Taste*. Translated by Richard Nice. Cambridge: Harvard University Press, 1984.

Brown, Jacqueline. "Black America, Black Liverpool, and the Gendering of Diasporic Space," unpublished paper, 1996.

Brubach, Holly. "The rites of spring." *The New Yorker* (June 6, 1988): 92.

Buck-Morss, Susan. *The Dialectics of Seeing: Walter Benjamin and the Arcades Project*. Cambridge: MIT Press, 1989.

Bürger, Peter. *Theory of the Avant-garde*. Minneapolis: University of Minnesota Press, 1984.

Butler, Judith. *Subjects of Desire: Hegelian Reflections in Twentieth-Century France*. New York: Columbia University Press, 1987.

_____. *Gender Trouble*. New York: Routledge, 1990.

_____. *Bodies That Matter*. New York: Routledge, 1993.

Carnet de notes sur vêtements et villes. (*Notebook on Cities and Clothes*.) Wim Wenders, director. Road Movies Filmproducktion GmbH, in cooperation with Centre National d'Art et de la Culture Georges Pompidou, 1989.

Case, Sue-Ellen. "Performing Lesbian in the Space of Technology: Part I." *Theater Journal*. 47.1 (March 1995): 1–18.

Case, Sue-Ellen, ed. *Performing Feminisms: Feminist Critical Theory and Theater*. Baltimore: Johns Hopkins University Press, 1990.

Case, Sue-Ellen, Philip Brett, and Susan Leigh Foster, eds. *Cruising the Performative: Interventions into the Representation of Ethnicity, Nationality, and Sexuality*. Bloomington: Indiana University Press, 1995.

Case, Sue-Ellen, and Janelle Reinelt, eds. *The Performance of Power*. Iowa City: The University of Iowa Press, 1991.

Certeau, Michel de. *The Practice of Everyday Life*. Berkeley: University of California Press, 1984.

Chan, Sucheng. *Asian Americans: An Interpretive History*. Boston: Twayne, 1991.

Chau, François. Actor, director. Personal interview, March 1992.

Chouy, Lee San. "The Land of the Rising Voices." *The Straits Times*. August 11, 1993.

Chow, Rey. "The Dream of a Butterfly." In *Human, All Too Human*, edited by Diana Fuss. New York: Routledge, 1996.

_____. "The Politics and Pedagogy of Asian Literatures in American Universities," *differences* 2.3 (Fall 1990): 29–51.

Chung, Phillip. "Clouds Hover Over Rising Sun." *Asian Week* 14. 4 (June 4, 1993).

Clément, Catherine. *Opera, or the Undoing of Women*. Translated by Betsey Wing. Minneapolis, University of Minnesota, 1988.

Clifford, James. *Person and Myth: Maurice Leenhardt in the Melanesian World*. Berkeley: University of California Press, 1982.

Cocks, Jay. "A Change of Clothes." *Time* (January 27, 1986).

_____. "Showroom at the Top." *Time* (May 19, 1986).

Coleridge, Nicholas. *The Fashion Conspiracy*. New York: Harper, 1988.

Commission on Wartime Relocation and Internment of Civilians. *Personal Justice Denied*. Washington, DC: U. S. Government Printing Office, 1982.

Cornyetz, Nina. "Fetishized Blackness: Hip Hop and Racial Desire in Contemporary Japan." *Social Text* 41 (Winter 1994): 113–140.

Crichton, Michael. *Rising Sun*. New York: Knopf, 1992.

Cunningham, Bill. "Couturist Class." *Details* (November 1988): 119–135.

Davis, Angela. "Reaping Fruit, Throwing Seed: Women of Color and Community-Building Practices." Lecture, Hewlett Series on Pluralism and Unity, Pomona College, February 2, 1996.

Dent, Gina, ed. *Black Popular Culture*. Seattle: Bay Press, 1992.

Derrida, Jacques. *Of Grammatology*. Translated by Gayatri Chakravorty Spivak. Baltimore: Johns Hopkins University Press, 1974.

Derrida, Jacques. "Signature, Event, Context," In *Limited, Inc.*, edited by Gerald Graff, translated by Samuel Weber and Jeffrey Mehlman. Evanston: Northwestern University Press, 1988.

"Designer Won't Sell Pajamas." *The Japan Times* (February 9, 1995): 3.

Dolan, Jill. *The Feminist Spectator as Critic*. Ann Arbor: University of Michigan Press, 1988.

_____. " 'Lesbian' Subjectivity in Realism: Dragging at the Margins of Structure and Ideology." In *Performing Feminisms*, edited by Sue-Ellen Case. Baltimore: The Johns Hopkins University Press, 1990.

_____. "Geographies of Learning: Theater Studies, Performance, and the Performative." *Theater Journal* 45.4 (December 1993): 417–442.

"Doughball an Uneven Outing at East West." *Los Angeles Times*, December 21, 1990.

Dower, John. *War Without Mercy: Race and Power in the Pacific War*. New York: Pantheon, 1986.

Drusedow, Jean. Curator, Costume Institute, Metropolitan Museum of Art. Personal interview. November 1989.

Ewen, Stuart. *All Consuming Images: The Politics of Style in Contemporary Culture*. New York: Basic Books, 1988.

"The Fallout Over *Miss Saigon.*" *Los Angeles Times*, August 13, 1990: F3.

Foucault, Michel. *The History of Sexuality*. Translated by Robert Hurley. New York: Vintage, 1980.

Garber, Marjorie. "The Occidental Tourist: *M. Butterfly* and the Scandal of Transvestism." *Nationalisms and Sexualities*, edited by Andrew Parker, et al. New York: Routledge, 1992.

Geertz, Clifford. *The Interpretation of Cultures*. New York: Basic Books, 1973.

Gilroy, Paul. *The Black Atlantic: Modernity and Double Consciousness*. Cambridge: Harvard University Press, 1993.

Gluck, Carol. *Japan's Modern Myths*. Princeton: Princeton University Press, 1985.

Gregory, Steven. *Black Corona: Race, Class and the Politics of Space*. Princeton: Princeton University Press, forthcoming.

———. "Time to Make the Doughnuts: On the Politics of Subjugation in the 'Inner-City'," *PoLAR: Political and Legal Anthropology Review* 17.1 (May 1994): 41–54.

Gregory, Steven, and Roger Sanjek, eds. *Race*. New Brunswick: Rutgers University Press, 1995.

Groos, Arthur. "Lieutenant F. B. Pinkerton: Problems in the Genesis of an Operatic Hero," *Italica* 64 (1987): 654–675.

Hagedorn, Jessica. "Introduction to Tenement Lover." In *Between Worlds*, edited by Misha Berson. New York: Theater Communications Group, 1990.

Hall, Stuart. "What is this 'Black' in Black Popular Culture?" In *Black Popular Culture*, edited by Gina Dent. Seattle: Bay Press, 1992.

Haraway, Donna. *Simians, Cyborgs, and Women: The Reinvention of Nature*. New York: Routledge, 1991.

Hart, Lynda and Peggy Phelan, eds. *Acting Out: Feminist Performances*. Ann Arbor: University of Michigan Press, 1993.

Haug, Wolfgang. *A Critique of Commodity Aesthetics: Appearance, Sexuality, and Advertising in Capitalist Society*. Minneapolis: University of Minnesota Press, 1986.

Henriques, Julian, Wendy Hollway, Cathy Urwin, Couze Venn, and Valerie Walkerdine. *Changing the Subject: Social Regulation and Subjectivity*. London: Methuen, 1984.

Hollander, Anne. *Sex and Suits*. New York and Tokyo: Kodansha International, 1994.

hooks, bell. *Feminist Theory: From Margin to Center*. Boston, South End Press, 1984.

———. *Yearning*. Boston: South End Press, 1990.

Hu, Ying. *Tales of Translation: Imaging the Woman in Late Qing China*. Stanford: Stanford University Press, forthcoming.

Hutcheon, Linda. *A Poetics of Postmodernism*. London: Routledge, 1988.

Huygen, Christian. "Han Ong writes himself." *Outlook* 17 (Summer 1992): 35–40.

Huyssen, Andreas. "Mass Culture as Woman: Modernism's Other." *Studies in Entertainment.* Edited by Tania Modleski. Bloomington: Indiana University Press, 1986.

Hwang, David Henry. *M. Butterfly.* New York: Dramatists Play Service, 1988.

_____. *As the Crow Flies.* In *Between Worlds*, edited by Misha Berson. New York: Theater Communications Group.

_____. *Face Value.* Unpublished play, 1993.

_____. "Foreword." In *The State of Asian America*, edited by Karin Aguilar-San Juan. Boston: South End Press, 1994.

Ishihara, Shintaro. *The Japan That Can Say No.* New York: Simon and Schuster, 1991.

Ivy, Marilyn. "Tradition and 'Difference' in the Japanese Mass Media," *Public Culture* 1.1 (Fall 1988): 21–29.

_____. " 'Popular Theater' and Representations of Difference in Contemporary Japan." Paper presented at Annual Meeting of Society for Cultural Anthropology, Santa Monica, California, 1991.

_____. *Discourses of the Vanishing: Modernity, Phantasm, Japan.* Chicago: University of Chicago Press, 1995.

JanMohamed, Abdul, ed. *Minority Discourse.* Oxford: Oxford University Press, forthcoming.

Johnson, Barbara. *The Critical Difference: Essays in the Contemporary Rhetoric of Reading.* Baltimore: Johns Hopkins University Press, 1991.

Kaplan, Caren. "Deterritorializations: the Writing of Home and Exile in Western Feminist Discourse." In *The Nature and Context of Minority Discourse*, edited by Abdul JanMohamed and David Lloyd. Oxford: Oxford University Press, 1990.

Kaplan, Joel, and Sheila Stowell. *Theater and Fashion: Oscar Wilde to the Suffragettes.* Cambridge: Cambridge University Press, 1994.

Kanai, Jun. Representative, Miyake Design Studio. Personal interview. July 1989.

Kawakubo, Rei. Interview. *Ryūkō Tsūshin* 276 (January 1987): 88–92.

_____. President and Head Designer, Comme des Garçons. Personal interview. August 1990.

"Kawakubo Rei: *"Jiyū o Oru Shokunin Katagi."* "(The Artisanal Spirit Weaving 'Freedom.')" *Nihon Keizai Shinbun.* February 15, 1988: 1.

Kawata, Jan. International Press Representative, Comme des Garçons. Personal interview. August 1990.

Kellner, Douglas. *Jean Baudrillard: From Marxism to Postmodernism and Beyond.* Stanford: Stanford University Press, 1989.

Kelly, Kevin. *Boston Globe.* February 17, 1993, Living Section: 25.

Kim, Elaine. "Defining Asian American Realities Through Literature." In *The Nature and Context of Minority Discourse*, edited by Abdul JanMohamed and David Lloyd. Oxford: Oxford University Press, 1990.

Kingston, Maxine Hong. *The Woman Warrior.* New York: Vintage, 1977.

Kozasu, Akiko. "Rei Kawakubo and Her Stylish Atmosphere," *Marie-Claire Japon* 3 (March 1989): 159–174.

Krauss, Rosalind. *The Originality of the Avant-Garde and Other Modernist Myths.* Cambridge: MIT Press, 1985.

Kristeva, Julia. *About Chinese Women.* New York: Urizen Books, 1977.

Koda, Harold. Curator, Fashion Institute of Technology. Personal interview. July 11, 1989.

Kondo, Dorinne K. "Dissolution and Reconstitution of Self: Implications for Anthropological Epistemology." *Cultural Anthropology* 1.1 (February 1986): 74–88.

———. *Crafting Selves: Power, Gender, and Discourses of Identity in a Japanese Workplace.* Chicago: University of Chicago Press, 1990.

———. "Bad Girls: Theater, Women of Color, and the Politics of Representation." In *Women Writing Culture*, edited by Ruth Behar and Deborah Gordon. Berkeley: University of California Press, 1995.

———. "*Miss Saigon* is a Celebration of Stereotypes." *Los Angeles Times*, February 18, 1995.

———. "Poststructuralist Theory as Political Necessity." *Amerasia Journal.* 21.1, 2 (1995): 95–100.

———. "Theory at the Intersections: Ethnography as Feminist and 'Minority' Discourse." In *Minority Discourse*, edited by Abdul JanMohamed. Oxford: Oxford University Press, forthcoming.

Kumagai, Tokio. Interview. *The Tokyo Collections.* Edited by Shizuyo Kusunoki. 1986: 142.

Kushner, Tony. *Angels in America: A Gay Fantasia on National Themes.* New York: Theater Communications Group, 1993.

Kusunoki, Shizuyo, ed. *The Tokyo Collections.* Tokyo: Graphic-sha, 1986.

Kwong, Dan. Closing Remarks, Treasure in the House: Performance Festival of Asian Pacific Art. Highways Performance Space, Santa Monica, California, 1991.

Laclau, Ernesto, and Chantal Mouffe. *Hegemony and Socialist Strategy: Towards a Radical Democratic Politics.* London: Verso, 1985.

Lannon, Linnea. "You See Holes, She Sees Lace." *Detroit Free Press*, May 15, 1983.

Lee, Lissa Ling. Actress. Personal interview. October 4, 1991.

Lemelle, Sidney, and Robin Kelley, eds. *Imagining Home: Class, Culture, and Nationalism in the African Diaspora.* London: Verso, 1994.

Lemoine-Luccioni, Eugénie. *La robe: essai psychoanalytique sur le vêtement.* Paris: Seuil, 1983.

"Les Japonais: incompris ou admirés?" *Le Vif* (March 1, 1987): 95–7.

Lipovetsky, Gilles. *The Empire of Fashion: Dressing Modern Democracy.* Translated by Catherine Porter. Princeton: Princeton University Press, 1994.

Lipsitz, George. *Dangerous Crossroads: Popular Music, Postmodernism, and the Poetics of Place.* London: Verso, 1994.

———. "Review of *The Black Atlantic: Modernity and Double Consciousness*," *Social Identities* 1.1 (1995): 193–200.

Lowe, Lisa. *Critical Terrains.* Ithaca: Cornell University Press, 1991.

Lye, Colleen. "*M. Butterfly* and the Rhetoric of Antiessentialism: Minority Discourse in an International Frame." In *The Ethnic Canon: Histories, Institutions, and Interventions*, edited by David Palumbo-Liu. Minneapolis: University of Minnesota Press, 1995.

Mani, Lata. "The Construction of Women as Tradition in Early Nineteenth-Century Bengal." *Cultural Critique* 7 (Fall 1987): 119–156.

———. "Multiple Mediations: Feminist Scholarship in the Age of Multinational Reception." *Feminist Review* 35 (Summer 1990): 24–41.

Mani, Lata and Ruth Frankenberg. "Crosscurrents, Crosstalk: Race, 'Postcoloniality' and the Politics of Location." *Cultural Studies* 2 (1993): 292–310.

Mann, Paul. *The Theory-Death of the Avant-Garde*. Bloomington: Indiana University Press, 1991.

Martin, Biddy and Chandra Mohanty. "Feminist Politics: What's Home Got to Do with It?" In *Feminist Studies, Critical Studies*, edited by Teresa de Lauretis. Bloomington: Indiana University Press, 1986.

Martin, Richard and Harold Koda. *Jocks and Nerds: Men's Style in the Twentieth Century*. New York: Rizzoli, 1989.

———. *Orientalism: Visions of the East in Western Dress*. New York: Metropolitan Museum of Art, 1994.

Mauss, Marcel. "A Category of the Human Mind: The notion of person; the notion of self." In *The Category of the Person: Anthropology, Philosophy, History*, edited by Michael Carrithers, Steven Collins, and Steven Lukes, translated by W.D. Halls. Cambridge: Cambridge University Press, 1985.

Mercer, Kobena. "Black Hair/Style Politics." In *Out There: Marginalization and Contemporary Culture*, edited by Russell Ferguson, et al. Cambridge: MIT Press, 1990.

Miyake, Issey. Speech at Japan Today Conference in San Francisco, September 1984.

Miyake, Perry. *Doughball*. Unpublished play manuscript, 1991.

———. Letter to the author. January 30, 1991.

———. Personal interview. May 1991.

Miyoshi, Masao. *Accomplices of Silence: The Modern Japanese Novel*. Berkeley: University of California Press, 1974.

Modleski, Tania. *Loving with a Vengeance: Mass-produced Fantasies for Women*. Hamden, Connecticut: Archon Books, 1982.

Moraga, Cherríe and Gloria Anzaldúa, ed. *This Bridge Called My Back*. Watertown, Massachusetts: Persephone Press, 1981.

Morley, David and Kevin Robins. "No Place Like *Heimat*: Images of Home(land) in European Culture." *New Formations* 12 (Winter 1990): 1–24.

Morris, Bernadine. "From Japan, New Faces, New Shapes." *New York Times*. December 14, 1982: C10.

Moy, James. "David Henry Hwang's *M. Butterfly* and Philip Kan Gotanda's *Yankee Dawg You Die*: Repositioning Chinese American Marginality on the American Stage." *Theater Journal* 42.1 (March 1990): 48–56.

———. *Marginal Sights: Staging the Chinese in America*. Iowa City: University of Iowa Press, 1993.

Muto, Sheila. "APA Activists Say 20th-Century-Fox Trying to Divide APA Community." *Asian Week*. 15. 1 (August 27, 1993).

267

Nelson, James. Editor, *Magazine House*, Tokyo; Freelance consultant. Personal interview, August 12, 1989.

Ong, Aihwa. "Women Out of China: Traveling Tales and Traveling Theories in Postcolonial Feminism." In *Women Writing Culture*, edited by Ruth Behar and Deborah Gordon. Berkeley: University of California Press, 1995.

Outlaw, Lucius. "African philosophy: Deconstructive and reconstructive challenges." In *Contemporary Philosophy: A New Survey*, edited by G. Fløistad and G. H. von Wright. Dordrecht: Martinus Nijhoff, 1987.

Pao, Angela. "The Critic and the Butterfly: Sociocultural Contexts and the Reception of David Henry Hwang's *M. Butterfly*." *Amerasia Journal* 18.3 (1992): 1–16.

Park, Steve. Actor. Personal interview. September 1991.

Parker, Andrew and Eve Sedgwick, eds. *Performativity and Performance*. New York: Routledge, 1995.

Parker, Andrew, Mary Russo, Doris Sommer, and Patricia Yeager, eds. *Nationalisms and Sexualities*. New York: Routledge, 1992.

Pernet, Diane. Designer. Personal interview, July 1989.

Phelan, Peggy. *Unmarked*. New York: Routledge, 1993.

Poggioli, Renato. *The Theory of the Avant-Garde*. Cambridge: Harvard University Press, 1968.

Pret-à-Porter. Robert Altman, director. Miramax Films, 1995.

Quon, Jody. Comme des Garçons representative. Personal interview, Paris. March 1989.

Radway, Janice. *Reading the Romance: Women, Patriarchy, and Popular Literature*. Chapel Hill: University of North Carolina Press, 1984.

Reinelt, Janelle, and Joseph Roach, eds. *Critical Theory and Performance*. Ann Arbor: The University of Michigan Press, 1992.

Román, David. *Acts of Intervention: U. S. Theater and Performance, Gay Men, and AIDS*. Bloomington: Indiana University Press, forthcoming.

Rosaldo, Michelle. "Toward an anthropology of self and feeling." In *Culture Theory: Mind, Self, and Emotion*, edited by Richard Shweder and Robert LeVine. Cambridge: Cambridge University Press.

Rosaldo, Renato. "Imperialist Nostalgia." *Culture and Truth*. Boston: Beacon Press, 1989.

Russell, John. "Race and Reflexivity: The Black Other in Contemporary Japanese Mass Culture." *Cultural Anthropology* 6.1 (1991): 3–25.

Ryūkō Tsūshin. 306 (July 1989): 18–47.

Ryūkō Tsūshin Homme. 6 (July 1989): 28–65.

Said, Edward W. *Orientalism*. New York: Pantheon Books, 1978.

Sainderichin, Ginette. *Kenzo*. Paris: Editions du May, 1989.

Sakai, Naoki. "Modernity and Its Critique: The Problem of Universalism and Particularism." In *Postmodernism and Japan*, edited by Masao Miyoshi and H. D. Harootunian. Durham: Duke University Press, 1989.

Sandoval, Chela. "U. S. Third World Feminism: The Theory and Method of Oppositional Consciousness in the Postmodern World." *Genders* 10 (Spring 1991): 1–24.

Saussure, Ferdinand de. *Course in General Linguistics*. New York: McGraw-Hill, 1966.

Savigliano, Marta E. *Tango and the Political Economy of Passion*. Boulder: Westview Press, 1995.

Schechner, Richard. *Performance Theory*. New York: Routledge, 1977.

_____. *Between Theater and Anthropology*. Philadelphia: University of Pennsylvania Press, 1985.

Schechner, Richard and Will Appel, eds. *By Means of Performance: Intercultural Studies of Theater and Ritual*. New York: Cambridge University Press, 1990.

Schudson, Michael. *Advertising, the Uneasy Persuasion: Its Dubious Impact on American Society*. New York: Basic Books, 1984.

Servan-Schreiber, Franklin. Editor, *Elle Décor*. Personal interview, July 28, 1989.

Shimakawa, Karen. "Who Is to Say? Or, Making Space for Gender and Ethnicity in *M. Butterfly*." *Theater Journal* 45.3 (1993): 349–362.

_____. "Swallowing the Tempest: Asian American Women on Stage." *Theater Journal* 47.3 (October 1995) 367–380.

Shore, Elliot. *Talkin' Socialism*. Lawrence: University Press of Kansas, 1988.

Sidorsky, Gail. "From East to West: A New Breed of Japanese Designers." *Image NYC* (1983): 17–20.

Sigmund, Suzanne. "Chinese-Hawaiian Performance Artist Enlivens Local Arts Scene." *Asian Pages* 3.3 (October 1–14, 1992): 13.

Silverberg, Miriam. "Remembering Pearl Harbor, Forgetting Charlie Chaplin, and the Case of the Disappearing Western Woman: A Picture Story." *positions: east asia, cultures, critique*. 1.1 (Spring 1993): 24–76.

Silverman, Kaja. "Fragments of a Fashionable Discourse." In *Studies in Entertainment*, edited by Tania Modleski. Bloomington: Indiana University Press, 1986.

Smith, Anna Deavere. *Twilight: Los Angeles 1992*. New York: Anchor Books, 1994.

Smith, Barbara. *Home Girls*. New York: Kitchen Table Press, 1983.

Spivak, Gayatri Chakravorty. *In Other Worlds: Essays in Cultural Politics*. New York: Routledge, 1988.

Spivak, Gayatri Chakravorty. "Introduction." In *Selected Subaltern Studies*, edited by Ranajit Guha and Gayatri Chakravorty Spivak. New York: Oxford University Press, 1988.

Stanlaw, James. " 'For Beautiful Human Life:' The Use of English in Japan." In *Remade in Japan: Everyday Life and Consumer Taste in a Changing Society*, edited by Joseph Tobin. New Haven: Yale University Press, 1992.

Steedman, Carolyn. *Landscape for a Good Woman*. New Brunswick: Rutgers University Press, 1987.

Steele, Valerie and Claudia Kidwell. *Men and Women: Dressing the Part*. Washington, DC: The Smithsonian Institution Press, 1989.

Stegemeyer, Anne. *Who's Who in Fashion*. New York: Fairchild Publications, 1988.

Stincheum, Amanda Mayer. "The Japanese Aesthetic: A New Way for Women to Dress." *The Village Voice*, April 19, 1983: 70–76.

Sudjič, Deyan. *Rei Kawakubo and Comme des Garçons*. New York: Rizzoli, 1990.

Tambiah, S. J. "A Performative Approach to Ritual." *Proceedings of the British Academy*. Volume LXV, London: Oxford University Press, 1979.

Tanaka, Stefan. *Japan's Orient*. Berkeley: University of California Press, 1993.

Tobin, Joseph. *Remade in Japan: Everyday Life and Consumer Taste in a Changing Society*. New Haven and London: Yale University Press, 1992.

Trinh, Minh-ha. *When the Moon Waxes Red: Representation, Gender, and Cultural Politics*. New York: Routledge, 1991.

Tsing, Anna Lowenhaupt. *In the Realm of the Diamond Queen: Marginality in Out-of-the-way Places*. Princeton: Princeton University Press, 1993.

Turner, Victor. *The Ritual Process: Structure and Anti-Structure*. Chicago: Aldine, 1966.

_____. *From Ritual to Theater: The Human Seriousness of Play*. New York: Performing Arts Journal Publications, 1982.

_____. *The Anthropology of Performance*. New York: Performing Arts Journal Publications, 1986.

Verdery, Katherine. "Beyond the Nation in Eastern Europe." *Social Text* 38 (Spring 1994): 1–20.

Visweswaran, Kamala. *Fictions of Feminist Ethnography*. Minneapolis: University of Minnesota Press, 1994.

Weaver, William, translator. *Seven Puccini Librettos*. New York: W. W. Norton, 1981.

Washida, Kiyokazu. *Mōdo no Meikyū* (The Labyrinth of Fashion.) Tokyo: Chūōkōronsha, 1989.

Weedon, Chris. *Feminist Practice and Poststructuralist Theory*. London: Basil Blackwell, 1988.

Weinstein, Jeff. "The Man in the Gray Flannel Kimono," *Village Voice*. April 19, 1983.

_____. Writer, *Village Voice*. Personal interview. November 10, 1989.

Weiser, Barbara. Vice-President, Charivari, New York. Personal interview. November 13, 1989.

West, Cornel. "Beyond Eurocentrism and Multiculturalism." In *Black Popular Culture*, edited by Gina Dent. Seattle: Bay Press, 1992.

Williamson, Judith. *Decoding Advertisements: Ideology and Meaning in Advertisements*. New York: Marion Boyars, 1978.

_____. *Consuming Passions: The Dynamics of Popular Culture*. New York: Marion Boyars, 1986.

Wilson, Elizabeth. *Adorned in Dreams: Fashion and Modernity*. Berkeley: University of California Press, 1988.

Wolff, Janet. *The Social Production of Art*. New York: St. Martin's Press, 1981.

Yamada, Mitsuye. *Camp Notes*. Latham, NY: Kitchen Table/Women of Color Press, 1992.

Young, Iris. *Throw Like a Girl and other essays in feminist philosophy and social theory*. Bloomington: Indiana University Press, 1990.